Beyond the River and the Bay

Beyond
the River
and
the Bay

Some Observations on the State of the
CANADIAN NORTHWEST
IN 1811
with a View to Providing the Intending Settler
with an Intimate Knowledge
of That Country

Eric Ross

UNIVERSITY OF TORONTO PRESS

© University of Toronto Press 1970
Printed in Canada by
University of Toronto Press, Toronto and Buffalo
ISBN 0-8020-5223-1

To the memory of my father
DAVID
DeWITT
ROSS

Preface

Ian Alexander Bell Robertson, the imaginary writer of this book, was invented by the author to describe the Canadian Northwest in 1811 in order to overcome a number of technical difficulties as well as to provide a means by which remarks of contemporary observers might be easily integrated into the text. Presented in the form of information for the intending settler, the work is a study in the historical geography of the old Northwest of the fur trade at the time of the arrival of the first Selkirk settlers. Biographical information about Robertson has been imagined as follows:

Born in Lady Stair's Close, Edinburgh, in 1771, of prosperous parents, Robertson was educated privately at home before being sent to the Royal High School, where he displayed a lively mind although he was perhaps better remembered for his successes in the yards than in the classroom. Between 1786 and 1790, he attended lectures in Edinburgh University but left without taking a degree. While there, he was a founding member of "The Club," whose purpose was the discussion of social and political questions of the day. Among its members were Thomas Douglas (later Lord Selkirk) and Walter Scott, the novelist. All three were to remain lifelong friends.

Following university, Robertson read law with a view to becoming an advocate. However, he became increasingly drawn to the pen and wrote a number of short pieces for the *Edinburgh Review*. These received some public favour and he was encouraged to attempt several novels which did not, however, find wide acceptance.

Meanwhile, he fell increasingly under the influence of Lord Selkirk and came to share his concern for the poor of the Scottish Highlands.

Like Selkirk, he reached the conclusion that emigration would greatly assist in overcoming the economic difficulties of the Highlands. And so in 1811, when Selkirk was given his large land grant for a colony in the Red River, he resolved to offer his support by writing a description of the whole of the Northwest as it was at that time with a view to providing the intending settler with an intimate knowledge of the country. His manuscript was completed late in 1811. It was intended to be published under the title *Some Observations on the State of the Canadian Northwest in 1811*, but for a reason unknown today it was apparently set aside and eventually lost. Fortunately, in 1963, during the demolition of several old houses in George Square, it was discovered among a number of other papers in an attic and is now being published for the first time.

The method of approach to this as, indeed, to any problem in historical geography was largely dictated by the nature of the historical and geographical evidence available for study. Before detailed research was begun, the materials were carefully assessed and an approach decided upon. For the early period of the Canadian Northwest, evidence was found to be mostly in the form of journals, reports and letters of contemporary observers. It seemed that these could be most effectively used, as demonstrated by Ralph Brown with similar materials relating to the eastern seaboard of North America, by confining the study to a survey of the geography of a particular period and avoiding the use of a time sequence. In doing this, Brown had followed Hettner's dictum that "historical geography takes a limited cross section through reality at one particular point of time and utilizes temporal development only in order to explain the conditions at the time chosen."

Since the choice of time for the cross-section had to be based on the amount and type of contemporary evidence available, as well as upon its significance historically and geographically, the source materials had to be considered first. For the Canadian Northwest, the earliest period for which a substantial amount of material was available was the last two decades of the eighteenth century through the first two of the nineteenth. This was the golden age of Canadian exploration, the time of Pond, Hearne, Mackenzie, Turnor, Fidler and Thompson. The last three could be called geographers and their observations were especially useful. Many of their notes, journals and maps have come down to us in both printed and manuscript form. The greatest single source of the

latter is the archives of the Hudson's Bay Company in London. Here
also are the daily jottings in the journals of the traders which tell so
much of their lives and of the land they lived in. Another important
source of contemporary evidence is found in the material collected by
Roderick McKenzie of the Northwest Company, who had planned to
incorporate it in a book. He requested the bourgeois of the company to
send him information about the natural productions, animals and birds,
climate, natives, etc., of the areas in which they lived. Many of them
responded with quite remarkable reports, and in considerable detail.
Two members of the Northwest Company who apparently did not send
in their reports are nevertheless worthy of special mention. These are
Daniel Harmon and Alexander Henry, the younger, whose journals are
among the most valuable now available. Other useful information may
be found in contemporary pamphlets, newspapers and magazines, and
in the publications of the Royal Society, which had taken an interest in
the Northwest from a very early time.

Thompson and his great contemporaries passed from the western
scene in the early years of the nineteenth century. Their places remained
unfilled until Hind, Palliser and the other scientific observers began
their explorations some two generations later. Material for the years
between these two groups is probably too scattered and too scarce to be
of much use to the student of historical geography.

The period at the turn of the nineteenth century, so rich in material,
is also of considerable historical and geographical interest. It is the time
when the traders from Montreal merged and met the Hudson's Bay
Company's monopoly with a united front. These were exciting times,
and they have captured the attention of many historians who have told
their story well. But the fur trade also had a geography, the study of
which so far has been largely overlooked. Most of the trading posts can
be located geographically and the routes between them mapped. Much
can be told about the elaborate transportation system, upon which the
trade depended; about the goods carried, and about the Europeans and
natives who manned the canoes, pulled the toboggans and carried the
huge packs on their backs. Less reliably, perhaps, something may be
added about the ranges of animals, the distribution of vegetation and
about the climatic regime.

The year of the arrival of the first agricultural settlers in the Northwest (1811) was chosen as a suitable date for taking a geographical cross-
section. It marked the beginning of the end of the era of the fur trade

and the start of the period of settlement which was later to change the
face of the west, a face which had remained for many centuries virtually
unscarred by the hand of man. The Northwest of 1811, still in its
"natural state," is well worth knowing today, not only as a backdrop
against which to project the fur trade during its most exciting period,
but as a starting point for modern studies of the geography and history
of that region.

The style of writing and cartography are both designed to evoke a
feeling of the period. The footnotes are those of the author. Little of
the material documented would have been accessible to Robertson even
though most of it had already been recorded in some diary, notebook
or journal. A few citations refer to the works of recent scholars. Modern
geographical terminology has been avoided, enclosed in square brackets
or relegated to the footnotes. To avoid confusion, however, modern
spelling has been used for place names.

The study was made possible by a generous fellowship from the Canada Council. Helpful advice was given by Professors J. Wreford Watson
and G. A. Shepperson of the University of Edinburgh; by Professor A.
MacPherson, Simon Fraser University; Professor G. S. Graham, London;
Professor E. E. Rich, Cambridge; and by Dr. W. K. Lamb, Dominion
Archivist, Ottawa. Thanks are also due the Governor and Committee
of the Hudson's Bay Company for permission to use the company archives, ably run by a helpful staff headed by Miss Alice Johnson.

Acknowledgments for assistance must also be made to the staffs of
several Scottish institutions including the National Library of Scotland,
H. M. Register House, Edinburgh University Library, Royal Scottish
Geographical Society Library, and the Castle Douglas Public Library,
as well as the British Museum Library, Public Record Office, Royal
Commonwealth Society Library, Canada House Library, Royal Geographical Society Library, London University Library, and the Institute
of Historical Research Library in England, and the Library of the Geographical Branch and the Public Archives in Canada.

Special thanks must be given to John Bryant, of the University of
Victoria, who drew the maps.

North Hatley, Quebec   ER
July 1969

Contents

Illustrations

Maps (in envelope at back of book)

Beyond the River and the Bay

1
The Northwest

Those intending to join Lord Selkirk's expedition to the Red River
are directed to study carefully the enclosed copy of Arrowsmith's map*
(map 1) of North America which was published earlier in this year of
our Lord, 1811. It is a remarkable piece of work in that it includes most
of the latest discoveries made by explorers and adventurers. Yet it must
be pointed out that its author, unlike many other map makers, has not
travelled in the regions he has portrayed. Rather, he has chosen to follow
in the best traditions of Ptolemy by drawing together information from
diverse sources to create a work remarkable for its detail and accuracy.

The eye of the prospective settler will be delighted by the wealth of
detail in the area known as the "Northwest." Though now a place name
in common usage, perhaps it would be instructive to mention its origin.
For many years one of the most important fur trading posts was at
Michilimackinac, a small island situated at the western end of Lake
Huron. Throughout most of the eighteenth century the traders from
Montreal, first the French and then the British, stopped here to make
up their brigades before continuing on either to the lower countries
through Lake Michigan or to the upper countries by way of Lake
Superior. It was customary, among the men at the post, to refer to the
lower countries as the "Southwest," and the upper countries beyond
Lake Superior as the "Northwest." Both names found general acceptance and continued to be used even after the Southwest was closed to
the Montreal traders, when it passed under the control of the United
States during the final years of the eighteenth century, and the Northwest, thereby extending to the southern limits of the remaining British
territories, had actually become the "west."

* See envelope at end of book.

The exact limits of the Northwest cannot be stated with any accuracy. However, from the negotiations of 1807 it would seem that the southern boundary will follow along the forty-ninth parallel of latitude from Lake of the Woods to the Rocky Mountains. Eastward from Lake of the Woods to Lake Superior, the boundary will probably follow a line through several lakes and rivers including Rainy River, Rainy Lake and Pigeon River. From Lake Superior to Hudson Bay there is no real boundary dividing the Northwest from the remainder of the British territories but, for convenience, it may be taken to correspond with the border between the Northern and Southern Departments of the Hudson's Bay Company which runs along the eastern limits of the English-Winnipeg and Severn River basins. North and west of Hudson Bay, the Northwest is thought to be bordered by the "Frozen Ocean" although the actual position of that ocean is known at only two points – at the mouth of the Coppermine River and at the mouth of the Mackenzie River. West of the Mackenzie, the Rocky Mountains are thought to extend to the Frozen Ocean. From there the border may be said to run along the mountains to the United States boundary. Beyond the Rockies is the little-known New Caledonia, now being explored by David Thompson for the North West Company.

Probably Arrowsmith has drawn more from the work of David Thompson than of any other man. This remarkable Londoner, though virtually unknown in Europe, is probably the greatest living geographer. From 1784 until the present (1811) he has travelled some 50,000 miles by canoe, horseback and on foot,[1] and has accurately mapped the main travel routes through about 1,700,000 square miles of the Northwest, the United States and New Caledonia.[2] Until 1797, Thompson was employed by the Hudson's Bay Company and after that by the North West Company. It was during his stay with the English company that he learned surveying from Philip Turnor, the first man to be hired by that company specifically as a surveyor. Turnor also trained Peter Fidler, who became the chief surveyor of the Hudson's Bay Company in 1796, a position he still holds. Fidler has made surveys of the Saskatchewan and Assiniboine rivers, and of the northwest toward Lake Athabasca. His work, as well as that of Turnor and, of course, David Thompson, was incorporated in the first edition of Arrowsmith's map of North America published in 1795. The 1811 edition contains the results of further explorations and surveys by Thompson and Fidler only, since Turnor returned permanently to England in 1792.

Arrowsmith has also drawn freely from the journals of Samuel Hearne and Sir Alexander Mackenzie although neither man had the knowledge of surveying possessed by Thompson, Turnor and Fidler. In fact, after descending the river which now bears his name (when he was only 25 years old), Mackenzie admitted that he had been "deficient in the sciences of astronomy and navigation" and lacked the necessary books and instruments to make proper observations.[3] These deficiencies had not passed unnoticed by Turnor who had met Mackenzie at Cumberland House on his return from the Arctic. "Mr. Mackenzie says he has been at the Sea, but thinks it the Hyperborean Sea but he does not seem acquainted with Observations which makes me think he is not well convinced where he has been."[4]

In the preface to his *Voyages*, Sir Alexander has described some of the difficulties facing the explorers of the Northwest: "I do not possess the science of the naturalist; and even if the qualifications of that character had been attained by me, its curious spirit would not have been gratified. I could not stop to dig into the earth, over whose surface I was compelled to pass with rapid steps; nor could I return to collect the plants which nature might have scattered on the way, when my thoughts were anxiously employed in making provision for the day that was passing over me. I had to encounter perils by land and perils by water; to watch the savage who was our guide, or to guard against those of his tribe who might meditate our destruction. I had, also, the passions and fears of others to control and subdue. Today I had to assuage the rising discontents, and on the morrow to cheer the fainting spirits, of the people who accompanied me. The toil of our navigation was incessant, and oftentimes extreme; and in our progress over land we had no protection from the severity of the elements, and possessed no accommodations or conveniences but such as could be contained in the burden on our shoulders, which aggravated the toils of our march, and added to the wearisomeness of our way."[5]

Mackenzie has been a very celebrated personage both here in Great Britain and abroad since the publication, in 1801, of the journals of his two spectacular voyages. Meanwhile, Thompson and Fidler continue to toil in the Northwest against many frustrations with scant recognition. Like Turnor, Thompson and Fidler are employed as fur traders as well as surveyors and generally the exploration and surveying have had to be subjugated to the demands of the trade. In all his years in the Northwest, Thompson has been permitted to devote only one year to exploration alone.[6] Thus the work of these men, as reflected in Arrowsmith's map (map 1), is all the more remarkable when one considers not only the harsh circumstances under which it has been conducted but also the lack of encouragement given by their employers.

All of the explorers owe a great deal to the natives of the Northwest, the Indians and Eskimos. Without them as guides, it would be impossible to travel through the maze of lakes, rivers, carrying-places and passes which cover so much of the country. Their maps, too, have often proven invaluable. In praise of them, Fidler has said: "The Indian map conveys much information where the European documents fail; and on some occasions are of much use, especially as they shew that such & such rivers & other remarkable places are, tho' they are utterly unacquainted with any proportion in drawing them."[7] Of course, Fidler means proportion in the European sense. To the Indians, it is something quite different. To them, time and space are closely related and A is not so many miles from B but so many nights, or moons, on the road. This concept is carried over to their maps and time (rather than distance) is expressed according to scale; thus a difficult river route occupies more space on their maps than an easy one of the same length because it takes more time to travel over it.[8]

The Indian generally knows his own particular country extremely well, but beyond it the rivers and lakes fade into the unknown – an unknown, as likely as not, filled with the terrors of evil spirits and horrible beasts. The limits of the Northwest are far beyond his ken and so he cannot begin to visualize the area as a whole. This has remained for the European to do. With his knowledge of astronomy and surveying, and by following the native into the wilderness, he has been able to reduce much of the wisdom of generations to a number of scientific maps and notebooks.

Most of these maps and notes are the result of individual surveys carried out for a specific purpose with little thought for what has already been done or for what is likely to follow. Integrating them into a map of the whole area is extremely difficult, especially since the quality of the individual maps varies from the rudimentary surveys of Hearne to the highly sophisticated work of Turnor. Perhaps no man possesses the necessary skill for collating these divers sources, with the exception of Aaron Arrowsmith who has even made use of three Indian maps in delineating the area north of Fort Churchill.[9] Thompson, alone of the explorers, has conceived a plan for mapping the Northwest as a whole and has approached his work in a methodical way. Most of his surveys have now been completed although his maps have not yet been drawn.[10]

Thus Arrowsmith's map of 1811 (map 1) gives a good representation of the Northwest as known to the European fur traders at the present time. Even without making allowance for the lapse in time between surveying and mapping, made necessary by the slow communication between the new world and the old, the map is remarkably complete since little important work has been carried out during the past few years. Turnor, now dead, did not return to the Northwest after the first edition of the map was published in 1795.[11] Fidler, although now chief surveyor of the Hudson's Bay Company, is completely embroiled in fierce competition with the North West Company at Ile-à-la-Crosse and has had little time for exploration.[12] David Thompson, with other surveyors of the North West Company, has been working outside the Northwest across the Rocky Mountains in New Caledonia, where the company's attention is presently directed.[13] Those much-discussed American explorers, Lewis and Clark, passed below the southern boundary of the Northwest during their scientific expedition to Louisiana and the Oregon country in 1804-6. The results of their explorations are not yet available. However, while such information would have been invaluable to Arrowsmith in compiling his map of North America, it is unlikely that it would have altered his portrayal of the Northwest in any way.

The large white spaces on the map show that sizeable areas still remain unsurveyed, unexplored and unknown. Here and there, an Indian comment will be noted about a particular feature which partly fills the blank; a great lake is only a short distance away, or it is necessary to sleep eight nights in descending a river to the sea. Neither the river, the lake, nor other unsurveyed feature is delineated but by adding the Indian account, Arrowsmith has shown, in a very small way, how the land appeared to the Indian in the days before he was forced to share it with the white man.

To the white trader viewing the Arrowsmith map, one of the most striking geographical features of the Northwest is the "Valley of the Lakes" which extends from Lake Superior to Great Bear Lake and encompasses Winnipeg, Reindeer, Athabasca and Great Bear Lakes. It is considered to mark the boundary between the two principal regions of the Northwest – the "Great Plains" to the southwest and the "Stony Region" [Canadian Shield] to the northeast. A third region, much smaller than the other two, is the swampy, low-lying coastal plain bordering the southwestern side of Hudson Bay which, for nearly two centuries, has been known as "New South Wales."

All three regions (see map 2) possess a remarkable system of rivers and lakes which are distributed with an evenness and closeness that make it possible to travel by light canoe from any one point in the Northwest to almost any other with a minimum of interruption. It is these waterways, more than anything else, which has made possible the rapid exploration of the Northwest, and it is also they which have made practical the fur trade which, in turn, has greatly stimulated exploration. Without them, it is doubtful if much of the Northwest would yet be known. And because the lives of the explorers and traders have been intimately bound up with the waterways, most of the information portrayed is concerned with them. The innumerable rapids, water falls and "lakes" so characteristic of the rivers of the Stony Region are clearly shown; so, too, are the uninterrupted meanderings of the rivers of the Great Plains, the divides between the major drainage basins, and the large lakes comprising the great Valley of the Lakes.

Although the traders are well aware of the existence of the Great Plains, the Stony Region and New South Wales, it should not be thought that they view the Northwest primarily in these terms. Instead, they see it in terms of river systems, or of "countries" based on the areas drained by the major rivers and their tributaries (see map 3). The principal ones are the Red River Country, the Saskatchewan Country and, most important of all, the Athabasca Country, based on the Mackenzie drainage basin. There are also several "countries" along the routes from Hudson Bay and Lake Superior across the Stony Region which enable the traders to exploit these regions.

It will be noticed that most of the rivers of the Northwest flow in a northerly or northeasterly direction. That is, they flow from a severe to an even more severe climate. This means that the spring thaw generally comes to their upper reaches before their lower, and that frequently the headwaters of the rivers are in spate when their mouths are still frozen solid. Whenever this happens a great deal of flooding inevitably results, particularly along the rivers with low banks. The most notorious of these, the prospective Selkirk settler should note, is the Red which, in the spring of 1811, was flooded throughout its entire length. Above its junction with the Assiniboine, the waters rose fifty feet above the normal five-foot level, and spread to a width of eight miles instead of the usual eighty or one hundred yards.[14] The spring was very late in 1811 and the flooding was worse than usual. But every year, in most parts of the Northwest, rivers and lakes frequently overflow their banks and many of the innumerable swamps, for a few defiant weeks, return once more to their former state as lakes.

The processes which transform lakes into swamps would seem to operate particularly rapidly in the Northwest if one is to accept the testimonies of many travellers in that country. For instance, Mackenzie noted that "many lakes are draining and filling up by earth which is carried into them from higher lands by the rivers."[15] He mentions particularly Cedar Lake near the mouth of the Saskatchewan, whose increasingly shallow waters are well known to the canoemen who are now forced to pole their way through its dense grasses. In the course of time, he predicts that the lake will be converted into a pine forest.[16] Lake Winnipeg is also becoming more shallow but not, it would seem, entirely from the effects of silting, for the water appears to be receding from its former shorelines. When Alexander Henry visited the lake in 1808, he noticed that the woods in many places were nearly a mile from the beach, and that the intervening space was low-lying with many small lakes, marshes and stagnant ponds. The waters of the lake, he said, appeared to have washed the foot of the woods many years before, and then gradually to have receded.[17] Similar observations have been frequently made at the posts on Hudson Bay which led Superintendent Auld of the Northern Department of the Hudson's Bay Company to speculate recently that either the water of the bay is receding or the land is rising. As proof, he points out that since 1790 the grass immediately under the windows of Churchill Factory has grown upwards of 120 yards towards the channel.[18]

Mackenzie believes that the decreasing area of fresh water resulting from the shrinking and disappearing lakes may be having a moderating effect on the climate of the Northwest.[19] He arrived at this conjecture while searching for the reason why the winters of the new world are so much more severe than those in comparable latitudes of the old. Mackenzie is not alone in his speculations. In fact, the striking differences in climate between the two worlds has long been a topic of debate. Probably the most popular theory to emerge is that the clearing away of the woods has had a moderating effect on the climate in Europe and that now North America, as a result of more and more land being opened up, is beginning to enjoy similar change. This theory has found a strong supporter in Richard Kirwen (1787) who, in attempting to explain why temperatures of eastern North America are lower than those in similar latitudes in Europe, argued that "living Vegetables alter their temperature very slowly and with difficulty, but that evaporation from their numerous surfaces, is much greater, than from the same space of land uncovered with vegetables; if they are tall, and close as forests, they prevent the sun's rays from reaching to, and warming the earth, besides protecting the Winter's snow for several months. Hence wooded countries are much colder than those that are open and cultivated ..."[20]

Mackenzie agrees that the climate is moderating but disagrees with Kirwen's explanation. He believes that the amount of land cleared so far is too trifling in proportion to the whole to have had much, if any, effect on the climate and thinks that the change must "proceed from some predominating operation in the system of the globe which is beyond my conjecture" although he suggests that the fact that many lakes are draining and filling up with earth "may have some partial effect."[21] Mackenzie's suggestion will not find favour among all of the traders. In fact, many will not agree that the climate is moderating at all, let alone with his reason for it, particularly those who managed to survive the past winter of 1810-11, one of the most severe in living memory. They would be more likely to support Samuel Hearne who wrote that the climate is actually getting colder. In 1772, when he travelled across the Stony Region to the Frozen Ocean, he saw the wind-blasted remains of large trees well beyond the northern limits of the forest at that time, and concluded that the cold must have been increasing "in those parts for some ages."[22]

It is not possible to show whether Mackenzie is right in thinking that the climate is becoming warmer or Hearne in believing it is becoming colder. Both claim Indian support for their observations but neither have produced any reliable evidence. Temperatures have been recorded at a number of posts for many years, but none long enough to indicate a general pattern. Moreover, there is no reason to suppose that the thermometers used are reliable or that they have been properly exposed.

Hearne is possibly the only European to have seen the retreating northern boundary of the vast forest belt which stretches diagonally across the Northwest (map 4). Known as the "Great Western Forest," it is also retreating along its southern edge as well. But while Hearne could only guess that a climatic variation was responsible for the change in the north, the reason for the alteration in the south is all too obvious. Man is clearly to blame. Year after year, through carelessness[23] and by design,[24] the Indians set fire to the long grasses of the plains. The flames frequently spread into the forest, killing the trees along its southern flank. Before new trees can replace them, the flames invade once again until now only the grasses, which can survive the fires, flourish in many places where once the forest had stood.

Thus the grasses are gaining an easy victory over the retreating forest. However, the forest does not present a united front to the advancing grasslands. In most places along its flank, patches of trees are detached and scattered far out onto the grasslands. To the Canadians, these seem like so many islands scattered over a sea of grass, and so they call them the "Ilets de Bois."[25] To the north, the thick spruces of the Great Western Forest gradually thin into the dwarfed clumps of the "Land of Little Sticks," before giving way grudgingly to the windswept stumps seen by Hearne, and finally to an endless, rolling, treeless land of sedges and mosses – the "Barren Grounds."

Nature has given to each area its own particular animals: to the grasslands, the buffalo and wolf; to the Great Western Forest, the moose, deer and beaver; to the Barren Grounds, the caribou and muskox; and to New South Wales, seals, white whales and waterfowl. These animals, more than anything else, have determined the way of life of the natives of each area. On the grasslands the buffalo outrank all animals in importance. They congregate in vast herds and enable the Indians who follow them to enjoy a life of ease and luxury unknown elsewhere in the Northwest. In the forest the moose occupies a position similar to the buffalo in the native economy, but it is by no means as numerous or gregarious. It tends to live a solitary life which forces the natives who depend upon it to dwell in small bands scattered throughout the forest. In the Land of Little Sticks and on the Barren Grounds, the caribou takes the place of the buffalo and the moose. Unlike the moose, the caribou are extremely sociable and travel in huge herds, constantly moving between the forest belt and the Arctic Ocean. Several tribes of Indians and Eskimos depend upon their annual migrations for food, but these peoples are always in danger of starvation, for in some years the caribou do not come. Unlike their southern neighbours, these tribes are familiar with fishing and on many occasions turn to the lakes and rivers when the caribou fail. Fish are plentiful throughout much of the Northwest, but many of the southern Indians consider it below their dignity to catch them. It is a tragic fact that many of them die of starvation rather than degrade themselves by fishing in some nearby lake or river.

It is strange that many Indians will not condescend to supplement their meat diet with fish, for they know all too well that no species of animal can always be depended upon. Years of plenty are suddenly followed by years of scarcity, and even during periods of plenty, the animals often mysteriously disappear for weeks, and even months, at a time. Apart from these periodic variations in the animal population, it is generally believed by Indian and white man alike that all animals were more plentiful in the past, and that their numbers were suddenly reduced at the time of the great smallpox epidemic which killed off most of the natives back in 1782. Despite this speculation, how they were reduced remains a complete mystery. Even David Thompson, who has been in the Northwest since 1784, can offer no explanation. Before the epidemic, he says, the Indians were numerous "and the Bison, Moose, Red and other Deer more so in proportion and Provisions of Meat, both dried and fresh in abundance. Of this all the Traders and Indians were fully sensible, and it was noted by Traders and Natives, that at the death of the latter, and there being thus reduced to a small number, the numerous herds of Bison and Deer also disappeared both in the Woods and in the Plains, and the Indians about Cumberland House declared the same of the Moose, and the Swans, Geese and Ducks with the Gulls no longer frequented the Lakes in the same number they used to do; and where they had abundance of eggs during the early part of the Summer, they had now to search to find them."[26] It might be supposed that some new disease or diseases (similar to the smallpox which decimated the Indians) had been inadvertently introduced into the animal population from Europe by means of the cattle and other animals which arrived regularly from Britain both in Canada and at the bayside posts. However, Thompson believes that "no disorder was known among the animals."[27]

To date, little agriculture has been conducted in the Northwest and so both white and native are almost completely dependent upon the animal kingdom for their sustenance. Thus the habits and ways of the various creatures are assiduously studied by all who live there. The intending settler would do well to begin his own study before leaving for the new world. To this end, his attention is directed to Thomas Pennant's *Arctic Zoology*, published in 1784. Like Arrowsmith, Mr.

Pennant owed a great debt to several explorers and fur traders. Among these were Samuel Hearne (whose "liberal communication of many zoological remarks" are acknowledged in his preface) and Andrew Graham, Hearne's friend and fellow employee of the Hudson's Bay Company, who not only provided him with many observations on the Northwest but with many specimens of animals as well. These had been sent by Graham to the museum of the Royal Society.[28] Included among these are probably some of the birds described earlier by John Reinhold Forster in his *An Account of the Birds sent from Hudson's Bay ...* published in 1772.[29] Hearne included some of his own observations about the animals of the Northwest in his *A Journey from Prince of Wales's Fort, in Hudson's Bay, to the Northern Ocean.* His work shows the influence of Pennant. It is unfortunate that Hearne did not illustrate his observations with drawings, for he was something of an artist as shown by the several sketches he did publish of various Indian implements, of a view of Great Slave Lake, and a view of Fort Prince of Wales.

2

The Inhabitants of the Northwest

The natives of America have been a source of great curiosity from the date of their discovery by Christopher Columbus in 1492. He had been searching for a short route to India and so when he came upon the dusky inhabitants of the islands which later came to be known as the West Indies, he called them Indians. The name soon passed into the languages of the civilized world. But even as it did so, it was realized that Columbus had not discovered a new route to Asia, but a new world, and that the natives were not Indians, but a people unknown. Who they really were, and where they had come from, became a favourite topic of speculation (if not of investigation) on both sides of the Atlantic and, indeed, continues to be right down to the present time.

Although it is true that there is now general agreement that (with the probable exception of the Eskimo) all of the natives from the Northwest to Cape Horn are one people,[1] there is still a measure of disagreement on their place of origin. Writing in 1797, Professor Benjamin Barton of the University of Pennsylvania said that the theories of all writers on the subject could be "distributed into two great classes." The first class embraces all those writers who suppose that the countries of America derived their inhabitants from Asia, from Europe, from Africa, or from the unknown Atlantis. The second class includes those who think that the Americans are in strict language the aborigines of the soil and not emigrants from other parts of the world. The advocates of the first opinion, he said, are "much the most numerous" and, in general, are the "men of the most learning and research."[2] Among them, theories of trans-Siberian migrations are the most popular,[3] although other theories are also considered. For example, James Adair, in 1775, devoted over two hundred pages in an attempt to prove (by a comparison of languages, customs and religions) that the natives were descended from the Jews,[4] while Hugh Williamson, as late as this year, argues for a Hindu origin.[5]

Professor Barton has read much of what has been written on the Indians and, on the basis of similarities in language and appearance, has come to the same conclusion as a majority of his colleagues, that the natives of America and Asia must have a common origin.[6] But unlike them,[7] he believes the establishment of many of the American nations in the new world to be extremely remote.[8] Thomas Pennant (1784), like Barton, thought that different peoples, "at several periods," had arrived from eastern Asia by way of the Bering Strait. For proof, he turned to the customs and dress common to the inhabitants of both worlds. Some, he said, had been long extinct in the old world, while others remained in full force in both.[9]

If Pennant's conclusions are correct, then the last peoples to migrate would probably still have more in common with their relatives in Asia than those who left earlier. Among the late arrivals must be the Chipewyans "and the numerous tribes who speak their language" [that is, the Athapaskan linguistic family which included the Sarcee, Beaver, Chipewyan, Yellowknife, Dogrib, Hare and Slave Indians] for according to their own tradition, they came from Siberia, and in dress and manner are still similar to people found on the coast of Asia.[10] These peoples are still moving eastward to this day. South of them are the several tribes of another great [Algonkian] family. [Included in the Algonkian linguistic family were the Cree, Ojibwa, Blackfoot, Blood, Piegan and Gros Ventre tribes.] According to Mackenzie, they were once inhabitants of the Atlantic coast but are now progressing westerly and have reached as far west and north as Athabasca. South of them are yet another [Siouan] people, the Assiniboine, who have been pushing in from the southeast. They are now inhabiting the plains on and about the source and banks of the Saskatchewan and Assiniboine rivers. Far to the north are the Eskimos. The extent of their lands is not known, although they are thought to extend along the coasts (which Mackenzie says the Eskimos never leave) from Fort Churchill to the mouth of the Coppermine and on to the mouth of the Mackenzie. They probably extend westward of the Mackenzie as well.[10]

The origin of the Eskimos is still the subject of a great deal of speculation. Captain W. Coats, who had spent many years in Hudson Bay between 1727 and 1751, thought them to be "of the lineage of the Chinase,"[11] whereas David Thompson, who met a number of Eskimos while working at Fort Churchill, is firmly convinced that they are of European descent.[12] Mackenzie observes that they are similar in appearance, manners, language and habits to the inhabitants of Greenland,[13] but he does not speculate on their origin, or the direction of their migration, or indeed, if they are moving at all.

These great sweeping migrations referred to by Mackenzie and others reach far back into the ages, beyond memory. In the lifetime of a man, the movement had been scarcely perceptible. But within each group, and even between two groups, there had been smaller, more obvious migrations as one tribe had pushed into the lands of another either through mutual agreement or, as was more likely, through force of arms. These would have been more easily recognized, although they, too, often had taken place over long periods. But with the coming of the white man, all this began to change. It seems that no sooner had a tribe gained European fire-arms than it began to push back its neighbours until they, in turn, obtained weapons and attacked their own, yet-unarmed neighbours. Moreover, in order to acquire the arms and other European goods, the natives (see map 5) have often been tempted to enter neighbouring areas in search of food and furs to trade. For instance, the Ojibwa (having exhausted the furs in their own country between Lake Winnipeg and Lake Superior) are now pushing into the beaver country of the upper Assiniboine, while the Chipewyan (now living in peace with their southern neighbours, the Cree) are slowly extending their hunting grounds southward from the Barren Grounds and the Land of Little Sticks. The Cree in turn are pushing still further south toward the open plains.[14] Some of the Cree have already adopted the easier way of life of their affluent neighbours, the Assiniboines of the plains, and have left forever the lonely drudgery of life in the forest. Here again can be seen the effect of the European, for one of the great attractions of life on the plains has been the availability of the horse which was introduced to America by the Spaniards.

Elsewhere in the Northwest, similar migrations have been taking place. In the forested areas where animals are scarce, it has usually been found necessary to subdivide a tract of land belonging to a tribe or nation among the several families who make up the nation. Rivers, lakes and mountains mark the limits of the lands of each family and are respected by all members of the tribe. This has encouraged a measure of natural conservation among the more prudent Indians, who generally kill only sufficient animals for their own needs and for trading for such articles as they can no longer get along without.[15] Yet in spite of their caution, at the time of writing many hunting areas have been ruined. The beaver, particularly, have been destroyed and great hardship has resulted for the local population. To suggest that this misery is the native's own making would be to ignore its principal cause – the invasion of Indians from the east. These were mostly Iroquois, Nipissing [Objibwa] and Algonquins who first pushed into the Northwest toward the close of the century, after exhausting the beaver in their own country through imprudent hunting with steel traps. They had followed the canoes of the fur traders from Canada, and had brought with them their steel traps, to extend their reckless exploitation of the fur lands from Lake Winnipeg, across the Northwest to the Rocky Mountains, and even beyond.[16] Resistance from the western tribes on whose lands they hunted, seems to have been remarkably slight,[17] probably because many of the intruders have contracts with the North West Company.[18]

The number of intruders is unknown as is the total native population of the Northwest. But from the estimates of several traders, the total can be taken as being between 40,000 and 60,000. Some of the "natives" are actually "halfbreeds," children of European fathers and Indian mothers who have been brought up as Indians. Other halfbreeds are brought up as Europeans at the trading posts and are often considered as white. No less than 21 of the latter are employed by the Hudson's Bay Company in 1811. Many more are employed by the North West Company.

The large halfbreed population has been largely attributed to the almost complete absence of white women in the Northwest. So far as is known, there are only two at the present time. One is the Canadian wife of Baptiste Lajimonière, who came to the Red River from Trois-Rivières in 1806,[19] and the other is Mary Fubbester, an Orcadian girl who, disguised as a man, had hired on with the Hudson's Bay Company at Stromness in the same year.[20] She had worked "at anything & well like the rest of the men" and her sex had remained unknown to anybody "except to one John Scart her paramour on whose account she came out,"[21] until 29 December 1807, when she gave birth to a boy at Pembina River House.[22] Her son is probably the first white child to be born in the Northwest.

Young Scart is almost certainly the only native wholly of European extraction now living in the Northwest. All other whites will have originated outside the area and, with the possible exception of a handful of settlers now wintering near York Factory (of whom more will be said later) , all are engaged, directly or indirectly, in the fur trade. It is difficult to state how many traders are now working in the Northwest since their numbers tend to fluctuate from year to year, and even from season to season, with the ever-changing demands of the trade. However, since virtually all of them are now employed by either the North West Company or the Hudson's Bay Company, who together monopolize the trade, a combined list of the personnel of the two companies would give a fairly complete census of the white population of the Northwest at the present time. The only whites who would be excluded from such a census would be the small number of "freemen," or independent traders, who continue to work on their own.

At the end of 1811, after the ships departed for Great Britain, the Hudson's Bay Company was left with 320 employees in the Northwest.[23] Of these, at least 21 are halfbreeds,[24] leaving less than 300 whites. Eighty-three of the latter went out this year and, because the ships had been unusually late, are now wintering near York Factory at Seal Island.[25] Among the newcomers are a number of men acquired through the new arrangement with Lord Selkirk. In the spring, it is planned to send 35 of them to establish the proposed colony on the banks of the Red River. The remaining 48 are to be distributed among the five factories of the Northern Department. The rival North West Company is thought to have about 1,200[26] men in the Northwest at the present time. However, since as many as ten per cent of its employees may be halfbreeds, the number of whites probably total less than 1,100 men. The "freemen" who remain outside the companies include in their numbers Iroquois, Nipissing and Algonquin Indians from the east as well as whites. The latter are mostly Canadian. Just how many of each there are, is impossible to say (their numbers fluctuate sharply from year to year) , but it is unlikely that there are now more than one or two hundred all told. These, together with the employees of the two companies along with the women and the child, would bring the total white population of the Northwest up to about 1,500 men, two women and one child.

At the present time most of the whites are Orcadian, Scots, English, or French Canadian although it is believed that the establishment of Selkirk's colony and the new employment policy of the Hudson's Bay Company will diminish the number of Orcadians and increase the number of Highland Scots and Irish. For many years, the Orcadians have been hired by the Hudson's Bay Company to fill its rank-and-file posts although many of them, in the course of time, have risen to positions of considerable responsibility. Nevertheless, many of the better jobs have been held by the English minority in the company. The French Canadians tend to be the counterparts of the Orcadians in the North West Company although they seldom rise in the ranks, and consequently few French names ever appear in the lists of "bourgeois," or partners, of the company. These are mostly English and Scottish, and particularly Scottish.[27]

Interestingly enough, the earliest employees of the Hudson's Bay Company were not Orcadian. They came from England, Ireland and Scotland. Then, in 1741, a few Orcadians were hired. They were found to be "submissive and industrious" and soon the company began to hire virtually all its tradesmen and contracted servants in Orkney.[28] Other sources of men have been largely neglected, as generation followed generation from Orkney to the Bay, until by now, the Orcadians have come to regard employment with the Hudson's Bay Company as their own exclusive right.[29] Most of the tradesmen have come from Kirkwall and Stromness but some have come from the country districts where they combined farming with their trade.[30] The contracted servants have been drawn from the common people who came under the acute observation of Murdoch Mackenzie, their fellow-countryman, in 1750: "The Commonalty are healthy, hardy, well-shaped, subject to few Diseases, and capable of an abstemious and laborious life at the Same Time; but, for want of profitable Employment, slow at Work, and many of them inclined to Idleness. In sagacity and natural Understanding, they are inferior to few of the Commons in Britain; sparing of their Words, reserved in their Sentiments, especially of what seems to have a Connection with their Interest; apt to aggravate or magnify their Losses, and studious to conceal or diminish their Gains; tenacious of old Customs tho' never so inconvenient, averse to new, till recommended by some successful Examples among their own Rank and Acquaintance, and then universally keen to imitate; Honest in their dealings with one another, but not so scrupulous with respect to the Master of the Ground; often running deeply in Arrears to him, while they punctually clear Credit with every one else ... Tho' in the Neighbourhood of the Highlands of Scotland, yet they have neither the Language, Dress, Custom of wearing Arms, clannish Adherence and Subjection to their Masters, or Violence of Resentments, for which the Highlanders are remarkable;

Their Manners and Customs resemble those of the southern, rather than of the northern Parts of the Kingdom, their Traffic and Correspondence being with the former only ... The Religion is Presbyterian as established in Scotland, without Bigotry, Enthusiasm, or Zeal; and without any Dissenters, excepting a very few of episcopal Persuasion. The Mirth, Diversions and reciprocal Entertainments of the Christmas, and other Holy-days, are still continued, tho' the Devotion of them is quite forgot."[31]

"Want of profitable Employment" at home has been the main inducement for the Orcadian to foresake the smoky but familiar comfort of his peat-fire in some low, dark house on a rocky island,[32] to seek a connection with the Hudson's Bay Company in an unknown savage land. Other offers have come his way as well. There has been a steady demand for seamen for the Iceland and Greenland fisheries, for the coal trade, and for the Royal Navy.[33] But none of these has been particularly attractive, least of all, perhaps, the navy. The navy, however, has always greatly admired the hardy Orcadians and, during the long years of the present war with France, has periodically sent press-gangs to the islands to force them into her service. No able-bodied man over five feet five inches tall[34] has been safe from her insatiable demands. To get beyond her reach, many an Orcadian has rushed into the arms of the Hudson's Bay Company.[35] Thus the navy, initially at least, helped the company's recruiting by stampeding men into its service. But as the war has worn on, the supply of tall men has dried up and only the short remain. Now even some of these have been sent to the bay much to the bewilderment of the Indian wife of one of the traders. Sitting in a canoe with her husband, and watching the new arrivals disembark from the ship, she looked steadily at them and then at her man, and at length said, "James have you not always told me, that the people in your country are as numerous as the leaves on the trees, how can you speak such a falsehood, do not we all see plainly that the very last of them is come, if there were any more would these dwarfs have come here."[36] James Spence could only remain silent, for he knew there was much truth in what his wife had spoken.

The connection between the company and the Orkneys has now entered its seventieth year. The length of the relationship, together with the strain imposed upon it by war, is beginning to tell on both parties. The islanders are starting to complain about the large number of men who go to the bay "instead of offering an honourable service to their King and country, or staying at home to cultivate their lands, and protect their wives, their children, and their parents . . ."[37] There are also complaints about the low wages paid by the company. However, these are still higher than those offered by the farmers who, in turn, complain about the resulting shortage of servants. Of course, the farmers realize that the company is not alone to blame, and that the Greenland and Iceland fisheries, the coal trade, and the navy (as well as the raising of 200 fencibles in the islands) have all contributed to the shortage of men; but the company, being the largest employer (and because it makes an annual demand and at once, it is therefore the more noticeable), has been made to bear most of the criticism.[38] The farmers (and would-be farmers) have been further irritated by the number of men who, after eight or ten years on the bay, have returned with their savings to over-bid them for farms.[39] However, some of the returning men have had no interest in farming and have preferred to be simply "idle and useless," although this trait was not necessarily developed in the Northwest for, according to the minister of the united parishes of Sandwich and Stromness, "several of them are perhaps so before they go there, and that this is what often induces them to go."[40] His colleague in the parish of Ophir is far more definite about the corrupting influence of the Northwest. Many of these men, he says, "bring home with them all the vices, without any of the virtues of the savages, indolence, dissipation, irreligion, and at the same time a broken constitution."[41]

The Hudson's Bay Company had at first been attracted to the Orcadians because they were more "sober and tractable" than the Irish or the English.[42] Moreover, unlike many of the Irish and Scots, they spoke the language of the company, English, and only English, their own language, Norn, having gone out of use by the middle of the eighteenth century.[43] Besides, their homeland made a convenient rendezvous on the voyage between London and Hudson Bay. But as the years have worn on, the shortcomings of the Orcadians have become ever more apparent. Most annoying to the company has been their tendency to take the employment it offers for granted. No longer has it been thought necessary to please with good service and it seems never to have even occurred to them that the company might look elsewhere for its servants.[44] With scandalous disrespect, the Orcadians in the Northwest have actually conspired with their relations, and with former employees in the islands, to prevent the company from hiring the number of men it has wanted, in order to force the factory chiefs on the bay to raise their wages. In this, they have been aided and abetted by the company's opponents who are employing "malicious tricks" to discredit its service and so prevent it from "getting the necessary annual supply of useful hands" to pursue its business with success.[45]

The Orcadians have further tried the patience of their masters by sometimes re-engaging for service in some new area of the Northwest after having been sent home as unfit or for misconduct.[46] By 1810, their vices seem to have at last obscured their virtues, for the company decided to turn to other fields for its servants in addition to Orkney. Agents are to be posted in Glasgow, the Hebrides, and, for the purpose of hiring French Canadians, in Montreal.[47] At the same time, the company has entered into an agreement with Lord Selkirk and has provided him with a large tract of land about the Red River for the purpose of establishing an agricultural settlement, in return for his undertaking to supply the company with 200 men per annum for ten years.[48]

Judging from the experiences of a lone Irishman and three Highlanders who were recently sent out by the company, the new policy will not be popular with the Orcadians and the intending settler would be well advised to prepare himself for a hostile reception in the Northwest. The Irishman was sent out to Churchill where he has been so maliciously treated by the rest of the men that the governor, in order to protect him, has been forced to engage him as his personal servant.[49] The three Highlanders, who were sent out from Stornoway in 1810, have fared no better and to screen them from similar treatment two of them have had to be kept at the factory.

These incidents appear to have been only the first clouds in a coming storm. For this fall, when the first large contingent of non-Orcadians arrived[50], the Orcadians became furious. They felt that they had been betrayed and, in a pique, many have refused to renew their contracts.[51] There even have been murmurings about quitting the country altogether.[52] Many of the newcomers are from Glasgow, the Highlands and Ireland. To make matters worse, at least some of them are Roman Catholic and there is even a priest among them.[53] Part of the men are to remain with the company while others are to be sent to the Red River to prepare for the arrival of the first large group of settlers in 1812. The Superintendent of the Hudson's Bay Company's Northern Department, William Auld, foresees "insurmountable difficulties in getting the Orkneymen to mingle with the Irishmen"; but he is more optimistic about the reaction of the company's few French Canadians for, as he puts it, "the Canadian servants being of the same religion will evalesce more readily with the Irish."[54]

Until now, at least, religion does not seem to have played an important role in the Northwest. In fact, the priest is probably the first clergyman to enter the area since the French period.[55] What effect he will have on the French-Canadian servants of the North West Company (who would all be Roman Catholics), Auld cannot predict, but he ventures to speculate that should he be an intriguing Jesuit, "he would find little difficulty in performing some severe strokes of retaliation on our pitiless oppressors."[56] Possibly Auld over-estimates the amount of control which the church has over the French Canadians for, although they come from devout families,[57] most of them set aside their religion when they enter the Northwest. They are usually young when they come and, because they are generally illiterate, they tend to forget the little religion they ever had when there is no church to remind them of it,[58] so that, after many years in the country, they do not seem to observe the Sabbath (or any manner of worship) any more than do the savages themselves.[59] In fact, the savages on the whole seem to take their own rudimentary religion more seriously, although contact with the whites has tended to weaken its hold. Referring to the Crees, who have been longest under European influence, Thompson says that he has "found many of the Men, especially those who had been much in company with white men, to be all half infidels, but the Women kept them in order; for they fear the Manito's."[60] The "gloomy superstition of Calvinism," as Auld puts it,[61] borne lightly by the Orcadians at home,[62] seems to have been even less demanding in the Northwest. For the most part, then, religion (if practised at all) has been practised without fervour, which goes a long way towards explaining the absence, to date, of religious strife in the Northwest. Seldom, if ever, are there references in the traders' journals to disputes involving religion. But with the arrival of a more zealous Catholicism from Ireland, all this might change. Not only has it already brought out the latent bigotry of the Orcadians,[63] but it might in future cause the company to suffer a decline in favour with the natives should they think the company was swerving from their simple religion.[64] However, even if this should happen the effect need not be very serious since the traders could always (as Auld has optimistically pointed out) put the blame for the change on the comet which appeared in the sky about the same time as the Irish appeared at York Factory.[65]

The French Canadians have been referred to as the "Orcadians" of the North West Company. But here the comparison ends. For according to William Auld, the nature of the Canadians is "as opposite to that of the Scotchmen or Orkneymen as black is to white."[66] The Orcadians, by nature cautious and careful, are noted for their prudence in managing their own property even if they tend to be somewhat indifferent in their care of that of others.[67] They also have a reputation for being sordidly avaricious[68] and it is said that only the pursuit of money will induce them to take the risks to life and limb which are a daily part of the fur trade. The volatile French Canadians, on the other hand, are as indifferent about themselves as they are about their masters and their masters' property.[69] They delight in the dangers in running rapids and cataracts in their frail canoes, caring little about their lives or their cargoes, and with little thought of gain. For money means nothing to them and, besides, they are usually in debt in advance to their employers anyway.[70] To the Orcadian, however, money is nearly everything and scarcely anything else will induce him to take similar risks.[71]

For the most part, however, the cautious and prudent (if self-interested) nature of the Orcadians has worked to the advantage of the company. For when they have been scattered about the country in small parties among the Indians, the general tenor of their behaviour has been such that not only has it won the respect and protection of the natives, but it has enabled them to enrich their employers as well as themselves. Writing in 1790 in praise of the "prudent demeanor" of the Orcadians, Edward Umfreville, a disaffected former employee of the Hudson's Bay Company, observed that although "they have annually exposed themselves to all the dangers incident to the trade, for fifteen years past, they have not sustained the loss of a man; and the principal advantage of the Company over the Canadian traders, is more to be attributed to the laudable efforts of their servants, than even to the superior quality of their goods." Umfreville, who claimed the honesty of the company's men to be incorruptible, went on to say that the Canadian servants were so "far from being actuated by the same principles" that few of them could be trusted with even a small assortment of goods to trade for their master's profit. For, ten to one, the master would find himself defrauded of everything through "commerce with Indian women, or some other species of peculation." Many of the Canadians, he said, spend the greater part of their lives among the savages and "being devoid of every social and benevolent tie" became slaves to every vice which could corrupt and debase the human mind. The result was that most of them were held in contempt by the natives. Nevertheless, Um-freville admitted, there were also many Canadians who were possessed of abilities capable of aggrandizing their masters and promoting their own welfare. Moreover, they were very apt at learning the Indian languages and in acquiring a knowledge of the necessary Indian cere-monies and customs to be observed in prosecuting the trade. These talents have been generally appreciated and made use of by their Scot-tish and English masters in the North West Company. In 1804, for example, not a single interpreter of the newly combined North West Company and xy Company bore other than a French name.[73]

Although excellent linguists, the French Canadians are not regarded as brilliant conversationalists. "All their chat," once moaned the loqua-cious Daniel Harmon of the North West Company who has been iso-lated among them for months at a time, "is about Horses, Dogs, Canoes, and Women, and strong Men who can fight a good battle."[74] Probably because they are without the least education (and appear to set no value on it)[75] their own language seems to be becoming corrupted. Before the conquest of their country by the British, it has been said that they spoke "as pure and correct French as in old France."[76] But an Eng-lish visitor to Canada in 1806-8, noticed than many Anglicisms have crept into their language and that several antiquated phrases are in use. He thought this might be due to their intercourse with the new settlers. "For *froid* (cold)," he said, "they pronounce *frête*. For *ici* (here) they pronounce *icite*. For *prêt* (ready) they pronounce *parré*: besides several other obsolete words which I do not at present recollect." Another common practice he observed is that of pronouncing the final letter of their words which, he added, is contrary to the custom of European French. This might also have been acquired in the course of fifty years of contact with the British settlers; if not, he concluded, "they never merited the praise of speaking pure French."

The Canadian who can read is considered "a sort of phenomenon."[77] There are few schools in Canada and most of these are kept by nuns or other women. This has led to a situation, perhaps unique in the whole world, where far more women than men can read. Yet the men who go west are far from ignorant for, according to Harmon, after they have been in the Northwest for a few years, they are more knowing or have a better knowledge of the world and human nature, than do the lower class of people in most other countries.[78] Yet, as already seen, they usu-ally prefer to put their knowledge at the service of others rather than use it for themselves. For unlike the Orcadians, few aspire to positions of leadership in the trade. In fact, they place little confidence in one of themselves and, according to Thompson, always prefer to work for an Englishman.[79]

Thompson, of course, used the term "Englishman" to describe all those who spoke English regardless of whether they were English, Scots, or American. The French Canadians probably refer to them in the same manner although, unfortunately, surprisingly little is known about how this colourful group views the fur trade and the Northwest. This is because most of them are illiterate and because persons interested in the Northwest, and even in the French Canadians themselves, have had to rely largely on the journals of English-speaking traders. Among the more important of these are the journals of Sir Alexander Mackenzie and Alexander Henry, the younger. It is true that these observers have been more interested in the fur trade itself, than in the men who conducted it. Nevertheless, their brief asides about the Canadians are often quite penetrating. Their colleague David Thompson, a man of much wider interests, has contributed a great deal more. But for the most complete portrait, it is necessary to turn to Daniel Harmon, the gossipy, gregarious clerk of the North West Company. It is to be hoped that his journal, along with those of Thompson and Henry, will some day be made available to the general reader. For many years Harmon has kept his journal so that his people back home in Vermont might know how "their long absent Relative has been employed both as to Body and Mind while in this Savage Country."[80] One of the early entries, written only a few months after his arrival in the Northwest, records a marriage "in the manner of the country" of one of his French Canadians. Harmon, still bearing the heavy conscience of New England, was obviously shocked. "In the evening," he wrote, "Monsr. Mayotte took a Woman of this Country for a Wife or rather Concubine, and all the ceremonies (as I am informed) attending such a circumstance is, when a person is desirous of having one of the Natives Daughters to live with him, he makes a present to the Parents of the Damsel, of such articles as he may suppose that will best please them for Rum always forms a principal part of the donation, for this is what Savages in general are most fond of, and should they accept the articles offered, the Girl remains at the Fort with her lover, and is clothed after the fashion of the Canadians, with a Shirt, short Gown, Petticoats & Leggins &c. and the most of them I am told are better pleased to remain with the White

People than with their own Relations. But should the newly joined couple not agree, they are at full liberty to separate whenever either chooses – however no part of the property that was given to the Girls Parents will be refunded."[81]

Life in the Northwest has gradually changed Harmon and, two years later, when a Cree chief offered his daughter to Harmon, he was sorely tempted for, as he put it "I was sure that while I had the Daughter I should not only have the Fathers hunts but those of his relations also." Such a connection would undoubtedly have promoted the interests of the company and, as a result, Harmon's as well. But, "thanks to God alone," Harmon managed to sidestep this snare "laid no doubt by the Devil himself."[82] Three more years passed and then temptation reared its ugly head again. One day in October 1805, a girl of about 14 years of age, the daughter of a Canadian father and a Snare [Interior Salish] Indian mother, was offered to the loney trader who "after mature consideration" concluded that it would be best to accept her because (as he rationalized his actions at the time) "it is customary for all the Gentlemen who come in this Country to remain any length of time to have a fair Partner, with whom they can pass away their time at least more sociably if not more agreeably than to live a lonely, solitary life, as they must do if single."[83] If he found that they could live together in harmony (and there seemed to be no reason why they should not since the girl was said to be of a "mild disposition and even tempered") he intended to keep her as long as he remained in the Northwest. But when he returned to his native land, he would try to place her into the hands of "some good honest Man, with whom she can pass the remainder of her Days in this Country much more agreeably, than it would be possible for her to do, were she to be taken down into the civilized world, where she would be a stranger to the People, their manners, customs & Language."

Harmon's "marriage" illustrates well the difficulties which face the unions between the traders and their dusky partners. No provision has been made for former employees of either the North West Company or the Hudson's Bay Company to retire in the Northwest and so, sooner or later, it becomes necessary for the man to either abandon his "wife" in the country she knows, or to take her to a land where she will always be a stranger. If there are children from the union, they must be separated from at least one of the parents. Most of the traders choose to abandon their women, although a few have taken their wives east,[84] usually to a farm where less adjustment for the wife is necessary and where the small savings of the couple can be made to go further. It is thought that no Indian wives have yet been taken to Orkney.

Harmon's "fur trade marriage" is quite different from the casual connections which are openly, even flagrantly, encouraged by the Indians (men and women alike) of most tribes. One reason for their lascivious behaviour is their belief that children borne by their women to Europeans are bolder warriors and better hunters than they are themselves.[85] Probably the most sought after women are the beguiling Crees whom Mackenzie has described as being the "most comely" he has seen in North America. "Their figure," he says, "is generally well proportioned, and the regularity of their features would be acknowledged by the more civilized people of Europe. Their complexion has less of that dark tinge which is common to those savages who have less cleanly habits."[86] But beauty is in the eye of the beholder and to the Chipewyan, the Cree woman would hold little appeal. Ask him what beauty is, and he will answer "a broad flat face, small eyes, high cheekbones, three or four broad black lines a-cross each cheek, a low forehead, a large broad chin, a clumsy hook-nose, a tawny hide, and breasts hanging down to the belt. Those beauties are greatly heightened, or at least rendered more valuable, when the possessor is capable of dressing all kinds of skins, converting them into the different parts of their clothing, and able to carry eight or ten stone in Summer, or haul a much greater weight in Winter."[87]

The easier and relatively civilized way of life at the trading posts has often allowed the more ambitious women to develop their talents far more than they ever could have done among their own people. For example, Icany, the wife of George Sutherland (a great drunkard and when in his cups a perfect mad-man),[88] not only can speak English "tolerably well" but is said to be able to read and write it too. She can also speak Cree and Ojibwa. For recreation, she enjoys playing cribbage.[89]

Unmarried white women will find a warm welcome in the new colony on the Red River, for the Hudson's Bay Company, at least, is now discouraging unions with the natives. One officer has recently gone as far as stating that "for the sake of the rising Generation" neither officers nor men should be allowed to marry "unless with the Daughters of Englishmen and then only with the previous Concurrance of the Superintendent."[90] Miles Macdonell, the leader of the new colony, who is now wintering near York Factory, finds it surprising that the company has never encouraged its men to bring their families to the Northwest. A few families could have been accommodated at each of the different factories, it seems to him, and the women could have found sufficient employment in making and mending clothes, washing, cooking, and so on. The men would have felt more attached to the country and the children growing up there would have been better suited to carry on the trade than those imported.[91]

Macdonell does not seem to realize that many of the Indian wives are already performing the tasks he mentions and that many of the half-breed children grow up in the trade and eventually find employment with one or other of the large companies. In fact, several of the half-breed children (and a few Indians as well) are now being educated to become "useful Members of the Community,"[92] at the new schools opened by the Hudson's Bay Company in 1807. They are the first schools in the Northwest and were founded in response to a request by parents (who have offered to contribute towards the expenses of establishing them), as well as a desire on the part of the company to train the children to "become useful to themselves and the Company."[93] At first the surgeons at the factories, "who could not have their times busily occupied," were to have undertaken the teaching for a "proper remuneration" in addition to their existing salaries.[94] This, apparently, had been considered only as a temporary expediency for soon the company was looking for proper teachers.[95] At least some of the posts requested clergymen as teachers, but none could be found who would leave Great Britain "on any terms" to promote the object which the company had in view. The first teachers were sent out in 1808 and were "to be placed in a state of respectability" at the factories.[96]

It had been intended to have a school at each of the principal factories for the children of the factory and of its inland dependencies.[97] But it was soon decided to remove the school at York Factory to Cumberland House because of its more central location, its superior food supply, and because that part of the country afforded "the means of occupying the Attention of the Inhabitants by some useful Pursuits."[98]

Instruction is given in reading, writing, arithmetic and "the fundamental Principles of Religion."[99] Servants' children of five years of age are admitted "without distinction" but they must be christened by the chief of the factory, or person acting in that capacity, at the time of admission. The children may remain in the school for seven years from the time they are admitted, or until they have completed their education and are fit to be employed in the service of the company, provided their father has not meanwhile quit the company for other employment. In the beginning, older children were also to be admitted to classes, but it was felt that early instruction would be a more successful means of implanting habits of industry, duty and utility.[100]

Before the establishment of the school, the only education available in the Northwest was that which the fathers could offer their children during odd moments of leisure. A few men, with better than average incomes, have been able to afford to send at least some of their children to Great Britain to be educated. But it has been the fate of most of the children of the Hudson's Bay Company employees to remain in ignorance in the Northwest. Many have been brought up by well-meaning fathers to be prepared for neither civilized life nor for life in their savage land, and when their fathers have left them behind to return to Europe, they have been unable to fend for themselves like the Indian children could.[101] An exception to this, were the children of Ferdinand Jacobs. Jacobs, for many years a chief at York Fort, realized that he could not bring all of his children to England when he retired there, and so had some of them brought up entirely among the natives, so that when he left the country they were fully capable of providing for themselves.

No ocean separates the men of the North West Company from Canada, the home, or adopted home, of most of them. The children of their fur trade marriages can, in theory at least, always make their way to Canada; they are not dependent on a passage in a company ship as are those of the Orcadians. But in practice most of the halfbreeds choose to remain in the familiar surroundings of the Northwest. The exceptions are the children of ambitious fathers, like Daniel Harmon and David Thompson, who have sent their children to Canada or the eastern United States to be educated.[102] The North West Company apparently has made no provision for educating the children of its employees within the country. According to Harmon, most of the children of the Northwest are blessed with "a retentive memory and apt to learn."[103] He mentions particularly a five-year-old boy to whom he taught English. The child, the son of a Gros Ventre mother and an English father, could already speak Cree and Ojibwa and could make himself understood in Assiniboine and French. Another child, the one-year-old daughter of a Hudson's Bay Company employee, was made to learn English by being isolated completely from Indians, including her own mother.[104]

The Hudson's Bay Company's schools are also to be available to the children of the chiefs of trading tribes friendly to the company. Should any of these chiefs "express a decided wish" to have any of their children educated at the factory, such children are to be admitted as a "means of cultivating the Friendship and Goodwill of the Parents and Children and thereby promote very essentially the objects the Committee [of the Hudson's Bay Co.] have in view."[105] Here is another attempt to tighten the bonds uniting the Indians and fur traders. Already, they are closely allied (albeit unofficially) through marriage, and through an ever-growing economic interdependence. Increasingly, the Indians have tended to gather about the trading posts as much as the demands of the hunt will allow. During the long periods when the chase makes it necessary for them to be absent, they frequently leave their aged and infirm behind at the posts.[106] Before the advent of the traders, such people could not have been looked after because of the necessity of almost constant travel, and would almost certainly have been doomed to perish when they could no longer keep up with the movements of the tribe.

Socially, the Indians and the traders have mixed unexpectedly well. But perhaps this is not so suprising when it is remembered that a man of David Thompson's experience, considers the Indian to be "fully equal to those of his class in Europe." Thompson believes that those writers who express contrary opinions do so because they always compare the Indians with themselves, and since they are usually men of education, the Indians lose by comparison.[107] The Indians' capacity for drunkenness is becoming legendary, but Harmon, at least, considers them no more offensive when in their cups than intoxicated French Canadians. In fact, he says that he would "rather have fifty drunken Indians in the fort, than five drunken Canadians."[108]

The Indians have often joined in the various "social occasions" of the posts – especially at the balls which are frequently given to mark special events such as the New Year, St. Andrew's Day, and Christmas,[110] as well as the gala affairs held during the annual meeting, at Grand Portage (and after 1804 at Fort William), of the North West Company men from the Northwest with those from Montreal. These famous balls take place in the dining hall of the fort. The gentlemen dress for the occasion. Music is provided by any instrumentalists who happen to be present. This has led to some oddly composed orchestras like the one in 1800 which consisted of a bagpipe, violin, flute and fife. On this occasion, as was usual, a number of native women attended. Harmon, who was attending his first Northwest Ball, was surprised to find that they could not only behave themselves, but that they "danced not amiss."[111]

Five years later, a more experienced Harmon attended a dance at the North West Company's Fort Assiniboine. As was common when relations were good, the men from competing trading posts were also invited. The next day, Harmon described the event in his journal: "Last evening Mr. Chaboillez invited the People of the other two Forts to a Dance and we had a real North West Ball, for when three fourths of the People were so much intoxicated as not to be able to walk straight, the other fourth put an end to the Ball or rather Bawl! And this morning we were invited to breakfast at the Hudson's Bay House with a Mr. McKay and in the evening to a Ball, which however ended in a more decent manner than the one we had the preceding evening at our House – not that all were sober, but we had no fighting.[112]

Sunday is little observed in the Northwest. It is true that at the Hudson's Bay Company's factories, it is customary for a sermon to be read to the men,[113] and that at the North West Company's posts a flag is flown on that day[114] and sometimes, at least, the men change their clothes,[115] but otherwise, business is much as usual, for the Indians come to trade regardless of the day and it is frequently necessary to travel about the country on the Sabbath. Indeed, every phase of life in the Northwest is dominated by the fur trade. At the present time it is the only enterprise in the country and all of the activities of every white man, as well as those of most of the Indians, are directly or indirectly concerned with it.

3

The Fur Trade

The gentle nature of the English countryside, with its proportions so nicely adjusted to the needs of man, makes it exceedingly difficult for the Englishman to form a just idea of the vast spaces of the Northwest, where all appears to have been designed for a much larger race of beings. The highest peaks of Scotland are but hills against the western mountains, the English plains but garden plots to the boundless prairies, and even the mighty Thames but a bubbling brook alongside the Peace, the Mackenzie, or the Saskatchewan. Indeed, so vast are the dimensions of the Northwest that one writer has observed that were the whole of the British Isles placed into Hudson Bay there would still remain ample room for its seas.

Bearing in mind the vastness of the Northwest, it is suggested that the reader turn again to Arrowsmith's map of North America. From the positioning of the heights of land, it will be seen that the northern part of the continent resembles an enormous saucer with Hudson Bay occupying its shallow bottom. At only one place, Hudson Strait, is it low enough to allow access to the sea. Elsewhere, its gentle slopes are lined with rivers carrying their waters down to the bay. It was two Frenchmen, Radisson and Groseilliers, who first saw in this grand design possibilities for commercial enterprise. They reasoned that if the products of European manufacturers were shipped into the bay each year, they could be exchanged for valuable furs brought down the rivers by natives who were already demanding European goods. Radisson and Groseilliers were met with indifference when they approached their own government with their plan, and so they came to Great Britain and petitioned His Majesty King Charles ii. British enterprise was quick to recognize the commercial advantages which would accrue to the Kingdom from such a plan and soon a body was formed called "The Governor and Company of Adventurers of England Trading into Hudson's Bay" on which His Majesty, in 1670, graciously bestowed a charter which granted the company exclusive right to trade through the bay. Since then, this privilege has been challenged many times both at home and abroad: there was the Parliamentary enquiry of 1749: there have been several armed attacks by the French (the latest in 1782)[1]: and there was even an invasion of the bay by British traders from Canada as recently as 1803.[2]

Shortly after its establishment, the Hudson's Bay Company planted trading posts at the mouths of the principal rivers draining into the bay, the Churchill, Nelson, Hayes and Severn being the most important of those in the Northwest (see map 6). From time to time, men were sent inland with a selection of trade goods to prime the flow of furs. Guns, kettles, knives and other tools were demonstrated to the Indians to show them how their harsh living conditions might be eased. The Indians were quick to perceive the advantages offered by the trade and soon large quantities of furs were being taken each year from the bay. At first, most of the furs came from the tribes living near the bay, but before long many of the natives living near the trading posts found it more profitable to become what is known in the trade as "middlemen." That is, they ceased to be hunters and trappers but became carriers for the more remote tribes who in turn often traded with still more distant tribes. In this way, goods of European manufacture quickly penetrated into the most distant corners of the Northwest. Indeed, many an Indian has been familiar with the white man's goods long before he has ever laid eyes upon a European. For instance, Hearne found several long beads of European design among the effects of some Eskimos massacred by his Indian companions near the mouth of the Coppermine River. These are thought to have been first traded by the Danes at Davis Strait[3] and then to have made their way from Eskimo to Eskimo across the unknown wastes of the Barren Grounds and the Land of Little Sticks to reach the Coppermine. Here, as elsewhere in the Northwest, it was found that a demand for European goods existed among the Indians before the trader had actually visited them.

The value of the goods tended to increase with distance from the trading posts. In fact, the price of some goods increased by tenfold in passing through the hands of the Indian middlemen who carried them into the Northwest. To some remote tribes this seemed unreasonable and so they attempted to avoid the middleman by making the long and dangerous journey to the bay themselves.[4] In this, they were often frustrated by the middlemen who blocked their way and frequently robbed them in order to protect their highly profitable position in the trade, as well as to prevent their inland neighbours from obtaining arms at the posts and thus becoming their equals in any future battles.

There can be no doubt that the fur trade quickly disrupted the lives of the natives and was responsible for unleashing a great deal of dissension among them; but for the English company it brought handsome profits for many years. However, its fortunes began to change when the French from the St. Lawrence started pushing ever further into the Northwest by way of the southern waterway. In spite of the distances they were forced to travel, the French were able to cut heavily into the Hudson's Bay Company trade by taking their goods directly to the Indian trappers and middlemen and thus saving them the long perilous journey down to the bay. With the British conquest of Canada, the company had hoped for relief, but soon the French Canadians were back again, this time with British leaders and with British trade goods, and before long competition was even more severe than it had ever been before. In fact, so severe did it become that the Hudson's Bay Company was forced to abandon its century-old practice of remaining close to the bay and, in 1774, established its first interior post, Cumberland House, at Pine Island [Cumberland] Lake in the Saskatchewan country. The Canadians reacted to this initiative by building a house of their own beside the English. This event marked the beginning of face-to-face competition between the traders from the river and the traders from the bay, competition which by now has reached into even the most distant parts of the Northwest. Over the years as competition increased, rivalry between posts intensified until a state of trade has been reached that would shock an Englishman raised in the refinement of the commercial enterprises of his own country. The lands closer to the river and to the bay were rapidly denuded of their furs, forcing the traders to move ever further into the Northwest until today the trade has been extended even to the Arctic circle on the Mackenzie River and to the mouth of the Columbia on the Pacific Ocean. This rapid expansion over such incredible distances has been made possible by the remarkable river system which connects the various countries of the Northwest. But as the distances have increased, so too have the costs of transportation,

making necessary much greater amounts of capital investment on the
part of the trader. A large enterprise like the Hudson's Bay Company
has been able to meet these costs but the smaller traders from the St.
Lawrence have found it necessary either to retire from the trade or to
take part in the series of agreements or mergers which led eventually to
the emergence of a single monopoly in 1804, the North West Company.
Since then, each entrance to the Northwest has been dominated by a
single monopoly – the St. Lawrence-Great Lakes route by the Northwest
Company and the Hudson Bay route by the Hudson's Bay Company.

The Hudson Bay route is shorter, easier, and more economic than
the St. Lawrence route.[5] Since both companies obtain the bulk of their
trade goods in England and sell most of their furs in the same markets,
possession of the better route by the Hudson's Bay Company has given
it an enormous advantage over its rival. Sir Alexander Mackenzie recognized the economic advantages of the bay route at least as early as 1794,[6]
and in recent years has tried on several occasions to have it opened to
the traders from Canada. In 1801, he sought popular support by stating
his case in the last few pages of his journals which were published in that
year. He advocated a "junction" between the Canadian traders and the
Hudson's Bay Company which would enable the Canadians to enjoy
"the privilege of the Company's charter."[7] It will be noticed that Mackenzie refers to the "Canadian traders" rather than to the North West
Company. This is because, in 1801, the succession of mergers which had
led to the final emergence of a single monopoly on the St. Lawrence
had not yet been completed. Two factions still continued to operate. The
larger was the North West Company but it had a powerful rival in a
smaller company headed by Mackenzie himself, which was known vari-
ously as the XY Company, the New North West Company, and finally,
as Sir Alexander Mackenzie and Company. During the period between
1801 and late 1804, before the North West Company absorbed its smaller
rival, both companies had made separate attempts to get transit rights
through the bay. Most ambitious of these was the XY Company's unsuccessful bid for control of the Hudson's Bay Company by attempting to
buy a majority of its stock. While this was going on, the North West
Company made a double approach to the English company. On the one
hand, it attempted to reach an amicable agreement with the company,
while at the same time it sent a ship into the bay to establish trading
posts in defiance of the Hudson's Bay Company's charter.[8] Negotiations
between the Hudson's Bay Company and the North West Company

continued until 1806, when they were broken off without an agreement having been reached. Meanwhile, the Canadian posts on Hudson Bay had not done well because the Indians had remained loyal to the old company and so, in 1807, the posts were quietly withdrawn. The Canadians, however, have not become discouraged by their setbacks and still look forward to the time when they will be able to trade through the bay. Perhaps the spirit of optimism which now pervades the North West Company was best expressed in the agreement by which it absorbed the XY Company in 1804, for a clause was included which provides for the purchase of either the whole of the Hudson's Bay Company rights or only for the right of transit through the bay and its territories. In fact as recently as last year, the North West Company did make an unsuccessful attempt to buy controlling shares in the Hudson's Bay Company.[9] At the same time, it approached the English company with a plan for partitioning the Northwest between the two companies.[10] Nothing has come of this proposal to date, although it is thought that correspondence concerning the proposed demarcation is still being exchanged.[11]

During recent years the Hudson's Bay Company's portion of the trade has greatly decreased. By 1810-11 (see map 7), it was reduced to a mere fraction of that of the Canadian company.[12] Moreover, it was recently forced to withdraw some of its more distant posts. Nevertheless, it is doubtful that it will agree to the Canadian proposal for it possesses the self-confidence of an old company which has come through many storms in the past and it undoubtedly feels that it can survive its present difficulties as well. And perhaps the company is at least partly justified in its optimism for, at last, it is taking steps to improve its competitive position in the trade. The first of these steps is of special interest to the intending settler, since it concerns the establishment of the colony under Lord Selkirk in the Red River country. It is hoped that the promise of land in the colony will induce many more men to go into the company's service. In addition, the areas for procuring men are being extended to include Canada and the Highlands of Scotland. That is, to include the areas from which its rival draws most of its men. In the years to come, the colony itself will also be a source of servants for the company. Moreover, the colony will supply provisions for conducting the trade and greatly reduce the amount of expensive European victuals used in the Northwest.

The company also hopes to improve its position by replacing its old rigid salary scale with a new system of payment based on the number of furs traded.[13] This change is undoubtedly inspired by a somewhat similar system used by the North West Company to induce its servants to greater efforts. However, there is some fear that the new emphasis on personal initiative may also have an adverse effect on the company's affairs. Employees will be subject to the temptation of competing with one another, rather than co-operating for the common good of the company. This has already been a problem in the past, particularly between the posts under the command of York and those under Churchhill.[14] To reduce this temptation in the future, the whole of the Hudson's Bay territories is to be divided into two great districts for administrative purposes (see map 8). One, to be known as the Northern Department, is to comprise all of the lands in the Northwest; the other, the Southern Department, is to include the remainder of the company's territories in British North America. Each is to be headed by a single superintendent with a great deal of local autonomy, who is to see that no intra-company rivalry develops.[15] The considerable authority given to the superintendents also demonstrates the company's desire to overcome the rigidity of organization which has always characterized its operations. All directions for pursuing the trade have had to come from the company's headquarters in London. These have almost invariably been drawn up by men with no local knowledge of conditions in the Northwest. Before any but the most insignificant changes could be made, approval had to be obtained in London. This meant that nearly two years passed from the time a proposal was made until a decision on it could reach the bay. In recent years, this direction-from-afar proved to be increasingly unsatisfactory in enabling the company to meet the challenges of its opponents, and in coping with the rapid geographical shifts in the patterns of trade. Now, with all of these changes, the company hopes that before long it will be in a position to extend its activities beyond its chartered limits into the Athabasca country and across the Rockies into New Caledonia. Athabasca will be its first objective, for not only is it closer to Hudson Bay than New Caledonia but it is accessible from both York Factory and Churchill Factory.

The Hudson's Bay Company's determination to enter the Athabasca country will almost certainly lead to a further deterioration in its already strained relations with the North West Company. Open clashes may well result which, the intending settler is warned, could involve him in a great deal of inconvenience. Some idea of the recent decline in cordiality between the servants of the two companies may be gained from Peter Fidler's treatment at Ft. Ile-à-la-Crosse, the chief staging post along the route to the Athabasca country. Only two decades ago when he was on an exploratory expedition with Philip Turnor, he wintered at Lake Ile-à-la-Crosse where he was treated "very kindly" by the Canadians.[16] Yet during this past summer he was dealt with so harshly there that he was forced to abandon his company's post which was burned to the ground immediately following his departure.[17]

Fierce competition has been largely responsible for the deterioration in relations throughout the Northwest. Perhaps the greatest strains occurred in the early years of the century when the xy Company entered the trade. In many places, three posts only a few yards apart could be seen competing for the furs and provisions of the natives. Nevertheless, as recently as 1807, Harmon could write at Cumberland that "the greater part of the Northwest and Hudson Bay people, live on amicable terms; and when one can with propriety render service to the other, it is done with cheerfulness."[18] But it should be noted that most of Harmon's experience in the Northwest has been at posts on, or near, the open plains where the Indians have tended to be difficult and often dangerous to deal with. Under these circumstances, the whites have inclined to band together in friendship and mutual defence. In the forested areas, where the natives are usually less of a threat, relations between white factions have tended to be less cordial. Oddly enough, the very competition which has divided the whites has also indirectly brought them together. For fierce competition has tended to debauch the natives and make them unruly, which in turn has forced the whites together for protection. Mention of personal friendships are quite frequent in the journals and diaries of the traders. So, too, are their animosities. Unfortunately the most serious disputes between the traders seem to take their origins in mere trifles.[19]

The settler would be well advised to exercise considerable caution in his intercourse with both the traders and Indians lest he should become involved in their disputes. Perhaps he should follow the lead of the small number of "free traders" who still manage to eke out a living in the Northwest. For them, good relations with the natives as well as with one or both companies is a matter of absolute necessity. Otherwise they would have great difficulty in procuring furs and provisions from the Indians, and in exchanging their furs at the trading posts for the small necessities which they require. Most of the free traders are former servants of the North West Company who have chosen to remain in the west rather than return to the ways of civilization to which many of

them have become strangers.[20] Of course their trade is mostly with their
former employers although the Hudson's Bay Company has not been
insensitive to the advantages of favouring them with some encouragement. In fact, two years ago the London Committee of the company, seeing the potential value of this commerce, gave instructions to its servants
to entertain the connection with the free Canadians "to the utmost of
your power."[21] Perhaps it would not be out of place to mention that
the free traders are not without guile. For example, they have been
known to examine carefully the bales of furs being taken from the
Northwest to discover their origins and thereby the best places for trade.
However, in recent years, the North West Company, at least, has frustrated their attempts by having its agents at Grand Portage (and later
at Ft. William) annually give a sealed paper containing a code letter or
letters to be put on the furs of each department, thus making it impossible to tell where the bales come from without a key.[22]

The free trader is no more "free" than the future settler will be free.
Like the trader, he will find it necessary to have intercourse with one
or other or both of the companies. And should he have ambitions of
entering the trade himself, he should be cautioned that today this can
be done only with the greatest amount of difficulty. The day when a
Canadian with a few packs of goods on credit could enter the Northwest to winter among the Indians and leave in the spring with a small
fortune is past. So is the time when a handful of Englishmen could
establish themselves at the mouth of a great river on Hudson Bay and
wait for the natives to come down in the spring to trade the products
of their winter's hunt. Today, the fur trade has become a great enterprise
and only a man of considerable means should consider entering it – at
least as an entrepreneur. And even he should proceed with caution for
even assuming he succeeds in gaining access to the fur markets (and is
not discouraged by today's low prices), and has sufficient capital to meet
the huge expeditures now necessary to get established, a shortage of
skilled labour would almost certainly frustrate his efforts. For unlike
1798, when the xy Company was formed, no sizable pool[23] of men now
exists (outside the two monopolies) who are skilled in handling canoes
and boats, or who know the languages, customs and ceremonies of the
Indians, and the thousand and one other things so necessary in success-
fully conducting this unique enterprise.

How then, it might be asked, do the traders learn their trade? The
North West Company men are trained by being sent among the Indians

when they are still young enough to "acquire a perfect knowledge of their languages and habits." Not until then are they entrusted with carrying on the business of the company.[24] The Hudson's Bay Company also tries to recruit men young enough to learn the ways of the natives. For example, David Thompson was hired less than a month after his fourteenth birthday, and was sent on his first journey alone with the Indians (from Churchill to York on foot) when he was only 15 years old.[25] During the 26 years since then, he has spent many months at a time with only the Indians for companions and in many ways has become one of them. "I had always admired," he once said, "the tact of the Indian in being able to guide himself through the darkest pine forests to exactly the place he intended to go, his keen, constant attention on every thing; the removal of the smallest stone, the bent or broken twig; a slight mark on the ground all spoke plain language to him. I was anxious to acquire this knowledge, and often being in company with them sometimes for several months, I paid attention to what they pointed out to me, and became almost equal to some of them; which became of great use to me."[26] Thompson's fellow surveyor and employee of the Hudson's Bay Company, Peter Fidler, was 22 when he left to winter among the Chipewyans in 1792. He did not return to his base until the following April having been "absent from all European intercourse and alone with the Jepewyans ever since the 4th September last having acquired a sufficiency of their Language to transact any business with them. Upon the whole this has been rather an agreeable winter than otherwise ... "[27]

At first glance, it may seem singular that an Englishman would find living among the Indians an enjoyable experience. Nevertheless, his sentiments are shared by a great many of the traders who seem to delight in wintering among the natives because it removes them "from under the Eye of a Master" and the routine and discipline of civilized life at the trading post. By living with the Indians, they expect to have nothing to do. Indeed, they frequently seem unwilling to help their hosts in any way at all. This attitude was believed by the late Matthew Cocking, of the Hudson's Bay Company, to be the chief reason why their men did not get on well with the natives.[28] Peter Fidler, on the other hand, believes just as strongly that it is impolitic to help out in any way. "It is an invariable custom with all Indians ... " he says, "that the more an European does of work with them the worse he is respected by them and gets generally the worst victuals and frequently but little of it when he complys to do everything they bid him whereas if he stiffly refuses from the first that he is with them they will be very kind to him and will give him a larger allowance of provisions than had he listened to every request of theirs."[29]

The promise of regular allowances of provisions for their men has provided the companies' main incentive for sending men to winter among the natives, particularly in times of scarcity at the trading posts. To pay for their victuals, an assortment of trading goods is usually sent along with the winterers. Traders are also frequently sent out with Indians who have been outfitted by their company in the fall to ensure that they do not forget their commitment to trade with that company when spring comes. On other occasions, men have been dispatched merely to establish good relations with the natives.

The goodwill of the natives is, of course, absolutely necessary not only to enable the traders to obtain their furs, but in order for them to preserve their very lives while living among them, hopelessly outnumbered and completely at their mercy. It is true that many of the posts are protected by palisades with bastions and mounted guards, but these are designed largely to intimidate the Indians and are effective only against the short impetuous attacks which are characteristic of the natives. In any long sieges, the posts would almost certainly be taken. But long sieges are highly unlikely, since they would allow the Indians time to come to their senses and to reflect on how dependent they have become upon the white man for his goods, and to decide that it would be imprudent to destroy their source. It is melancholy to reflect that, with few exceptions, this desire for Europeans goods on the part of the Indians, and the European's desire for the Indians' furs, forms the only basis of "friendship" between the traders and the savages of the Northwest.[30]

Presents as well as credits are frequently advanced to strengthen the traders' hold on the more important and reliable of the natives. For instance, in 1807, the Hudson's Bay Company sent out badges "to be presented to the Chief Indian Officers according to their Rank," gilt ones for chiefs and silver for inferior officers.[31] In the same spirit the children of the chief Indians are to be admitted to the schools recently organized by the Hudson's Bay Company for the halfbreed children of its employees.[32] Far more important in bringing together the two peoples, however, are the ties of marriage between the traders and their native wives, especially those with the daughters of chiefs or other important Indians. Moreover, it is now the practice of both companies to support many aged and infirm Indians at their posts. Usually these are the dependents of Indians who have gone off to hunt, and of the wives of traders.

Yet it must be stressed that although the marriages, the gifts, the caring of the sick, and other overtures of friendship have tended to some extent to bring the two peoples together, the fact remains that essentially the relationship which exists between them is based almost solely upon need. Consequently, alliances are strongest in the forested areas where mutual need is greatest and weakest on the plains where it is least. One need only reflect for a moment upon the primitive life of the Indian forest dweller to know how greatly eased has been his harsh life with the acquisition of steel axes for cutting wood for fuel, copper kettles for cooking meat, or guns for shooting the elusive moose. His brother on the open plains, however, has far less use for axes. His fuel usually consists of buffalo dung or small trees from along the banks of rivers. A kettle would be useful though not vital since meat is often dried in the sun, pounded into a powder and mixed with melted fat to make "pemmican" which is eaten uncooked. Guns, too, are less useful, for the plains tribes have devised many ingenious methods of killing without guns the innumerable buffalo which inhabit their lands. The most common is to drive them into pounds where they can easily and safely be slaughtered with spears, and bows and arrows. Bows and arrows are also easier to handle on horseback than are cumbersome guns. Besides, should an animal be only wounded by the first shot, there might not be enough time to reload before it turns on its attacker. Moreover, the noise of the guns often frightens the buffalo and sometimes stampedes them, greatly endangering the life of the hunter. In contrast, the Indians of the forest hunt on foot. Their chief object is the wary moose, a difficult animal to approach closely enough to kill with a bow and arrow. Since its habits are usually solitary, there is little danger of frightening away other moose in shooting at one of them. Other animals of the forest also tend to live scattered during much of the year, which means that the tribes which depend upon them must also spread themselves thinly and widely. This differs sharply with the habits of the plains peoples who are enabled, by the vast herds of buffalo, to live in relatively large groups. This has given them a greater sense of community than their forest neighbours, and has also made them potentially a greater threat to the safety of the fur traders. And the fact that they are less dependent upon the traders has tended to make the plains Indians more reckless in their relations with them. The intending settler should therefore take notice that much of Lord Selkirk's tract is occupied by open plains and that frequent disputes between the Indians and traders could well disrupt the harmony of the proposed colony.

It might be instructive to observe for a moment the changing connection with the two Indian peoples. During the early years of the trade, the Europeans were far more dependent upon the forest tribes who produced furs and some provisions, than they were upon the plains Indians who produced mostly provisions and a few inferior furs. However, as the trade extended further and further into the Northwest, the traders became increasingly dependent upon the plains tribes for provisions to supply the ever-lengthening canoe routes. Meanwhile, the demand for wolves and other inferior furs produced by these tribes fell off sharply as a consequence of the wars with France and the closing of the continental fur markets. Thus the traders have become less dependent upon the plains for furs but increasingly so for food. So reliant, in fact, have they become upon the plains Indians for provisions that without them the North West Company, at least, would have to abandon the most lucrative part of its trade.[33] Yet if the success of much of the trade is now contingent upon provisions from the plains tribes, it cannot be said that these tribes have developed a similar dependence upon the whites. Indeed, most of their trade is in luxuries which they could easily do without, such as rum, tobacco, and ornaments. On the other hand, trade with the forest tribes, in the beginning at least, was mostly in necessities. But instead of being satisfied with the few goods which could have made their lives easier, most of these Indians used the new leisure these articles gave them to hunt for more furs, often merely to provide the means of getting still more furs. Soon, with their acquisitive instincts discovered and developed, they began ruthlessly ransacking their fur lands. As the number of animals was reduced, they became increasingly difficult to discover and kill, making it still more necessary to obtain the efficient tools of their destruction. And so it has gone on. The demand for European goods among the forest tribes has been increasing even as the number of animals has been diminishing. This has also been true on the plains, but to a far lesser extent: the buffalo population has not decreased significantly and, apart from luxuries, there does not seem to be the same demand for material goods. It has been said that the collecting of horses, often through theft, has largely satisfied the acquisitive instincts of these tribes. Meanwhile, in the forested regions, the old skills of hunting are being lost as the scramble for furs continues. Guns have now almost completely replaced the bow and arrow, and steel traps are taking the place of the native kinds. The Crees, who have had the longest connection with the whites, now admit that they could no longer live without guns and marvel at how their ancestors survived with only bows and arrows since the beaver was wiser, and the bear stronger, than they.[34] The plains Indians, on the other hand, have largely retained their traditional methods of hunting through constant use.

Because of its stationary habits, the beaver has been especially vulnerable to the introduction of European inventions, particularly the steel trap. In many of the more accessible areas it was virtually extirpated by the closing years of the eighteenth century. David Thompson has vividly described how the Ojibwa and other tribes using steel traps became very prosperous during the 1790s, living for a time in a type of fool's paradise. "For several years" he said, "all these Indians were rich, the Women and Children, as well as the Men were covered with silver brooches, Ear Rings, Wampum, Beads and other trinkets. Their mantles were of fine scarlet cloth, and all was finery and dress. The Canoes of the Fur Traders were loaded with packs of Beaver, the abundance of the article lowered the London prices. Every intelligent Man saw the poverty that would follow the destruction of the Beaver, but there were no Chiefs to control it; all was perfect liberty and equality. Four years afterwards (1797) almost the whole of these extensive countries were denuded of Beaver, the Natives became poor, and with difficulty procured the first necessaries of life, and in this state they remain, and probably for ever."[35]

The Ojibwa are a forest people and, like other forest tribes, they have not only become dependent upon the white man for the necessities of life, but addicted to his luxuries as well. The fact that the women and children shared in the prosperity is probably a reflection of the wives' influence in the background, for although they are in every respect servile to their husbands, they nevertheless exercise considerable control over them.[36] In any case, the women's partaking in the rewards of the trade was only just, since they have always played an essential role in it by preparing all the skins and furs before they leave the Northwest, so that they will not spoil on their long journeys to the markets of the world.

It is regrettable in a country renowned for its manufactures that many of the trading goods it sends to the Northwest are not of good quality. It was only a few months ago that William Guthrie candidly described their low standard in his *System of Modern Geography*. "The commodities we [Great Britain] exchange with the Indians for their skins and furs, are all manufactured in Britain; and as the Indians are not very nice in their choice, those things are sent of which we have great plenty, and which, in the mercantile phrase, are drugs with us. Though the workmanship too happens to be in many respects so deficient, that no civilized people would take it off our hands, it may be admired among the Indians ... "[37] In the early days of the trade (when the northern tribes still cut up their guns to make knives and chisels)[38] it is true that the Indians were "not very nice in their choice" of trade goods. But since then most tribes have had sufficient experience to know what they want. This is well illustrated by the tenor of the speeches made to the traders by the leaders of the bands of Indians when they come to the factories to trade. The following could serve as a model: "You told me last year to bring many Indians to trade, which I promised to do; you see I have not lied; here are a great many young come with me; use them kindly, I say; let them trade good goods; let them trade good goods, I say! We lived hard last winter and hungry, the powder being short measure and bad; being short measure and bad, I say! Tell your servants to fill the measure, and not to put their thumbs within the brim; take pity on us, take pity on us, I say! We paddle a long way to see you; we love the English. Let us trade good black tobacco, moist and hard twisted; let us see it before it is opened. Take pity on us; take pity on us, I say! The guns are bad, let us trade light guns, small in the hand, and well shaped, with locks that will not freeze in the winter, and red gun cases. Let the young men have more than measure of tobacco; cheap kettles, thick, and high. Give us good measure of cloth; let us see the old measure; do you mind me? The young men loves you, by coming so far to see you; take pity, take pity, I say; and give them good goods; they like to dress and be fine. Do you understand me?

As soon as the Captain has finished his speech, he with his followers, proceed to look at the guns and tobacco; the former they examine with the most minute attention. When this is over they trade their furs promiscuously ... "[39]

There have been many complaints about the poor quality of the guns sent out which have frequently burst when fired because the barrels were too thin.[40] The thin barrels were probably intended for convenience since a light weapon would be relatively easy to carry over long distances,[41] although false economy and even fraud on the part of the manufacturer could well have been factors. Fraud has also been suspected in other goods offered to the Indians – not to mention the supplies sent out for the use of the traders, themselves.[42] Hatchets supplied to Cumberland, for example, were so poor that during the winter of 1780 the men had to "labour hard to keep the house in firing."[43] The main trouble with these and other edge tools has been that the intense cold makes them brittle. After receiving many complaints, the Governor and Committee recently gave instructions that when this happens, the tools "may be softened by Fire and tempered so as to endure any degree of cold whatever," and added that the blacksmith and armourer at the factories could "easily remedy this defect when it occurs."[44]

The faulty tools, inferior trade goods and shortages of supplies are at least partly the result of the war in Europe. In 1809, to give but one example, very little merchandise was sent to the bay as a direct result of the war. Fortunately, there had been a considerable supply on hand from previous years.[45] Fur sales, as already intimated, have also been adversely affected by the war and the blockade. Indeed, there is at present little, if any, demand for several types of furs. Unhappily, none of these and the other effects of the war can be profitably explained to the Indians who have never understood why the white people possess such an insatiable desire for furs, let alone why they have now become so inconsistent in their demands for them.

Perhaps it would not be amiss to point out to those intending to venture into the Northwest that it is the custom of the country to cloak commercial transactions in ceremony and to disguise them as exchanges of gifts. To regularize these exchanges, the whites early adopted the "beaver" as the basic unit of exchange. All other furs are given a value in relation to it.[46] Thus, depending on its current price in the London market, a given fur might be worth three beavers or it might be worth only a half beaver. Until last year, when sterling was adopted, the Hudson's Bay Company had also kept its books in "made beaver," as the unit is commonly expressed. However, "made beaver" continues to be used when trading with the Indians "because they don't understand anything of money."[47] They do, nevertheless, have a clear idea of commercial competition and can frequently be seen carrying their furs from post to post looking for the best exchange. They are hard bargainers, too – not only with the whites but among themselves as well. As already pointed out, tribes well placed geographically have often succeeded in becoming "middlemen" and have conducted a profitable trade between the trading posts and the more distant tribes. Their profits have ranged up to one thousand per cent.[48] However, in some cases at least, this really has not been exorbitant since the "carriers," as the middlemen are called, often run the risk of death by starvation, or at the hands of their enemies, in carrying the goods and furs between the trading post and the distant lands of their customers.[49] Thus, the Indians who arrive at the posts are not necessarily the same Indians who trapped the furs which they carry or, indeed, even of the same tribe. Nor is the Indian in charge of the group necessarily their leader when in their homeland. Far more likely, he is a nonentity who has succeeded in gathering together his companions on the way down to the post. The more he can gather around himself, the greater is his prestige, and hence his bargaining power at the factory. While there, it is his disagreeable duty not only to speak for his companions, but to beg for their friends and relations, and even for those whom they fear.[50] The arrival of one of the most famous leaders in the Northwest, "Captain" Matonabbee, at Fort Prince of Wales in 1776 has been astutely described by Samuel Hearne who was then in charge of the fort: "When the usual ceremonies had passed, I dressed him out as a Captain of the first rank, and also clothed his six wives from top to toe: after which that is to say, during his stay at the Factory, which was ten days, he begged seven lieutenants' coats, fifteen common coats, eighteen hats, eighteen shirts, eight guns, one hundred and forty pounds weight of gunpowder, with shot, ball, and flints in proportion; together with many hatchets, ice chissels, files, bayonets, knives, and a great quantity of tobacco, cloth, blankets, combs, looking-glasses, stockings, handkerchiefs, etc., besides numberless small articles, such as awls, needles, paint, steels, etc., in all to the amount of upwards of seven hundred beaver in the way of trade, to give away among his followers. This was exclusive of his own present, which consisted of a variety of goods to the value of four hundred beaver more. But the most extraordinary of his demands was twelve pounds of powder, twenty-eight pounds of shot and ball, four pounds of tobacco, some articles of clothing, and several pieces of iron-work, etc., to give two men who had hauled his tent and other lumber the preceding Winter. This demand was so very unreasonable, that I made some scruple, or at least hesitated to comply with it, hinting that he was the person who ought to satisfy those men for their services; but I was soon answered, that he did not expect to have been *denied such a trifle as that was*; and for the future he would carry his goods where he could get his own price for them. On my asking him where that was? he replied, in a very insolent tone, "To the Canadian Traders."[51]

Dissatisfied bands have been known to transfer their trade to competing posts without the slightest compunction. However, dissatisfaction has not always been the only reason. Often they have done so to get out of paying for goods which had been advanced to them on credit. In fact, they have not been above travelling to another post of the same company to escape from their debts, and some have been even bold enough to disguise themselves and change their names, and appear at the same post where they were owing. With a change of governor at Churchill (and probably elsewhere as well) all outstanding debts have been lost, for the Indians have always declared before the new governor (and they bring plenty of witnesses to support them) that their debts had been paid long before and that it had been forgotten to remove their names from the book.

During their stay at the posts, the Indians have to be watched constantly to prevent them from stealing – particularly things made from metal which can be manufactured into useful objects. Iron hoops, small bolts, spikes and carpenter's tools are all coveted by them – either for their own personal use or for sale to other Indians who did not make the journey to the posts to trade.[52] When houses are left unoccupied they are, of course, completely open to the depredations of the natives. But on at least one occasion, the Indians failed to loot an empty cabin although many had passed near it. It belonged to the Canadians who had left some 900 pounds of goods in it, unguarded except by a wooden image about the size of a small child, placed over the house on a red painted pole. Not a single Indian dared go near the place for fear that the "Een coz zy," as they called the image, should tell the Canadians.[53]

When a band of Indians approaches a fort to trade, it is customary for them to send forward a few young men to announce their arrival and to procure a few small gifts – such as tobacco, paint, and powder – in accordance with a long-standing practice introduced by the Canadian traders.[54] When they have come to within a few yards of the gate, the Indians salute the traders with several discharges of their guns. This is answered by hoisting a flag and firing a few guns. On entering the house, the Indians are disarmed, treated to a few drams and a bit of tobacco. The pipe is then passed for some time and the Indians relate their news with great deliberation and ceremony, relaxing from their usual taciturnity in proportion to the amount of rum they have drunk until at length their voices are drowned in a general clamour. After the lodges have been put up by the women, a gift of rum is made to the Indians; its size depending upon the amount of competition in the area and upon the importance of the leaders and of the nations concerned. Upon its receipt, earnest drinking commences. When it at last subsides, trading begins.[55]

The "gift" of rum during the trading ceremony is made in cynical spirit for the traders know well that Indians under the influence of alcohol are easier to bargain with for their furs and provisions than are sober ones.[56] The custom of "giving" the rum to the natives has its origins far back in the days of the French regime when the traders were forbidden by their church, under threat of excommunication, to sell liquor to the Indians. Only a painful penance could restore the offender to the suspended rites of the sacrament.[57] It has also been said that the offence carried the penalty of being sent to the galleys as well. In any case, the law which could have been so beneficial to the natives soon had the opposite effect when the traders decided to "give" rather than "sell" the liquor to them.[58] With the Indians, the taste for rum seems to be an acquired one, for on first encounter they will not buy it, although they are usually quite happy to receive it as a gift. But soon the taste is acquired and then they are in the hands of the traders. "The love of Rum," says Duncan McGillivray, of the North West Company "is their first inducement to industry; they undergo every hardship and fatigue to produce a Skinfull of this delicious beverage, and when a Nation becomes addicted to drinking, it affords a strong presumption that they will soon become excellent hunters."[59] Although liquor is still being given away in 1811, it has been traded as well for many years. In fact, the Hudson's Bay Company (not being greatly concerned with the possibility of excommunication) has always sold it. In justice, however, it must be pointed out that during the quiet years before competition became fierce, liquor had been used sparingly. "To prevent the Natives from hurting themselves with brandy and strong water," wrote Andrew Graham, who had traded many years on the bay before retiring in 1775, "we at none of the settlements exchange that commodity for any furs but the following viz. Martins, Cats, Foxes coloured, Wolves and Bears; this had been the case from the time the Company had the charter, and wisely done. If the Natives were to receive brandy for whatever kind of furs they bring down, they would trade little or nothing else; which would end in their ruin and the Company's affairs."[60] Graham's retirement coincided with the establishment of the Company's first inland post. From then on, it has been meeting its opponents face to face, and any scruples it may have had about selling liquor to the Indians have largely disappeared in the resulting scramble for furs and provisions.

The harmful effects of liquor on the natives have become well known in England during the past few years through the attention drawn to the subject by Mr. Wilberforce in his attempts to curtail its use in the Northwest by Act of Parliament.[61] Of course, a far greater awareness exists in the Northwest itself. Every trader knows that most of the quarrels between the natives and the whites, and among the natives themselves, are precipitated by alcohol;[62] but he also knows that as long as competition continues to persist he, and all his fellow traders, will be powerless to stop the traffic, even should he be of a mind to do so, for in some areas the Indians will not trade furs for anything else.[63] Moreover, the trader knows that liquor can be very useful to get the natives to do many things they are not otherwise inclined to do. For example, the Hudson's Bay Company has frequently found that a few grogs will make reluctant Indians part with provisions, act as guides, or paddle canoes.[64] The trader is also aware that if liquor is held back from the independent tribes of the plains, much of their provisions may flow southward now that Louisiana is part of the United States.[65]

While alcohol is undoubtedly harmful to the natives, it is also admirably suited to the needs of the fur trade. The long, difficult, and expensive transportation system requires all trading goods to have a low initial cost, be easily carried, and be of great demand (and hence of high value) in the Northwest. Cheap rum from the West Indies can be sent into the Northwest in a concentrated form which can then be easily diluted and sold where the demand is great. The more accustomed a tribe has become to drink, the stronger is the mixture sold to them. For the Blackfeet, who have been trading a relatively short time, a nine-gallon keg contains only four or five quarts of high wine mixed with water. But for the western Crees and Assiniboines six quarts of high wine are added, and for the hard drinking Ojibways, eight or even nine quarts.[66] Unlike material goods such as kettles and awls, alcohol is not only used up immediately, but it creates a further demand as well. So, too, does tobacco.

It is well known that tobacco was used by the Indians long before the Europeans came to the Northwest. In fact, it had been grown on the plains until the introduction of a superior product by the traders eliminated the demand for it.[67] Brazilian tobacco is now the most prized by the natives. It reaches the Northwest by way of Portugal and Great Britain. Tobacco has long played an important part in most Indian ceremonies when pipes are solemnly passed among those taking part.[68] It is also smoked for pleasure and for allaying hunger during frequent periods of want.

Guns, too, create their own demand. Once accustomed to the gun, the warrior and hunter seldom return to the bow and arrow. Guns must be replaced from time to time and, once in the hands of the Indians, create a steady demand for shot and powder. Moreover, in the state of unrest which generally prevails among the natives, few tribes would feel safe without firearms.

The rum, the tobacco, the beads and cloth, as well as the hundred and one other items of trade, are made up into packages of ninety pounds for easy handling during shipment from Montreal or the bayside factories into the distant interior of the Northwest.

4

Transportation and Communication

Travellers to the Northwest may proceed either by way of the St. Lawrence and the Great Lakes, or by way of Hudson Bay (see map 9). The second route is probably the more convenient since ships of the Hudson's Bay Company sail each summer directly from London to the bay. Usually there are two ships – one destined for "the bottom of the bay" and the other for ports in the Northwest. It is generally about mid-August when the ships enter Hudson Strait. In picking their way through the tricky, ice-choked, island strown passage, they try to remain as close together as possible in order to be ready to render mutual assistance should any mishap occur. It is extraordinary that there are no charts to guide them, for, in spite of having used the strait for nearly a century and a half, the company has still not made a survey of it.[1] The vessel bound for the Northwest usually sails first to Churchill and then on to York, probably to take advantage of the northwesterly winds which prevail at that time of year.[2]

Because of the extreme shallowness of Hudson Bay, the ships must anchor off shore at both factories. On each tide, tenders ply between the storerooms and the ships, although at Churchill the tenders were recently replaced by a long, flat launch. It is about 28 feet long, from 14 to 16 feet wide but only three and one-half feet deep, and can carry about one-third to two fifths of the ship's cargo at one time. Its shallow draft permits it to be conveniently floated in on the tide to a place near the storeroom, while its low decks allow the cargo to be simply rolled ashore. At one end of the launch there is a crane to enable goods to be easily transferred to and from the ship. The launch has proved to be very convenient and has eliminated the need for building a new jetty which would have had to have been 120 yards long and 10 feet wide.[3]

The new launch was not used this year, however. Because of the advanced state of the season, the company ship *Eddystone* decided to by-pass Churchill and sail directly to York Factory where she finally arrived on 27 September, the latest arrival on record, after longest voyage ever, two months from Stornoway.[4] Following the exchange of the customary salutes with the factory, she proceeded to "five fathom hole" at the mouth of the Hayes River where she dropped anchor beside another ship which had arrived two days earlier.[5] She was the *Edward and Ann*, a newcomer to the bay chartered[6] to provide the extra space necessary for sending out the vanguard of the Selkirk settlers and their effects to the Northwest. Only in five fathom hole does sufficient water remain at low water to float the ships. Between each tide, the waters retreat toward the horizon to expose miles of glistening mud flats and forlornly isolate the ships from the factory. During the short periods of high tide, tenders hasten to the sides of the ships to unload the supplies and goods of the old world and replace them with those of the new. Ship time is always a period of great confusion. There is so much to be done and so little time to do it. But with the extra ship and the lateness of the season, probably never before had there been such chaos as in 1811. The sailors spoke of becoming ice-bound and being forced to winter on the bay. Indeed, ice was already forming along the shores and snow was being whipped in on the northwest gale.[7] As each hour passed, confusion increased. Goods for the various factories were hastily landed "promiscuously" from the tenders onto the narrow wharf near the factory only to get mixed up with the goods intended for the ships.[8] By 5 October, when the furs were put on board the *Eddystone*, so much ice was drifting about her sides that it was decided to leave without further delay. During the next 24 hours, the ship was put in order, and, accompanied by the *Edward and Ann*, sailed on the sixth at noon. So hurried was the departure that the *Eddystone* abandoned her ebb anchor and 75 fathoms of cable,[9] while the *Edward and Ann* left without completely unloading her cargo. The latter was largely the result of the *Edward and Ann* being so "miserably manned" and a shortage of small boats at York. In fact, there was not a single longboat at the factory and a schooner had to be pressed into service as a tender.[10] Fortunately, the *Eddystone* had on board a longboat and a yawl which were both used for her unloading[11] but apparently the *Edward and Ann* carried no similar boats. The *Edward and Ann* had been scheduled on her return journey to call at Moose Factory at the bottom of the bay to pick up timber[12] for the British markets where supplies are short as a result of the French blockade.[13] However, because of her late arrival at York, and the menacing appearance of the season, she returned directly to England with the *Eddystone*.

From York it is possible to travel to other posts along the bay by means of the factory schooner. The present schooner is probably the *Mainwaring*, a vessel of 80 tons built at Ipswich in 1807. Her main function is to supply Fort Severn, a dependency of York, but she conducts business with other posts along the bay as well. It is thought that the *Mainwaring* is a replacement for the *Beaver*, a brig which for many years was stationed at York. Built as a sloop in London in 1780, the *Beaver* was converted to a brig in 1789 before being sent on an exploratory expedition to the northern part of Hudson Bay in 1791 and 1792. She is now believed to be in service at Moose Factory at the bottom of the bay.[14] It is also possible to travel north from Churchill on board the sloop which is sent out each year from Churchill to trade with the Eskimos.[15]

To reach the Northwest by way of the St. Lawrence, the traveller must first make his way to Montreal, the grand emporium of the Canadian fur trade. It is here that furs from the Northwest are stored before being sent to Europe and it is here that trading goods are received for shipment to the Northwest. From Montreal, the traveller may proceed to the Northwest either by way of the Ottawa River, Lake Nipissing, Georgian Bay and Lake Superior, or by way of the St. Lawrence and Lakes Ontario, Erie, Huron, and Superior. On the western side of Lake Superior is Fort William, the North West Company's port of entry to the Northwest. It is more than a thousand miles from Montreal and this distance greatly adds to the cost of goods received in the Northwest. In 1804, for instance, an average of 23 per cent was added to their value at Montreal.[16]

The Ottawa route is more heavily travelled. It is reckoned to be 100 miles shorter than the lake route but its chief advantage is the comparative absence of fog and wind. Thus starting dates and dates of arrival can be accurately set in advance. This is of the utmost importance to the Montreal agents, who must have their furs from the interior at a precise period and ready to ship from the St. Lawrence before it freezes over. Only six weeks are required for the upward journey and probably even less time is needed for the downward trip since the current of the Ottawa greatly shortens the last 250 miles to Montreal. A grave disadvantage of the Ottawa route is its 36 portages[17] which have restricted its use to light craft that can be easily carried. To meet the conditions imposed by this route, the French early developed an astonishing vessel called the "canot-du-maître." Although due credit should be given French inventiveness, it must in justice be pointed out that their *canot* was largely an adaptation of the [Algonkian] Indian canoe, which consists fundamentally of a light cedar frame covered with birch bark. After the conquest, the British adopted the *canot-du-maître* and it is still regarded as the best possible craft for the Ottawa route. It is considerably larger than its native prototype, being approximately 36 feet long and about six feet wide in the middle.[18] Possibly the inspiration for the large craft came from the Ojibwa [an Algonkian tribe] who build canoes which can carry as many as twelve men.[19]

In the bottom of their canoes, the Canadians lay four poles, side by side. These are nearly as long as the canoe itself and about three or four inches in diameter at their thickest end. On this "grand-perch," as the poles are called, the cargo is arranged with great care so that nothing is allowed to press against the bare, unprotected sides of the canoe. For ease in handling, the cargo is made up into packages of 90 pounds each. According to Col. Landmann of the Royal Engineers, the canoes usually carry a weight of five tons. This includes sufficient provisions to support 10 men for from 20 to 22 days. Each canoe is provided with a mast and a lug-sail. There is also a ten-foot setting pole for each man. These are used to assist in towing the canoe up the rapids.[20] The eight or ten canoemen[21] must bring along their own paddles and camp kettles, but each canoe is supplied with a few towing lines, a bundle of *watap* (roots of the pine tree for stitching up any seams which might burst), a parcel of resinous gum for patching leaky seams, and a piece of birch bark for repairing holes. There is also a hatchet, a crooked knife, and a few other indispensable articles.[22]

The canoes are built at Trois Rivières and are brought up the St. Lawrence to Lachine, nine miles above Montreal, as early in the spring as the departing ice will allow.[23] The reason they are taken to Lachine instead of Montreal is because the very shallow rapids, which stretch for several miles immediately above the city, can only be navigated by the canoes when they are empty. The fully loaded canoes ride very low in the water, with the gunwales only six inches above the surface.[24] The goods and supplies for the Northwest are sent from Montreal to Lachine by road.[25] The carts are driven on the right side of the road, in accordance with the custom in Canada, which to the eye of the English traveller present "a very awkward appearance."[26]

Before leaving Lachine, the heavily-laden canoes are divided into brigades. The size of the brigades seems to vary considerably. In 1761, for example, they consisted of only three or four canoes, while in 1800, they were made up of ten. Each brigade is the charge of one or two guides, or pilots, whose duty is not only to point out the best way to steer, but to take command of the men and to be responsible for the goods carried as well. Shortly after departing from Lachine, the canoes reach the first obstacle to navigation, the rapids at Sainte-Anne, which are considered to mark the beginning proper of the long journey to the Northwest. Here the voyageurs take communion in the little Roman Catholic Church dedicated to Saint Ann, the patroness of the Canadians in all their travels by water.[27] Another custom observed on arriving at Sainte-Anne is the distributing of a gallon of rum to each canoeman for consumption during the journey. Moreover, it is also the custom to drink much of the rum on the spot so that saint, priest, and the relatives left behind are soon forgotten. The next day, the carefree Canadians, somewhat the worse for wear, pile into their canoes and to the rhythm of a song leave behind them the cares of civilization as they disappear around the sweeping bend and into the Indian country. Before they reach Georgian Bay about 25 days later,[28] there will be 35[29] back-breaking portages to cope with. But from there to Fort William, it will not be necessary again to remove the canoes from the water. The only remaining obstacle to navigation, the Sault-Ste-Marie, is now by-passed by a small set of locks built by the North West Company especially for its large canoes.[30]

The whole of the Ottawa route is justly renowned for the sublime grandeur of its many lively landscapes. From the rapids of Sainte-Anne, the brigades ascend the mighty Ottawa to the mouth of the picturesque Mattawa; then up the narrow gorges of the Mattawa to where a short portage leads to Lake Nipissing; and across the lake to the entrance to the French River; and finally down the swift French to island-strewn Georgian Bay.[31] If the winds are right, sails are raised and the canoes pass quickly through the bay and on into the North Channel until St. Joseph's Island is reached. Here the North West Company has had a post since 1783. From 1796, its importance has been greatly enhanced by the presence of a military post. This post or, more properly, fort was established by the British to replace their fort at Michilimackinac [Mackinac] which was turned over to the Americans. The new fort is beautifully situated on a rise of ground and, since the soil is good, has a promising future.[32] It is the most westerly military position in the country.

St. Joseph Island marks the junction of the Ottawa route with the lower Great Lakes route. From here onward both routes follow the same track past Sault-Ste-Marie and through Lake Superior to Fort William. Goods shipped by boat on the lakes travel more cheaply than those sent by canoe on the Ottawa, but the risk of their being lost is considered greater. Should a ship be sunk, a whole year's furs could disappear beneath the waves, whereas the loss of one, or even two, canoes would not be critical. However, the main disadvantage of the lake route is that the shortness of the open season will not allow a complete journey to be made in one year. To reach the Northwest in time to catch the brigades going into the interior, the supplies must leave Montreal the previous autumn. The goods go by boat from Montreal to Kingston where they are put on a vessel bound for Niagara.[33] Near Queenston, where additional supplies are sometimes picked up,[34] the goods are removed from the vessel for the portage around Niagara Falls. They are first carried ten miles by land and then at Chipewa Creek, a tributary of the Niagara River, put into boats which take them the remainder of the way to Lake Erie where they are again put into a vessel. This vessel carries them the rest of the way to Sault-Ste-Marie, possibly with stops for goods and supplies at Detroit, where the North West Company procures much of its flour and Indian corn, or at Michilimackinac, where it obtains maple sugar, tallow, gum and other goods. Some of the Detroit and Michilimackinac goods are deposited at St. Joseph Island along with part of the Montreal cargo, and the rest is sent through with the vessel to Sault-Ste-Marie.

Thus large quantities of provisions as well as the heavier and more bulky goods are shipped to the Northwest by boat,[35] while most of the furs are sent out by canoe.[36] This practice, along with the fact that the furs usually occupy more space than the goods traded for them, means that more canoes are required for the outward than for the inward journey. The additional canoes are bought from the Ojibwa Indians of the St. Joseph Island area, a people noted for their skill in making canoes.[37] Happily, their country is rich in the required materials[38] –

cedar, spruce and birch. Smaller canoes for the Northwest itself[39] are also obtained at St. Joseph Island. Like the *canots-du-maître*, they are used only one season.[40] It is fortunate for the Indians that they can take part in the trade in this way, for their country is not well inhabited by animals of the fur-bearing kind and so they tend to be very poor.[41]

From St. Joseph Island to Sault-Ste-Marie is but a short journey. Unlike the canoes, which can now by-pass the rapids of the Sault and proceed directly to Lake Superior, the lake vessels are forced to terminate their journeys within 300 yards of the quay belonging to the North West Company's establishment there. The post is built on the north side of the falls and consists of several stores for the Montreal goods and a number of houses. There is also a sawmill which seems to be driven by the waters of the Sault.[42] Undoubtedly lumber from this mill was used in building the 90-ton schooner *Recovery* which now plies between the Sault and Fort William.[43] A short distance above the Sault post is Pointe-aux-Pins. It was here that Harmon saw a predecessor of the *Recovery* in 1800.[44] That ship was probably the *Otter* which had been built at Pointe-aux-Pins in 1793 to replace the *Athabaska* which had then been floated down the falls for use on the lower lakes.[45] The Lake Superior vessels do not actually seem to call at the Sault, but rather terminate their voyages at Pointe-aux-Pins According to Harmon, they made four journeys per season between the Pointe and the Grand Portage. The post at Grand Portage is 35 miles south of Fort William, and, until replaced by Fort William in 1802-3, was for many years the North West Company's port of entry into the Northwest. Unlike Fort William, where the schooner ties up at the wharf beside the factory,[46] the post at Grand Portage had been located on the edge of a very shallow part of the lake, making it necessary for the vessels to anchor nearly a mile off shore.[47]

The Lake Superior schooner seems to serve primarily as the last link in the lake transportation system from Montreal. At least, its operations do not appear to be closely co-ordinated with the activities of the brigades from Lachine, since the canoes go right through to Fort William instead of terminating their journey at the Sault. As on the Ottawa route, the canoes, which depend mainly on paddling, are probably considered to be more reliable than the schooner. The huge lake is subject to severe storms and dense fogs[48] and, during these adverse conditions, the light canoes are considered to be more dependable; unlike the schooner, they can always be taken ashore during rough water and, in all but the densest fogs, can pick their way along the coast in places where the schooner would be in grave peril. An added advantage of the canoes over the schooner, during the days of the Grand Portage, was that they could bring their cargoes directly into the shore while the schooner had to anchor a mile off. At Fort William, not only has this disadvantage of the schooner been eliminated, but the new route has increased the usefulness of the *canot-du-maître* as well. For now the large Montreal canoes can be used to carry goods beyond Fort William and on into the Northwest itself. On the old Grand Portage, it had always been necessary to change to smaller canoes before proceeding into the interior.[49]

The Grand Portage route, which had led from Lake Superior to Rainy Lake, contained some of the most difficult carrying places in the whole of the Northwest (including the tortuous, nine-mile Grand Portage itself) as well as several exceedingly shallow rivers and lakes.[50] To traverse this route with the large Montreal canoes had been out of the question. Instead, smaller canoes of similar construction had been used. Called the *canot-du-nord*, they were and are, in their own way as brilliantly designed for the country in which they are used as is the *canot-du-maître* for the Ottawa route. Although originally developed for use in the eastern part of the Northwest, the *canot-du-nord* has proved to be ideally suited to the needs of the fur trade in much of the remainder of the country; and it has been this craft, more than any other, which has enabled the trade to be extended to nearly all parts of the Northwest.

The northern canoes are from 24 to 27 feet long, four feet eight inches to five feet wide, and 21 to 24 inches deep.[51] They have a carrying capacity of about 3,000 pounds of cargo plus a crew of five men. Yet they can be carried by only two men.[52] In doing so, the men walk one behind the other with the canoe, upside-down, supported on their shoulders. This means that the portage trails through the bush need be no wider than the width of a canoe, and the track itself no more than a foot or so. Considering its large capacity, the draft of the *canot-du-nord*, seldom more than 18 inches, is extremely shallow – an invaluable asset in an area where the absence of rain for months at a time frequently reduces even great rivers to mere trickling streams.

The men who man the *canots-du-nord* are the aristocrats of the canoemen. Because they remain in the Northwest throughout the year, they are known as the winterers, or *hommes-du-nord*. They look down on the "goers and comers" who man the Montreal canoes, and derisively refer to them as the *mangeurs-du-lard*, or pork-eaters, after their supposed diet.[53] The *canots-du-nord* come down each year to Fort William to ex-change cargoes with the *canots-du-maître* and the ship. An exception are the canoes from the distant Athabasca country which can come only as far as Rainy Lake if they are to return to their posts before the winter sets in. Before the move to Fort William, some of the pork-eaters had been chosen to carry the goods destined for Athabasca, with northern canoes, over the Grand Portage route to Rainy Lake.[54] Since the trans-fer, it has been possible to send some of the Montreal canoes right through to Rainy Lake to meet the winterers.[55]

Most of the *canots-du-nord* are built in the country between St. Joseph Island and Lake Winnipeg, an area which not only produces the neces-sary raw materials, but which is inhabited by skilled Ojibwa canoe-makers. However, since here, too, more canoes are needed for the down-ward than for the upward journey[56] (furs being more bulky than trading goods) and since many canoes are not in fit condition for a return trip, additional craft must be built in the interior as well. These come mainly from the Athabasca and Peace rivers where birch and pine[57] (but not cedar) fit for large canoes are available. These canoes are used only once, probably because of the heavy pine frames, which make carrying more difficult. On the Red and Assiniboine rivers additional canoes are also required but the conventional materials for building them are not avail-able. However, the North West Company has solved this problem by making a frame of willows, nearly the shape of a canoe, and stretching over it a raw buffalo hide or two, depending on the size of the craft. If two hides are used they are cut square at the shoulders and sewn to-gether with sinews. The sides are then brought over the largest willow, which serves as the gunwale, and lashed fast with leather cords. The hair is generally on the inside. These canoes are capable of carrying large cargoes, but it is necessary to unload them at least once a day, and dry them in the sun or over a fire – otherwise they will sink. They are only good for drifting down the current and so only make one journey.[58]

The canoes for the interior set off from Fort William in brigades, those bound for the most distant posts going first. Between each brigade a space of two days is allowed. This is to prevent a second brigade from reaching a carrying place before the first has completed the several trips necessary, back and forth, across the narrow portage.[59] As it is, the portages are accomplished with "astonishing expedition."[60] When a canoe reaches the beginning of a carrying place, the bowman instantly jumps into the water to prevent the frail craft from touching bottom, while the other members of the crew tie their slings to the packages in the canoe and swing them on their backs and in an instant are on their way over the portage. The canoe, itself, is carried by the bowman and steersman. The middle men are exempt from this task.

In calm weather the canoes generally travel at about six miles per hour. To lighten their labours, the men usually sing a simple melody, keeping perfect time to it with their paddles. When they arrive at a rapid, it is the guide's duty to determine whether it should be run with the full load, half load (the other half being carried by land), or not run at all. "It would be astonishing to a European observer," wrote a partner of the North West Company in 1804, "to witness the dexterity with which they manage their canoes in those dangerous rapids, carrying them down like lightning on the surface of the water. The bowman, supported by the steersman, dexterously avoids the stones and shoals which might touch the canoe and dash it to pieces, to the almost certain destruction of all on board. It often baffles their skill, when the water is very high, to avoid plunging in foaming swells on the very brink of the most tremendous precipices, yet, those bold adventurers rather run this risk, for the sake of expedition, than lose a few hours by transporting the cargo over land.

"When they are obliged to stem the current in strong rapids they haul up the canoe with a line, all hands pulling along shore and sometimes wading through the water up to their middle, except one man, who remains in the stern of the canoe, in order to keep it in the proper channel: this part of their duty is always accompanied with much labour."[61]

When the wind is favourable, sails are always used and, in a fresh gale, the canoes are carried along at eight or nine miles per hour.[62] However, care must be taken not to carry too much sail for the canoes are quite unstable and can easily be overturned. In places where portaging is unnecessary, such as on the Saskatchewan, boats are often used instead of canoes, since they are more stable and can be safely used with a sail.

Although the North West Company has been making increased use of boats in some parts of the Northwest during recent years, it nevertheless continues to rely mainly upon the canoe for transportation. Its English rivals, on the other hand, now favour the boat although it still uses many canoes. The reason for the differing preferences of the two companies may be discovered through a comparison of the country around Fort William with that in the region of York and Churchill factories. Near the northern factories there has been a lack of suitable materials, as well as (and probably as a result of) a shortage of skilled Indian canoe-makers. Cedar is not available at either York or Churchill. In fact, according to Mackenzie, it is not found northwest of Cedar Lake.[63] There is some birch, but trees large enough for canoes are very scarce and most of these have long ago been stripped of their bark. So acute has the shortage become at Churchill, for instance, that two years ago an appeal had to be made to Moose Factory, at the bottom of the bay, to send a shipment of "birch rhind."[64] The absence of cedar for frames has meant that pine (which is considerably heavier) has had to be substituted, while the shortage of birch bark has compelled the traders to either carry it to the factory from some distance, or to build their canoes inland near the source of supply. However, whenever the latter course has been taken, the company has run considerable risk of losing its canoes to the Canadians,[65] who have been encroaching on the preserves of both factories.

Fort William, on the other hand, is located in a country rich in birch, cedar and spruce. Moreover, the Ojibwa Indians who live there are renowned for their canoes, which range in size from small two-man craft to the large ones designed for Lake Superior which can carry twelve men.[66] Thus the Canadians have had little difficulty in getting the many large canoes which they require, and many of the Canadians themselves have become skilled canoe builders.[67] At York, the Indians are not only unfamiliar with large canoes but seem to be incapable of comprehending what the Hudson's Bay men have wanted when they have tried to persuade them to build them.[68] Unlike their Canadian counterparts, few English traders have learned to make canoes, in spite of attractive bonuses offered by their employers for every large canoe they constructed.[69] The Indians, who are not innocent of guile, have realized that the whites know little of canoe building and that, if they refuse to sell them even their small canoes, the company will be forced to hire them to transport its goods and supplies. They must also know that small canoes require more crew per pound of cargo carried than do large ones, and that to build large canoes would only result in less jobs being available. These jobs, in most cases, would necessarily go to themselves since few Hudson's Bay men, unlike their French-Canadian rivals, can handle canoes. The English company, on the other hand, has been anxious to avoid using Indians as much as possible because they are such notorious pilferers (especially when rum is concerned), and will, whenever the opportunity arises, blackmail the company for higher wages. Moreover, Indians engaged in manning the canoes are prevented from hunting for as much as six months of the year, and as a result many valuable furs are lost.[70]

The relatively few large canoes which the Hudson's Bay Company has been able to procure seem to come mostly from Cumberland House where they are built from birch bark brought down from the upper Saskatchewan.[71] Nevertheless, for the most part the company has been forced to use small canoes. These are very inefficient. In fact it is said that ten men are required to carry the same cargo which could be transported with only five men in the large Canadian canoes.[72] This has meant that the company must either remain largely dependent upon the Indians, or it must recruit twice the number of European canoemen if it is to compete with the Canadians for the inland trade. With the severe personnel shortage caused by the war with France, the latter course has been out of the question. Moreover, the few recruits the company has been able to get are nearly all, at best, reluctant canoemen. They seem to have little of the spirit of the Northwest for which the French Canadians are renowned and which causes each to emulate his mates in skill, bravery and endurance. Generally speaking, the French Canadians spend the whole of their adult lives in the Northwest, and so experienced canoemen are always available to train the newcomers as they arrive from the east. The Hudson's Bay employees, on the other hand, contract for definite periods, usually three years, and so are less likely to acquire much skill with a canoe even when they do have the inclination to do so. And since not many of them become skilled, there are few to teach the new men as they arrive from Europe. Nor has the company been able to look to the Indians to train its employees, for they will not take inexperienced men in their canoes.

No similar personnel shortage has faced the North West Company. On the contrary, the keen competition among rival Canadian factions at the turn of the century resulted in so many men going west that since the absorption of the xy Company in 1804, the North West Company has actually enjoyed a labour surplus. As already intimated, most of these men acquired great skill in handling canoes (and many in building them) by going into the Northwest with experienced men while still very young. Many of the Hudson's Bay men, on the other hand, spend their youth in the Orkney Islands where from early childhood they are accustomed to going out in boats. It is therefore not surprising that boats were early tried as a substitute for canoes by the Hudson's Bay Company. These were heavy craft with keels, somewhat resembling whaleboats and thus betraying the Orcadian origins of their builders. Miles Macdonell, the leader of the Selkirk settlers now wintering in the Northwest and a man who has had previous experience with boats on the St. Lawrence and in the United States, has complained that the company's boats are "better calculated for sea service than that of shoal rivers."[73] The size of the boats built at York and now in use there is not known, but they are probably similar to the ones sent this year from Churchill to York for use on the route to Lake Winnipeg. These can take six working men with 30 pieces of goods, each weighing 90 pounds, as well as provisions for the voyage and probably one or two officers as passengers.[74] In handling, they likely correspond to the boats in use at Churchill in 1798, which were said to row faster than canoes and to be much superior in coming down rapids.[75] Against this, however, is the fact that two experienced crews are required to manage one boat when descending rapids.[76]

One great advantage of boats is that, once built, they can be used for several seasons, whereas canoes are seldom serviceable a second year. This has been a small consideration to the North West Company, which has always had an abundant and ready supply of new canoes, but an overriding one with the Hudson's Bay Company, which has not. However, boats large enough to be practicable are much heavier than canoes and cannot be portaged. Instead, they must be dragged across the carrying places on skids of green timber like the ones strewn from one end to the other along the portage around Grand Falls at the entrance to the Saskatchewan.[77]

Boats reaching Grand Falls from York Factory travel by way of the Hayes and Hill rivers and Lake Winnipeg. It may seem strange that they do not follow the more direct route via the Nelson River. However, this track is seldom used, largely because it is very shallow below Hell's Gate, and "full of Gravelly shoals" which are difficult to spot before the canoes or boats have run upon them.[78] It has only been during the past few years that boats have made the complete journey from York Factory to Grand Falls and on into the Saskatchewan country.[79] Before that, they were used in conjunction with canoes. The boats would leave the factory by way of the Hayes but would go only as far as Rock Portage. Above the portage there is a stretch of almost continuous rapids and falls. From the beginning of the rapids to the head of Trout River canoes would be used. At Trout River, the goods would then be transferred to boats destined for the Saskatchewan.[80]

The North West Company's route from Fort William to Grand Falls is far more suited to canoe travel than is the Hudson's Bay Company's route from York Factory.[81] Besides a "much better" track, the Canadians enjoy the added advantage of entering Lake Winnipeg on the current during the upward journey when cargo is heaviest.[82] But against this advantage must be reckoned the adverse effects of the prevailing westerly winds since the cranky canoes cannot use sail with a headwind. To lessen this disadvantage, the canoes pick their way from the mouth of the Winnipeg River along the eastern side of the lake to Dog's Head, at the Narrows, where the lake is "hardly a league wide." Here they cross and then continue on a course up the western shores to the mouth of the Saskatchewan.[83] Care must be exercised in travelling on Lake Winnipeg, however, for not only is the wind a problem, but the lake is very shallow, especially along the shores where the canoes go,[84] so that there is constant danger of damaging the thin bottoms.

Once the boats have been dragged across the Grand Falls Portage, it is possible for them to travel all the way to the foothills of the Rockies without again leaving the water. In a sense they are now competing on at least equal terms with the canoes since their weight handicap is no longer a consideration. In many places, where poles and tow-lines are required, the boats may be more difficult to handle, but in other places, where sails can be used, they gain an advantage over the unstable canoes. Moreover, the greater stability and strength of the boats has made it possible to transport bulky articles which would be out of the question by canoe. For instance, this year two calves were shipped inland from York (where they had been born) "in a small boat very deeply loaded with Goods besides."[85] On another occasion, two horses were sent across the Northwest by boat from Fort Vermilion on the upper Saskatchewan to York Factory.[86]

In many ways, each company's preference for either canoes or boats symbolizes its character. The solid English joint-stock company has chosen the sound, heavy boat. It can be used year after year and represents capital investment. The more transitory nature of the Canadian partnership is reflected in its choice of the dashing, unstable canoe. It must be replaced each year and can be charged under annual expenses. The boat, too, typifies the stolidness of the Orcadians in the same way that the canoe characterizes the gay abandon of the French Canadians.

The French-Canadian canoemen have long been noted for their carefree attitude towards life. David Thompson, who must know them as well as anyone, claims that as long as they have full stomachs, they are happy.[87] Some idea of the enormous quantity of goods which they are capable of devouring may be gained from Alexander Henry's description of the provisions consumed by his men and himself during their upward journey in 1809: "I arrived at Fort Vermillion, having been two months on my voyage from Fort William, with a brigade of 11 canoes, loaded with 28 pieces each, and manned by five men and one woman. Our expenditure of provisions for each canoe during this voyage was: Two bags of corn, 1½ bushel each, and 15 lbs. of grease, to Lac la Pluie; two bags of wild rice, 1½ bushel each, and 10 lbs. of grease, to Bas de la Rivière Winnipic; four bags of pemmican, 90 lbs. each, to Cumberland; and two bags of pemmican, 90 lbs. each, to serve until we came among the buffalo – generally near the Montee, or at furthest the Elbow, of the Saskatchewan."[88]

Obviously such large quantities of food could not have been carried from Fort William without occupying a large part of the space necessary for cargo. For this reason, provision depots including those mentioned by Henry, have been established along the canoe and boat routes throughout the Northwest. Among the most important depots are those at Fort William, Lac-la-Pluie [Rainy Lake], Bas-de-la-Rivière-Winnipeg [mouth of Winnipeg River], and Cumberland House. Brigades proceeding northwest of Cumberland to the Athabasca country require an extra three or four bags of pemmican per canoe to carry them to Fort Chipewyan, the great supply depot of that country. Bas-de-la-Rivière-Winnipeg receives its pemmican from the Red and Assiniboine rivers, Cumberland from the Saskatchewan, and Chipewyan from the Peace River. All of it is collected with comparative ease from the huge herds of buffalo and deer which frequent the valleys of these rivers and, in each case, is floated down stream to the depots without encountering a single obstacle to navigation. For example, only two men and one boat have been required to carry about three tons of pemmican from the Assiniboine to Bas-de-la-Rivière-Winnipeg,[89] while three men in a large canoe have managed to carry two tons of dried provisions down the Peace to Fort Chipewyan.[90] Lac-la-Pluie is unique in that it supplies wild rice (gathered locally) rather than meat.

Canoes routed up the Saskatchewan from Cumberland carry only enough supplies to last until they "come among the buffalo."[91] Here they are met by hunters who bring extra horses for the clerks and partners who then happily give up their cramped quarters in the canoes and mount for the buffalo hunt. This they regard as the most pleasant time of their lives.[92] During the day, they gallop and race across the sun-drenched plains, and in the evening, with the results of their hunt, they join the crews of the slow moving canoes for a feast of fresh meat beside a roaring fire on the bank of the river. On the downward journey, however, there is no time to hunt. The canoes travel too quickly. And, of course, less food is necessary. In 1809, for example, it required two months for Henry's brigade to travel from Fort William to Fort Vermilion,[93] while in the spring of the same year, it had made the journey from Vermilion to Fort William in just under a month.[94] There are more than 1,500 miles of rivers, lakes and portages between the two points. The incredible speeds with which they are covered has only been made possible by the fantastic endurance of the French-Canadian voyageurs who are capable of working in a canoe, twenty hours out of every twenty-four, for two or three weeks at a time "without a day of rest or any diminution of labour."[95] During their paddling they smoke almost continuously and sing the songs which have been passed down from their fathers and grandfathers. They rest from five to ten minutes every two hours when they refill their pipes, and it is more common for them to describe distances as so many pipes than in any other way.

The number of days required for the brigades to travel from place to place during the upward journey are shown in figure 9. Downward trips, of course, take much less time. So, too, do the journeys performed by the partners of the North West Company who travel in light canoes with picked crews and with only their personal baggage and provisions. Simon McTavish's seven and three-quarter days from St. Joseph Island to Montreal is probably the record for the North West Company, although a 25-foot military canoe with a crew of 10 picked men has made the same journey in half a day less. The soldiers' baggage was arranged so that everything could be portaged in one trip, and there was a favouring wind on Lake Huron. Another North West Company partner, Roderick McKenzie, made the trip from Rainy Lake to Fort Chipewyan in one month and four days in 1799. He used a light canoe with six men.[96] Similar craft are used by the Hudson's Bay Company to carry important persons and documents. For example, the 1809 instructions from the London Committee to buy as few small furs as was possible and no more wolf skins, were rushed from York Factory to Fort Vermilion as quickly as possible. When the canoe carrying the Committee's message got stuck in the ice en route, Mr. Bird, who was in charge, came on by land on horseback, arriving October 23. He also brought with him, incredible though it may seem, London newspapers dated 13 June which told of the progress of the war in Europe.[97]

Apart from the fast canoes, there is another form of rapid communication known as "expresses." These carry correspondence, reports and news from post to post throughout the country. The North West Company has the more elaborate system. It operates two expresses annually. The winter express leaves Athabasca in December, travels throughout the whole of the Northwest, and reaches Sault-Ste-Marie towards the end of March.[98] Thus the men coming up from Montreal in the spring are able to get news of the preceding summer much sooner than they could otherwise do. There is also a summer express which hurries down with news of the winter's hunt, apparently in advance of the canoes with the furs.[99] In a similar way, the Hudson's Bay Company operates a useful line of communication between its bay-side factories. This consists of pairs of "packet Indians" sent on foot from each factory with letters to arrive at the next factory about the expected time of arrival of the annual supply ship from England. In this way, news of the safe arrival of the ships, together with information about the state of the factories, is made known all along the bay so that, wherever necessary, assistance may be rendered.[100]

The small canoes of the northern [Athapaskan] tribes (see fig. 1), although seldom used by the traders themselves, nevertheless play an important role in the trade since they are often used by the Indians in transporting their furs to the posts. In shape, these canoes somewhat resemble a weaver's shuttle – flat-bottomed, with straight upright sides, and pointed at both ends. They seldom exceed 12 or 13 feet in length and are from 20 to 24 inches wide at the stern which is by far the broadest part. It is here that the baggage is generally placed.[101] Although far less elegant in appearance than are the graceful eastern [Algonkian] canoes, the northern craft are, in their own way, just as admirably designed for the prevailing conditions of the land in which they are used. For the most part, the broken rivers of the northerly portions of the Stony Region have proved to be more of an obstacle than an aid to transportation; they are generally unsuitable for navigation, and yet their cold, deep waters block the way by land. Consequently, the northern Indian canoe was developed not so much as a mode of transportation, but as a means for crossing the rivers and lakes which are encountered when travelling by land. On occasion, they must be portaged 150 or even 200 miles and so are made light enough to be easily carried by one man. They are cranky and unstable and can carry only one person sitting upright. However, a second person can also be carried lying on the bottom. It is in this way that the Indians ferry one another across the rivers and narrow parts of the lakes.[102]

The northern Indian canoes are also used for chasing water-fowl during the moulting season and for pursuing deer as they swim across rivers and lakes. When they are used for this purpose, the single-bladed paddle normally employed is exchanged for a double-bladed one. This type of paddle is not usually used by the Indians of the Northwest and probably has been adopted by the northern [Athapaskan] tribes from their northerly neighbours, the Eskimo, who use a similar paddle with their own small hunting canoes, called kayaks.

The broad flat parts of the Eskimo paddles are generally inlaid with ivory in a very tasteful and imaginative way, epitomizing the high level of craftmanship which characterizes everything these people do. Their kayaks are ingeniously constructed of pieces of wood and whalebone, fastened together by means of the sinews of animals, and covered with seal-skin parchment. Only a small central aperture is left, just large enough to admit the body of a man. Into this the Eskimo thrusts himself up to his waist with his feet stretched out before him. To the central opening is fixed a flat hoop about two inches high. Attached to this is a skin fitted in such a way that it can be fastened tightly to the body of the Eskimo and so prevent any water from entering the kayak.

The kayaks are generally about 20 feet long and two feet broad at the widest place. The paddles are about 10 feet long,[103] and by dipping one blade and then the other, speeds of at least 16 miles an hour can be attained.[104] An English boat with 12 oars can not keep up with it.[105]

Supplementing the canoe routes in a number of places in the Northwest are overland trails. These usually run between two fur trading posts, such as the trail between Vermilion and the now defunct South Branch House, or they simply join together two waterways, as does the road between the two branches of the Saskatchewan at the Montée. Six days are required for the trip between Fort Vermilion and South Branch House;[106] less than a day is needed to cross at the Montée.[107]

When travelling on the trails through the buffalo country it is not customary for the traders to carry provisions since, with the aid of fire-arms, they can always "kill a sufficiency for a Day."[108] But while the almost limitless herds have removed the threat of starvation, they have added another hazard of their own, the danger of trampling. As the buffalo rove relentlessly across the vast prairies, they ignore almost every-

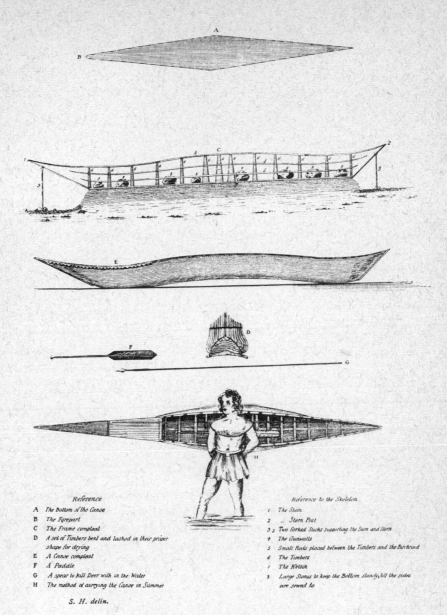

S. H. delin.

FIGURE 1   Northern Indian Canoe

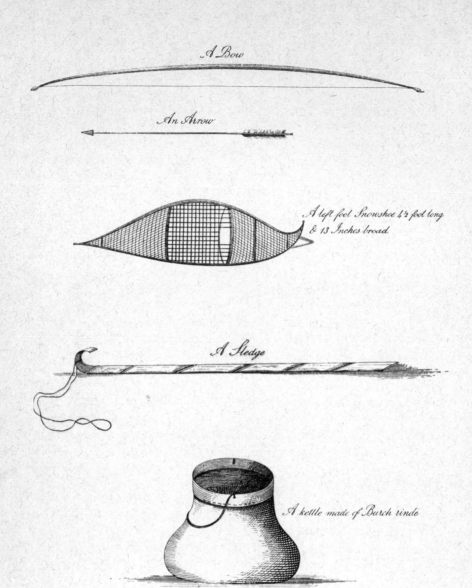

A Bow

An Arrow

A left foot Snowshoe 4½ foot long & 13 Inches broad

A Sledge

A kettle made of Burch rinde

FIGURE 2   Indian Implements

thing in their way, especially when they are being driven onward by a raging storm or being pursued by the packs of wolves which always follow in the wake of their migrations. Because of the ever-present danger of being trampled as well as the fear of being attacked by the marauding wolves, it is not safe to camp on the plains without a fire.[109] In places where there is no wood, fires must be made from buffalo dung.[110] Guns, of course, are also used to drive off the buffalo; so, too, are dogs.[111]

The buffalo are terrified of the native dogs. However, this is to be expected since the dogs are descended from wolves. In fact, according to Pennant, they still betray their savage descent by uttering only a howl instead of the significant bark of the genuine dog.[112] Nevertheless, they are faithful to their masters[113] and useful in frightening wild beasts into snares or traps, although they lack the sagacity of the European dog.[114]

There are several types of native dogs. The ones used for hunting are quite small but there are also larger breeds which are used by the Indians and Eskimos as beasts of burden. Probably the largest of them all is the breed introduced from Newfoundland by the Hudson's Bay Company which now has spread to all parts of the Northwest. These are used only as beasts of burden. In winter they draw their loads on sledges but in summer they carry them on their backs. The weight is placed near the shoulders and an experienced dog can carry 60 or 70 pounds a distance of 25 or 30 miles a day.[115]

During the first half of the eighteenth century,[116] the dog was joined as a beast of burden by the horse. In fact, before the Indians had learned to ride them, they were used exclusively for carrying baggage.[117] That is, they had been regarded as dogs, an attitude reflected in the Cree word for horse, *mistahtim*, which means "big dog."[118] Loads are carried by means of a *travois*, a device consisting of two poles. One end of each pole is attached to either side of the horse and the other ends are tied together and allowed to drag on the ground behind the animal. It is used mostly in winter. The *travois* was undoubtedly derived from a similar device used with the small indigenous (as opposed to Newfoundland) dogs, which in turn probably developed from the practice of making the dogs carry the poles for the tent.

Once the Assiniboine Indians had mastered the art of riding their horses during the final decades of the eighteenth century, they tended to use them mostly for hunting buffalo, and most of their baggage was once again carried by the dogs.[119] However, these were probably not their own small dogs but rather the large Newfoundland breed which must have reached them about this time. In any case, the Assiniboine most likely did not have enough horses for hunting as well as for use as pack animals. They have been chronically short of horses, probably as a result of rough usage[120] and the harsh climate in their part of the Northwest.

The use of the horse has ensured the plains tribes of an abundant supply of buffalo meat which, in turn, has enabled them to keep a large number of dogs. In other areas, where meat has been less easy to get, and where horses could not be used,[121] the tasks of land transportation have fallen mostly upon the natives themselves – and particularly upon the women who are almost universally treated as beasts of burden. Matonabbee, who had been Hearne's guide to the mouth of the Coppermine in the early 1770s, lived in an area where horses were unknown, and the rivers were generally unsuitable for cargo canoes, and where dogs were scarce and too small to carry heavy articles,[122] the Newfoundland dog not yet having reached them. He explained to Hearne why women made such useful beasts of burden. "When all the men are heavy-laden," he said, "they can neither hunt nor travel to any considerable distance; and in case they meet with success in hunting, who is to carry the produce of their labour? Women were made for labour; one of them can carry, or haul, as much as two men can do. They also pitch our tents, make and mend our clothing, keep us warm at night; and, in fact, there is no such thing as travelling any considerable distance, or for any length of time, in this country, without their assistance. Women, though they do everything, are maintained at trifling expense; for as they always stand cook, the very licking of their fingers in scarce times, is sufficient for their subsistence."[123]

Matonabbee was a Chipewyan, a tribe noted for the harsh treatment of its women. If more than a few of the men would take the trouble to make sledges, the work of the women could be made much easier. For they have several types of sledges well suited to their country. The simplest of these is made and used on the Barren Grounds. It consists merely of the skins of deer legs sewn together and is pulled over the snow, hair side down, until the woods are reached and proper sledges can be made.

The wooden sledges (see fig. 11) are called *bafe-hoth* by the Chipewyans and *mo-co-toggan* [toboggan] by the Crees. They are made from thin boards of larch, lashed together and turned up slightly at one end to form a vehicle from 12 to 14 inches wide and eight or nine feet long. The boards are fastened together with thongs of parchment deerskin. Several crossbars of wood are sewn onto the upper side which both strengthen the sledge and provide a means for attaching the load to it. The front is turned up to form a semi-circle of at least 15 or 20 inches in diameter. This prevents the craft from driving into the light snow and enables it to glide smoothly over the hard snowdrifts which are so characteristic of the Barren Grounds and open plains.[124]

The *mo-co-toggan* was early adopted by the traders. They often pull them by hand, but horses are also used in areas where the snow is not deep, particularly on the open plains. In places where the snow is generally deeper, dogs are employed since they are relatively light and tend not to sink far into the snow. The North West Company also makes use of a Canadian sledge called a *carriole* which is likewise drawn by either horses or dogs, depending upon the condition of the snow.[125]

On the open plains, where there is seldom much snow, horses can generally be used throughout the year. As a result, the natives of the area are becoming so dependent upon their mounts that they seldom travel anywhere without them – even when going only short distances from their tents. On some occasions, however, they ride as far as 70 miles in 12 hours, but 40 or 45 miles is a more common day's ride. The Indians rarely use bridles, but rather guide their horses with halters made of strong, durable ropes manufactured from buffalo hair. On the horse's back is placed a dressed buffalo skin and over that a pad from which are suspended stirrups made of wood. The Indians do not shoe their horses and so particular attention is paid to the colour of the horses' hooves. Since a yellow hoof with white hair is brittle and easily worn away, the natives place a greater value on black-hoofed animals, and only they are taken on war expeditions.[126]

It is a curious fact that the wheel was unknown to the Indians. Consequently, there were no carts in the Northwest before the coming of the white man. The exact date of their introduction cannot be fixed with certainty, but it is known that at least as early as 1734 carts were being used by the Hudson's Bay Company in the building of Fort Prince of Wales. They were pulled by oxen which had apparently been sent out the year before.[127] The French also had carts in the Northwest. These had been used in the Red River area where the ground is so smooth and level that they could travel in any direction. More recently, the North West Company has re-introduced carts into the same area. The first of these seem to have been built at Pembina River House in 1801. The wheels of the first North West Company models were simply solid discs of wood, three feet in diameter, which had been sawn from the ends of trees, these were soon replaced with four-foot, four-spoked wheels. In 1803, these were in turn replaced by proper wheels "on the plan of those in Canada."[129] However, carts are not widely used in the Northwest and the traders continue to rely for the most part on modes of conveyance adopted from the natives.

5

Supporting Enterprises

The settler proceeding to the Northwest can profit greatly from an examination of the many ingenious ways in which the white traders there have learned to cope with natural conditions which seem at once strange and harsh to those who have been raised in the peaceful English countryside. To survive and prosper, the traders have necessarily devised new types of food, clothing and shelter, as well as their extraordinary system of transportation. To provide these things, a number of secondary activities or supporting enterprises have been developed over the years. In addition to these enterprises, the Hudson's Bay Company has also experimented with ventures such as lumbering and whaling in an attempt to defray its heavy expenses during recent years when the fur markets have been depressed as a result of the war with France.

FOOD

Transportation costs are far too high to allow much food to be imported into the Northwest from Great Britain or Canada and so most of it must be provided locally. Moreover, imported provisions are not popular because the only types which are practical to send must be dried or salted and these are known to be injurious to health when they constitute a large part of the diet over a considerable time. Consequently, techniques for living on the produce of the country were early adopted by the traders. They acquired skill with the gun, the fishing net and the hoe; they employed native hunters and fishermen; and, perhaps most important of all, they developed a huge trade in provisions with the Indians, particularly those of the plains.

Practically none of the Indians of the Northwest are engaged in agriculture. An exception are the Ojibwa around Lake of the Woods,[1] who, now that their fur animals are depleted, recently turned to growing Indian corn and potatoes to supply the passing traders.[2] They have been able to do this because their lands straddle the all-important Fort William to Lake Winnipeg route of the North West Company. These tribes also gather large quantities of the wild rice which grows along the waterways between Rainy Lake and Lake Winnipeg. This is mostly traded at the company's provision depot at Rainy Lake where it is later supplied to the canoes going into the interior. According to Harmon, wild rice is not produced anywhere else in the Northwest. It grows in water about two feet deep where the bottom is muddy. In appearance it resembles oats, although it generally grows to a height of eight or more feet above the water. It is gathered towards the end of September by beating the heads of rice over canoes which are moved beneath them. So much is gathered in this simple way that the North West Company is able to buy from twelve to fifteen hundred bushels annually, and it is "the principal article of food" at the posts in this area.[3]

Like Indian corn, rice is especially valued as food for the canoemen, and like corn, rice for the following day is usually put to boil after supper and taken from the fire (while still boiling) when the canoes depart at 4 o'clock in the morning. Two hours later, it provides a hot breakfast. Rice has the advantage over corn of not going sour, as the latter tends to do, during the heat of summer.[4] The Hudson's Bay Company, which is not advantageously situated for procuring either corn or rice and which hires a large number of Orcadians and Scots, has imported oatmeal for the same purpose, but at least one post factor (Thomison of Cumberland) regarded it as "not a wholesome food alone for men on long Journeys."[5]

Corn, beans, pumpkins and other crops are also grown beyond the borders of the Northwest for use in that country. The most important suppliers of these products are the Mandans of the Missouri, and the Ojibwa beyond Michilimackinac, who also supply maple sugar.[6] These foods add variety and interest to the traders' otherwise monotonous diet consisting largely of meat.

Most of the meat used in the trade is supplied by the Indians. This is either "green" (as fresh meat is known in the trade) or it is preserved. Preservation is almost invariably performed by cutting the meat into thin slices and then drying them – either over a fire or in the sun. Dried meat is not only very portable but it is considered palatable as well, particularly that dried very slowly in the sun, or by means of a large slow fire. The latter method is preferred by the northern tribes whose lands do not always provide a hot sun. In the south, fires are also used, but they are much larger and the meat is dried more quickly. Hearne considered the result inferior to the northern fare, although most of the traders prefer it.[7]

The most important prepared meat is pemmican, the main staple of nearly all those engaged in the fur trade during the open season. It is made from the lean and fleshy parts of the buffalo which are dried, smoked and pounded into a state known as "beat meat." Forty pounds of melted buffalo fat is poured over 50 pounds of beat meat to make 90 pounds of pemmican. This is then tightly packed in bags made from buffalo hide with the hair left on. These are about 30 inches long, 20 inches wide and about four inches thick – a convenient size and shape for stowage and carriage. Berries are sometimes dried and mixed with the pemmican to give added flavour. According to Thompson, pemmican is wholesome, tasty and nutritious, and affords the greatest nourishment for the least possible bulk and weight. Even the gluttonous French Canadians, who devour eight pounds of fresh meat every day, he says, are content with a pound and a half of pemmican per day.[8]

Pemmican will keep indefinitely. Stocks of it are frequently put aside at the posts for use in emergencies. But apparently some of the men of the Hudson's Bay Company have been negligent in maintaining their reserves for, in 1807, a strongly worded circular letter was sent to the officers and traders inland from Churchill urging them to get as much dried provisions from the natives as they could; at the same time, it warned them that the provisions were not to be used as they had been in the past. Instead, they were to be "religiously preserved" for use in case of a scarcity of fish or fresh meat, although they might be given to the men sent after the natives in winter, and to the men who took the furs down to the factories in boats.[9] But in spite of these instructions, a serious shortage of dried provisions has developed during the severe winter of 1811, and an urgent request has gone out to the provision depot at Bas-de-la-Rivière-Winnipeg for pemmican for Churchill and other factories.[10]

Country provisions have been chronically scarce at Churchill and

York, and both factories have always depended heavily upon European provisions.[11] But with the war, these have become more difficult to obtain and the quality has deteriorated.[12] At the same time, the company has tried to economize by reducing the consumption of European provisions in favour of the products of the Northwest. With this end in view, instructions were issued by London in 1810, that Bas-de-la-Rivière-Winnipeg and the Saskatchewan factories were to supply York, Churchill and other factories with pemmican and dried meat.[13]

The pemmican and dried meat come mostly from the plains. For the Indians of this area, preparing it has become a major industry, especially for the Assiniboines. They trade luxuries such as liquor, tobacco, powder, balls, knives, awls, brass rings, brass wire, blue beads and other trinkets.[14] In spite of the increasing importance of the horse in hunting buffalo, Alexander Henry of the North West Company maintains that the Assiniboine, at least, still capture most of their buffalo in pounds. The reason for this is probably because that tribe suffers from a chronic shortage of horses.[15] In building pounds and in driving the buffalos into them, the Assiniboine are considered to be the most expert on the plains. Their pounds are of various dimensions depending upon the number of tents in one camp. The most common size is from 60 to 100 yards in circumference and about five feet in height. To construct a pound, trees are cut down, laid on top of one another, and woven together with branches and green twigs. Small openings are left to enable the dogs to enter to devour the carcasses of the bulls, which are not normally used by the Indians. The pounds are usually constructed between two hummocks on the downward slope or at the foot of rising ground. The entrance is about ten yards wide and always fronts on the plains. On each side of the entrance is the beginning of a range of fascines which spread outward, away from the opening, for about 300 yards. The initial 100 yards are solid but the last 200 yards become increasingly open as they extend away from the pound. Beyond the fascines, the lines are continued, here and there with three or four crosssticks to resemble dogs or other animals, for another two miles out onto the plains. Double rows of them are also planted in several other directions to an even greater distance.

Young men are sent out to perform the tedious task of collecting and bringing in the buffalo. This is done by setting fire to the dung and grasses on the plains. The herds are driven slowly at first but when the ranges come into sight the speed is increased. As soon as the herd enters the ranges, a sure-footed person disguised with a buffalo robe, who has been stationed there, leads the animals towards the pound. Young men at the rear of the herd then appear and drive them on with all possible speed. The remaining men, together with the women and children, take up positions between the cross-sticks and in the openings among the fascines in order to direct the buffalo onward by waving their robes. The Indian leading the herd rushes into the pound and out the other side either by jumping over the wall or by crawling through an opening left for that purpose. The buffalo tumble in pell-mell at his heels where they are quickly slaughtered with bows and arrows.[16]

The Europeans apparently have not imitated the Indians in using pounds, probably because of the great amount of skill and number of men involved. Nevertheless, they do frequently hunt buffalo on horseback, partly for amusement and partly for profit.[17] This has been resented by the Indians who regard it as an infringement of their "right" to supply provisions. To protect this right, they have frequently set fire to the plains near the posts to drive the buffalo out of the range of the white hunters.[18]

Pounds for deer are made by the Indians of the forest. These are always placed along well-used deer runs. They are similar to buffalo pounds except that they are often a mile or more in diameter and snares are set for the deer which become imprisoned within them.[19] Snares are also used for capturing caribou. These are placed in the openings in a long hedge constructed across the animals' migration path for this purpose.[20] Water-fowl are caught in a similar manner. A number of hedges or fences, about two or three yards apart, are placed at right angles along the edge of the water where the birds generally come to feed. Small openings, large enough for the birds to swim through, are left in the hedges. In these are placed the snares. Much the same type of trap is set to catch partridges as they hop along the edges of the willow groves. The natives also have another simple, but ingenious, way of capturing partridges in winter. Noticing that the snow makes it difficult for them to get pebbles for their gizzards, they have devised a method of catching them in nets with no other bait than a heap of gravel.[21]

Geese are the most important of the water-fowl,[22] and make up a large part of the provisions at the bayside factories.[23] They are killed by both white and native hunters who use a combination of European and Indian techniques. When the geese arrive in the spring, about ten of the best shots at the factory, with several Indians, are sent to the marshes to shoot them. Each man carries two guns and erects a blind, about three feet high and six feet in diameter, made from driftwood and pine branches. This is to provide shelter from the elements as well as to conceal the hunter from the birds' view. The blinds are placed about 120 feet apart along a line across the main flight path of the geese, which is always near the sea or lake-shore. Each hunter has about ten decoy geese. These are sticks made and painted to resemble the head and neck of the grey goose, to which is added a piece of canvas for a body. These are placed about 20 yards from the blinds, with their beaks to the windward, the position in which geese feed. When the geese first arrive, they readily answer the call of the hunter. In fact, the Indians imitate them so well that they would probably land among the decoys, if the shots of the hunters did not prevent them from doing so.[24]

The geese are all shot on the wing. They are too timid, and the marshes too level, to allow the hunters to approach them when they are on the water. According to Thompson, some good shots kill from 70 to 90 geese during the spring hunt, but the general average is from 40 to 50, depending upon the season.[25] This tallies closely with Umfreville who said that a good Indian hunter, in times of plenty, could get from 50 to 60 geese a day.[26] The natives generally bag more than the Europeans[27] but not, perhaps, because they are better shots so much as because they are better able to withstand the long hours of waiting in the cold.[28]

On the plains, the huge flocks of passenger pigeons are hunted during the annual migrations of these birds. Henry mentions "great numbers" of them at the mouth of the Assiniboine in 1800. "The trees were every moment covered with them," he said, "and the continual firing of our people did not appear to diminish their numbers."[29]

A number of other foods are gathered by the natives and whites, and add interest to the traders' table. Some of these, such as dandelion greens and hazel nuts,[30] are familiar in Europe while others such as maple sugar and *wish-a-capucca* "tea" are quite new. Dandelion greens are especially valued at Churchill where they make an early salad long before anything can be produced in the garden.[31] Maple sugar, made by boiling down the sap of the maple tree, is used as a substitute for cane sugar. It has long been produced by the Indians, who sell large quantities to the traders, who have also adopted their practice of making it.[32] *Wish-a-cappuca* is the name given by the natives of Hudson Bay to a plant from which they make a "tea." It is good tasting and used as a beverage by all Europeans living in that part of the Northwest. Many berries are also gathered and used. Gooseberries make excellent pies and tarts; strawberries "of a considerable size and excellent flavour" are known as far north as Churchill River; and cranberries, found in great abundance near Churchill, are annually sent to England in considerable quantities as presents. Other berries used are the heathberry, whose juice makes an exceedingly pleasant beverage; the juniper-berry, which is sometimes used with brandy to make a cordial; currants, and the *bethago-tominick* or dewater-berry. All of these berries are wholesome and act as a preventive against scurvy.[33]

Fish is the main staple at many posts. In fact, most of the posts have been located on lakes and streams noted for their fisheries to ensure that there will be a steady supply of food when provisions from other sources are scarce. Fish are generally caught in nets set near the house, so that a minimum of labour and transport is necessary. The best fish are caught in the autumn and early winter. These are either dried or frozen, but seldom, it would seem, salted. Where fish is plentiful, it is intended to form the main item of diet. Dried provisions are reserved for emergencies although some may be given to the men going down in the canoes since fish is not a suitable food for travelling because it is perishable, awkward to carry and, unlike dried provisions, has to be cooked which requires precious time. The men who go to fetch furs from the Indian tents in winter are also allowed pemmican. Their object is to keep their sled-loads as light as possible, and so they do not wish to be encumbered with a kettle and bulky fish.[34] Far less bulky, and therefore more suitable for long journeys, is the roe of the fish. When dried it is easily carried and a small amount of it will serve many people. For example, two pounds of whitefish roe, when well bruised, will make four gallons of broth.[35]

The Chipewyans are probably the most skilled fishermen. They angle for trout and pike with hooks, some of which they buy from the traders, but for large fish they prefer their own hooks made of bone. Fish caught on their bone hooks seldom get away; such is not always true when European hooks are used. They use a variety of baits whose nature is kept secret. However, Thompson has spied a few of these and reports that eagle's fat, red rag, beaver castorum and red woodpecker feathers are among the things used. For catching large trout which are taken only at depths of from 120 to 240 or more feet, the head of a whitefish is used. No hook is necessary. Instead, a small round stick of birch, well dried and hardened in the fire, is loosely attached to the underside of the bait. The trout grabs the bait head first and a system of slip knots enables it to be swallowed before its progress is arrested by a sudden jerk which causes the piece of wood to become vertical in the mouth – thus catching the trout. This technique has been adopted by the traders.[36]

Both the traders and natives set nets under the ice. The traders' nets are made from twine in the European manner. The Chipewyans make theirs from small thongs cut from raw deer-skins. These seem very good when dry, but after being soaked in water for some time, grow so soft and slippery that when large fish strike the net, the hitches are very apt to slip and allow them to escape. Moreover, these nets are liable to rot unless regularly removed from the water and dried. The Dogrib Indian nets are superior and do not suffer these disadvantages because they are manufactured from twine made by twisting the inner bark of willows.[37]

AGRICULTURE

Hunting, fishing and gathering provide most of the food used at the trading posts. But the produce of the kitchen gardens which are kept at many posts often augments the food supply. Wherever possible, these gardens are planted within the stockades to protect them from the depredations of the Indians and the wild animals. The gardens, too, are a blending of the European and the North American. Indian corn, squashes, pumpkins, beans and potatoes from the new world, are grown beside barley, oats, wheat, cucumbers, peas, onions, turnips, beets, radishes, parsnips, cabbages, cauliflowers, cresses and lettuce from the old. With the exception of the potato (which has now become well known in Europe), the native vegetables seem to be raised only along the Red, Assiniboine, and Rainy rivers; that is, only in the more temperate parts of the Northwest. Barley, oats and wheat have been tried with varying degrees of success in many parts of the country. However, information is too limited to indicate future prospects for these or, for that matter, any other crops. But it is known that barley has been grown with excellent results at Dunvegan, on the Peace River.[38] It has also been successful at Bas-de-la-Rivière-Winnipeg,[39] and Ile-à-la-Crosse,[40] but has failed at Churchill.[41] Wheat came to maturity at Ile-à-la-Crosse.[42] It probably has been tried elsewhere as well, but no reports have yet been received. Root crops, particularly potatoes, have been grown in most of the areas inhabited by the traders. The most notable exception is the coastal strip of New South Wales, where, apart from radishes, only hardy "greens" like cabbages, cauliflowers, cresses, and perhaps beans and peas, can be grown.[43] Inland from the bay, the climate improves considerably so that potatoes, turnips and cabbages can be raised at Split Lake on the Nelson River,[44] and turnips and potatoes at Oxford House on Knee Lake.[45]

ANIMAL HUSBANDRY

The Indians of the Northwest have only two domesticated animals – the dog and the horse. Their bushy-tailed, sharp-eared dogs, resembling foxes and wolves,[46] have been described in the preceding chapter. These are also used by the traders, although the Hudson's Bay Company, at least, has imported dogs of its own as well. These are the large animals from Newfoundland, already mentioned, and domesticated dogs from England. The latter have not always been a success. One that had been sent out to Churchill was badly frozen because of insufficient hair. As a result a request went out for a "Dog and Bitch of large make & thick long hair the younger they are the better & do not let them be lower than 3 or 4 feet high at least."[47]

Horses were introduced into North America by the Spaniards in Mexico and quickly spread throughout the plains;[48] and by the time the first white men entered the Northwest, the Indians were already using them.[49] Undoubtedly, the rapid spread of these animals has been accelerated by the frequent raids of one tribe upon another in search of horses. Indians have been known to travel hundreds of miles looking for this loot. Thompson reports one occasion when the Piegans (who live near the source of the Saskatchewan) made a journey of a distance of fifteen hundred miles in a direct line, and stole horses and mules from the Spaniards.[50]

It has already been seen how, at first, the horse simply replaced the dog as a beast of burden. Besides its size, its greatest advantage over the dog has been that it does not compete with the human being for food and in many areas it can, unlike the dog, fend for itself. On the plains, horses are usually kept near an "island" of trees where they can take shelter from storms.[51] They feed on the long grasses of the plains throughout the year, for the snow is seldom very deep, although at times the horses are forced to remove a foot and a half of it to find their food. The snow is usually blown from the hill tops[52] but the horses prefer the grasses of the valleys which grow to a great height. In this, they differ from the buffalo which prefer to feed on the hilly, dry ground, where the blades of grass are small, short and tender.[53]

Although small, the Northwest horse is bold and intrepid and so delights "in the pleasures of the chace" that when it sights a large band of animals, it can "scarcely be restrained from pursuing them." It is so full of fire that it can with ease out-run most of the large animals on which man depends for his subsistence.[54] According to Henry, a common horse can be bought from the Blackfeet and Piegans for a carrot of tobacco which weighs about three pounds and costs four shillings in Canada.[55] But some are apparently far more expensive, since Harmon mentions losing one in the Swan River department which had cost the North West Company goods to the value of 100 dollars. "Whenever an Assiniboine sells a racer", according to Harmon, "he separates from him in a most affectionate manner. Immediately before delivering him to the purchaser, he steps up to the favourite animal, and whispers in his ear, telling him not to be cast down or angry with his master for disposing of him to another, for, he adds, 'you shall not remain long where you are. I sold you to obtain certain articles, that I stood in great need of; but before many nights have passed, I will come and steal you away.' And, unless great vigilance on the part of the purchaser prevent, he generally fulfils his promise; for they are the greatest horse thieves, perhaps upon the face of the earth."[56] Thompson would agree with Harmon that the Assiniboines are the most notorious of the horse stealers and has said that whenever they appear in small numbers, the horses are immediately guarded. At great risk to themselves, they frequently steal from other tribes. All too often, this is done when the victims are visiting the trading posts. When the traders themselves leave the posts to take their furs down to the depots by boat or canoe, the horses are sent to places where there is plenty of food and water, as well as aspen and poplar, and where they can be easily guarded by two or three well-armed men. The aspen and poplar are used to make fires to relieve the horses from the torment of mosquitoes and horse-flies.[57]

The plains tribes to the westward of the Assiniboines, the Bloods, Piegans and Blackfeet are also notorious thieves, although they have not yet taken to stealing horses from the traders. This is probably because they have such vast numbers of their own. Some of the Blackfeet are said to have as many as 40 or 50 horses apiece, but the Piegans have even greater numbers, one man having been reported as having 300.[58] Most of these have been taken from the defenceless tribes to the south and west, the Snakes [Shoshon], Salish and Kootenay Indians, who own vast herds of horses but still lack guns and ammunition to protect them.[59] The Sarcees seem to content themselves with rearing their own horses.[60]

In the past a few horses seem to have been sent out from Europe to Hudson Bay[61] but recently even the bay posts appear to get their horses from the plains.[62] Besides horses and dogs, a number of other animals have been introduced from Europe. Among these are oxen,[63] hogs,[64] goats[65] and cattle.[66] Rats have also been introduced, unavoidably, as they have come from England "part owner of the cargo"; they have not yet travelled beyond the factories at the seaside.[67] Domestic fowl are now to be found as far west as Fort Vermilion,[68] and Hearne appears to have kept a canary during his stay in the Northwest.[69]

Attempts have been made to tame or domesticate several different types of animals and birds of the Northwest but with little success. The animals have ranged from the polar bear[70] to the field mouse and have included the mink,[71] moose,[72] horned owl,[73] arctic fox, and weasel. Among the more profitable attempts has been that with the Canada goose whose young have been taken in considerable numbers on several occasions at Churchill. These were easily tamed, but never learned to eat grain unless some old geese were taken with them. This was readily done when the birds were moulting and could not fly well. Efforts to domesticate grouse have been less successful. Many trials were made at York by placing the eggs of the grouse under domesticated hens. The eggs hatched and the hens became every bit as fond of the young grouse as they would have been of their own kind, but the grouse always died "probably for want of proper food."[74]

Having noticed that the beaver and the bee were "nearly alike in instinct Wonderfull in their Management of their Buildings and alike providing in the Summer for their Wants in Winter" a certain Frank Oakey of the Hudson's Bay Company, in 1806, humbly submitted to the London Committee a suggestion that the beaver, like the bee, could be domesticated. Even if the skins and castorum were worth nothing, he pointed out, the beaver would be worth breeding "as a Provision to the Servants at the Factories."[75] The Committee, well aware of the great distances which the company is "obliged to go to procure Beaver in consequence of the approaching annihilation of the Species in the Country adjacent to the Factory" eagerly seized on the idea of domesticating the animal and immediately wrote to William Auld to enquire if there were in his vicinity a "Situation adapted to put his plan into

Execution"; they also asked him to inform them of the advantages and disadvantages of the scheme.[76] Auld apparently made enquiries at York Factory which replied directly to London that "The least or even the greatest attempt, with the aid of all your servants at York Factory to execute the plan for propagating Beaver as a commercial concern here or we think in any part of the Country would shew in the Undertakers marks not only of Folly but signs of insanity."[77]

CLOTHING

Most of the clothing used by the traders comes from either Canada or England, usually as partial payment for services; but some is also bought from the Indians, particularly winter wear. This is inevitably made from furs and dressed skins, since none of the Indian tribes of the Northwest have wool, linen or cotton. Skins of the deer family are preferred, with moose being the most popular. Moose skin makes excellent tent-covers and shoe-leather and is used for all types of clothing. The Indians dress their skins by soaking them in a lather made of the brains and some of the softest fat and marrow of the animal, after which they are dried by the heat of the fire and then hung in the smoke for several days. The skins are then taken down, well soaked in warm water, wrung as dry as possible and finally dried by the heat of a slow fire, care being taken to rub and stretch them as long as any moisture remains. Because the skins are not dressed in oil, they always become hard after being wet unless great care is taken to keep rubbing them all the time they are drying. The same applies to all Indian-dressed leather except that made from the *wapiti* [elk] which washes as well as chamois-leather and always preserves its softness.[78] Because their own clothing is frequently stiff and uncomfortable after having been wet, the Indians often prefer European wear, especially for use during the wet weather of the spring and autumn. European clothing must have a special appeal for the women who must otherwise perform the tedious task of softening the leather of the family's clothing, particularly when the men are in camp. It also relieves them, of course, of the labour of making the clothing in the first place.

Some idea of the amount of work and material which goes into producing an Indian's clothing may be gained by examining the annual wardrobe for an adult. First in importance is the warm winter suit. To make it, the prime parts of the skins of from eight to ten deer are required. All of these should be killed during August or early September, for after that the hair is too long and at the same time so loose that it will drop off with the slightest injury. Light summer clothing, as well as stockings and shoes, are made from dressed leather. For these things, several more deer-skins are required. In addition, skins are needed in a parchment state, for making thongs, or *clewla,* as the natives call them for manufacturing netting for snow-shoes, snares for deer, sewing for sledges, fish-nets and so on. All in all, each person requires upwards of twenty deer skins for clothing and other uses, each year, exclusive of tent cloths, bags and a number of other things made from them.[79]

Among the most highly esteemed articles of native clothing are Eskimo boots. These are worn to above the knee by both the men and women. The foot is of moose-skin, and the upper part is of seal-skin with the hair off. Both are sewed neatly together so as to be perfectly watertight. These boots are much sought after by the people at the factories for use in the marshes where their European boots always leak. With care, a pair of Eskimo boots will last two years.[80]

MEDICINE

For the most part, the natives of the Northwest have strong constitutions and good health. Their diseases are few with dysentry and a violent pain in the chest, known as the "country distemper," being among the most prevalent.[81] The latter was supposed by Umfreville and others "to proceed from the cold air being drawn into the lungs; which impeding the vessels from spreading through that organ, hinders the circulation, and renders respiration extremely painful and difficult."[82] Mackenzie, however, considers this unreasonable. He believes that the complaint comes from the natives' "immoderate indulgence in fat meat at their feasts, particularly when they have been preceded by a long fasting."[83] A venereal disease is also very common among the natives, although Umfreville thought the symptoms to be "much milder than in Europe, perhaps owing to their diet, which is void of spices, or salt, and of spiritous liquors, when from the Factory."[84] According to Mackenzie, the progress of this disease is slow but it nevertheless gradually undermines the constitution and brings on premature decay.[85] In any case, few of the natives live to a great age, although they tend to enjoy all their faculties to the last.[86] Many of them die of consumption and of the "fevers" that frequently attack them.[87] They are also troubled with pains in their heads, breasts and joints, and many of them, especially the women, are subject to fits.[88]

For relief from nearly all of their diseases, the Indians resort to their favourite remedy – sweating. This is done in a structure designed especially for that purpose. "They make a Little hutt or tent, about four foot high and about 6 foot over, – which Done, they take as many Coats or skin's, as they can procure, and Cover itt up close, Leaving a small Vacancy to go in att, – they then take about 20 Large stones, and heet them hott in the fire, in another tent, when hott, they put them into their hutt or swetting house, as they Explain itt. (Mu tu tu san a'ke,) then they go Naked as they were born, their they sitt Like monkey's upon their Brich, tell they are in a perdigious sweat, – and when they think they have swetted Suffitiently, they then come out, and Run as they are in Such a heat into the River if Summer, if Winter they wash themselves with Snow, by Which I never knew itt did them Either good or harm; – Such methods with Some Europians wou'd be prest. Death, But these Natives are of such a Strong constitution as before mentioned that nought can hurt them."[89]

The sweat-house is supplemented by a fairly elaborate system of medicine. The Ojibwas, Woodland Crees and Plains Crees have a greater knowledge than other tribes of the medicinal qualities of the bark of trees, herbs, roots and so forth. This, together with their superior medical skill, has enabled them to charge high fees to members of other tribes who frequently call upon them for their professional services. Sometimes, for a handsome compensation, the medicine-men will give instructions on where to procure certain medicinal ingredients, and how they should be prepared and used in particular cases.[90] The usual method of administration of their *materia medica* is in the form of purges and clysters, but these remedies, like their rudimentary surgery, are blended with the mystery of magic and incantation.[91] Harmon is obviously impressed with their skill and has stated that it is well known "to those acquainted with the Indians, that their physicians frequently effect cures with their roots, herbs, &c in cases, which would baffle the skill and the drugs, of a scientifick physician,"[92] although he has cynically observed that it is very probable "that Indian doctors, like some apothecaries in the civilized world, sell some medicines, of little or no value."[93]

The Crees have certain simples which induce abortions, which they sometimes practise, and it is claimed that the act can be repeated without injury to the health of the woman on whom it has been performed.[94] For sprains, the dung of an animal just killed is considered to be the best remedy. To cure blisters on the feet caused by frost or chafing shoes, the Indians immediately open the blister and apply the heated blade of a knife to the affected part. As painful as it is, the treatment has been found to be effective. A sharp flint is used as a cautery for searing bruises and swellings; it also serves as a lancet for letting blood.[95]

The Indian procedure for letting blood has been found to be very effective and has been adopted by the traders on occasion.[96] Unlike the European method, it is not performed upon the arm but upon the back of the hand, after the wrist has been tied off "pretty hard." In praise of this technique, James Isham of the Hudson's Bay Company wrote that he had "never heard of any one that Losst their arm, or that came to any hurt by so doing."[97]

Chipewyan medicine is far less developed than that of their southern neighbours. In fact, Mackenzie claims that the uses of simples and plants are unknown to them because their country does not produce any. Consequently, they have had recourse to superstition for their cures; and charms have been their only remedies, except for the bark of the willow, which is burned and reduced to a powder and sprinkled on open wounds and ulcers.[98]

The use of the inner bark of the larch as a poultice, "which is generally us⁴ among the Natives to stop or Prevent a Mortification,"[99] has been adopted by the Europeans. They have also learned from the Indians the only "efficient cure yet known" for snow blindness. It consists simply of applying the steam of boiling water, as hot as the patient can bear, to the affected eyes.[100]

Probably the greatest elixir of the Northwest is *wish-a-cappuca* "tea."[101] Umfreville wrote that it grew "very plentifully in all parts of the country. The Indians make use of it by way of medicine; it makes a very agreeable tea, and is much used here both by Europeans and natives, not only for its pleasant flavour, but for its salutary effects. Its virtues are many; it is an aromatic, very serviceable in rheumatic cases, strengthens the stomach, relieves the head, and also promotes perspiration. Outwardly, it is applied to gangrenes, confusions, and excoriations; in the latter case the powder is made use of."[102] However, Samuel Hearne, who was a very keen observer, very much doubted if *wish-a-cappuca* tea "had the least medical quality," although it was "much used by the lower class of the Company's servants as tea; and by some . . .

thought very pleasant."[103] Thompson seems to be less sceptical and has found it a useful cure for dysentry.[104]

The cold of winter, which is thought to be "fatal to every species of contagious fever," seems in the case of scurvy to be "the most dreadful auxilliary."[105] To cure and prevent scurvy, many expensive articles have been imported including English porter, port wine, crystalized salt of lemon, and essence of malt.[106] Local cranberries have also been tried and have been found to be "nearly equal to oranges & lemons as a specific for Scurvy."[107] Spruce-juice has also proved very effective as an antiscorbutic.[108]

Apart from the usual sicknesses, epidemics have raged across the Northwest from time to time. Probably the most catastrophic of these was the smallpox epidemic of the winter of 1781-2. Thompson believes that the epidemic probably had its origin in an attack which some Sioux and Ojibwa made on a number of infected white settlers in 1780. From the Ojibwa, the disease spread among the tribes of the forest throughout the country, and from the Sioux, to all of the Indians of the plains and even to those beyond the Rockies.[109]

At first the Indians had been unaware that smallpox could be passed on from one man to another, any more than a wounded man could give his wound to another.[110] But after they learned of the infectious nature of the disease, they would immediately abandon even their closest relations as soon as the latter became ill. As a result, many Indians starved or were eaten by wild animals before they could recover their strength. However, the Hudson's Bay men, at least, took many of the victims into their forts and shared with them all that they had. Apparently none of the Europeans contracted the disease from the Indians. Although no information is at hand, it is possible that the Canadian traders behaved just as humanely. The Hudson's Bay Company men tried to prevent the disease from spreading by keeping the different tribes separated from one another,[111] and by smoking their clothes and other personal effects with flour of sulphur.[112]

Proportionately, more men died than women and children because the men, unable to bear the heat of the fever, rushed into the rivers and lakes to cool themselves, and the greater part of them perished. From the number of tents which remained after the epidemic of 1781-2, it appears that about two-fifths of the natives died, although the survivors believed that far more than half the population had perished.[113] After the epidemic, at least one tribe stopped the indiscriminate slaughtering of its enemies and began adopting the children, young women and male youths not yet bearing arms, whom they captured in attacks. In this way, they hoped to build up their own strength at the expense of that of their enemies.[114] Older Indians, of course, continued to be slaughtered.

FEMALE SERVANTS

The "adoption" or more properly the enslaving of Indians has not been restricted to the natives themselves. For a number of young women captives have been sold to the traders to be reared at the posts, where Umfreville claimed that they were "more happy than their slaughtered parents had ever been."[115] Some, like the one Hearne requested a war party to obtain for him, are brought up as domestics,[116] while others, like the two Sioux women Thompson's men bought from the Mandans in 1798, are later sold to other traders.[117] On one occasion, two women are reported to have been taken as far as Montreal to be sold.[118] During the past few years, however, this traffic has been discouraged. Since 1806, the partners of the North West Company have been forbidden to allow their men to take women from the Indians. Those who continue to do so have been made to pay a heavy fine.[119] Of course, the distinction between the taking of women from the natives and in taking a wife in the manner of the country is not always an easy one to make. Perhaps it is for this reason that the Hudson's Bay Company has always discouraged its men from having any sort of connection with the native women. This has not, of course, prevented a number of Indian wives and halfbreed children from collecting around the various posts. In many ways, these women have been the servants of the company, although they have not been recognized as such in London. To rectify this situation, the small committee at York Factory decided to throw caution to the winds and, in 1802, sent an address to the London committee on behalf of their wives and children. The address preceded the sending of an account of the company goods which had been supplied to the women and children, and was apparently intended to allay any protests which the London committee might have made by pointing out that the women were "deserving of some encouragement and indulgence" since they cleansed and put into a state of preservation all beaver and other skins brought in by the Indians as well as preparing line for snowshoes, making leather shoes and performing many other useful tasks. "In short," the address ended, "they are virtually your Honours Servants

and as such we hope you will consider them."[120] It is to be hoped that
the native women will receive generous consideration from London if
only because they have (in common with the Indian men) provided
the traders with a great deal of knowledge of how to live in the
Northwest.

USES OF TREES

The Indians have taught the traders the uses of many trees found in
the Northwest. The most important of these is the birch whose outer-
bark is widely used for covering canoes. It is also highly esteemed for
making tents because, unlike leather, it can be packed when wet without
rotting. But because it has the disadvantage of cracking if it is rolled
when cold, it often must be heated over a fire before being packed away.
As the bark is most easily removed from the tree during the early part
of the summer when the sap is rising, it is usually collected at that time
of year. The reddish inner-bark is used by the Indian women for
tanning leather.[121] Although the birch is the most important single tree
in the Northwest, the maple, cedar, pine, spruce and other trees are
widely used for a variety of purposes. The pine for example, is important
for its turpentine.[122]

MINERALS

Few minerals have yet been discovered in the Northwest, and those
which have have not been extensively used. Salt-springs are known to
exist in many places,[123] but they do not seem to have been used by the
natives for preserving food. This is probably not a result of ignorance
of the preserving qualities of brine, but rather, an expression of their
preference for drying food. In many ways, the latter method is superior
and it is well known that the traders always adopt the native way when
they are in the interior.[124] Salt provisions are still, however, carried
by the Nor'westers from Fort William; and the Hudson's Bay Company
annually puts down many barrels of ducks and geese in brine at its
bayside factories. Native provisions are often scarce on the bay, and
so the produce of the short water-bird season must be used throughout
the year. In that climate, salting would seem to be the only means
available for preserving the birds until they can be used. The salt being
sold to passing traders by the free traders at The Pas in 1808,[125] would
have been intended solely for flavouring.

Coal has been found in open seams at several places along the Saskatchewan[126] and Mackenzie rivers.[127] In its pure state it has been used by the smiths of the North West Company for the forge, with equal portions of charcoal made of birch or aspen, and has answered every purpose for making and repairing axes and other tools.[128] It does not appear to be used by the natives except for dying porcupine quills.[129]

Bitumen issues in "fountains" along the banks of the Athabasca River near the forks of the Clearwater and elsewhere.[130] It was probably from the natives that the traders learned to mix it with spruce gum to seal their canoes. The fountains would seem to be quite deep, since a twenty-foot pole can be inserted "without the least resistance."[131]

Copper appears to be the only metallic mineral employed by the natives (although Mackenzie saw several lumps of un-used iron ore on the banks of the Mackenzie River) .[132] It is found on the Coppermine River and on the south shore of Lake Superior.[133] It is only used by a few Indians and even then it is not smelted but merely beaten into shape.[134]

NATIVE CRAFTSMANSHIP

Stone is widely used by the Eskimos and by some Indian tribes for making utensils and other objects (see fig. 2) . The Chipewyans skilfully carve stone pipes for smoking tobacco, a habit which they have learned from the Europeans.[135] These pipes, along with the tobacco, a flint and steel, and touch-wood for making a fire, are often carried in a small bag called a "skiperton." Some of these are truly elegant, being richly ornamented with beads, porcupine quills and moose hair. They are made by the women and are highly esteemed by the Europeans for the neatness of their workmanship.[136] The porcupine quills are coloured with a number of different dyes which the Indians make from the roots of plants. So impressed was John Reinhold Forster with the quality of the natives' dyes, that he urged the Hudson's Bay Company to export some of the roots to England for dying cloth.[137]

ESKIMO CARVINGS

Ivory is much used by the Eskimos in making many of their utensils, weapons and tools. It is also employed for making toys for their children. These are mostly small carvings in the forms of their birds, beasts and fish; their men, women and children; and of their utensils. Their more recent carvings reflect what they have seen of the white man and his equipment. For there are now also carvings of European men, and of their ships, and boats. In short, nothing has escaped their keen powers of observation and imitation.[138] William Wales, the mathematician, believed that perhaps few people have a "greater genius for arts." He said that it is shown in every one of their implements, but particularly in their boats, harpoons, darts, bows and "snow-eyes." The latter is a device "excellently contrived" for protecting the eyes from the effects of the bright sun on the snow in the spring.[139]

WHALING

One of the most ingenious of the Eskimo implements is the harpoon, which is designed for use at sea. It is attached to inflated bladders by means of coiled ropes. The bladder not only marks the course of the wounded animal, but greatly slows it down as well, so that it might easily be taken. With these weapons, large white whales can be taken by the Eskimos in their frail little kayaks. The kayaks are ideally suited to the natural conditions of the area near the mouth of the Seal River where the white whales congregate for about a month each summer. At this place, the bottom of the bay is studded with huge rocks and is so level that the water retreats some six to seven miles at low tide. The whales swim among the rocks making them very difficult and dangerous to pursue in conventional boats. But the Eskimos, with their kayaks, can twist about in any direction with great dexterity to avoid the rocks and still capture their prey with their harpoons and bladders.

This method of whaling is safer than that employed by the men of the Hudson's Bay Company. They use small sail-boats with the bottoms painted white to resemble whales. The crews consist of "two of the worst hands in the factory." One man acts as both steersman and harpooner and stands, with the tiller between his legs and the harpoon in his hands, watching under the boat for any "silly whale" which might mistake the vessel for a companion.[140] The harpoon line is fastened to the boat (rather than to a bladder) and frequently a wounded whale has pulled the boat from three to five miles, at some five miles per hour, before the animal could be finally dispatched with a lance.[141] In an area with so many large rocks lurking beneath the shallow waters, the small boats and their crews are in constant danger of being pulled to their destruction. William Auld has stated that the whales range from 16 feet in length down to three or four feet,[142] while Thompson says that they average about 15 feet.[143]

Eighty or 90 whales have been taken by each of the company's boats during the season. This means that each boat produces some eight and a half to nine and a half tons of oil a year. The number of boats used depends largely on how many men can be spared from other tasks to man them.[144] With the shortage of personnel during recent years it is unlikely that more than one or two boats could have been fitted out for whaling in 1811, and probably the production was no greater than it had been during Hearne's time when eight to 13 tons of oil were sent to England each year. Because of the labour shortage and the financial difficulties the company is now experiencing, it is doubtful if the bounty offered to those engaged in whaling during Hearne's day,[145] is still in effect.

White whales are also taken by the Eskimos in the Mackenzie delta,[146] but only in New South Wales have they been hunted by Europeans. Whaling has never been popular among the whites, but at least it has provided a diversion for those who have been forced to live in what must be one of the least interesting regions in the whole of the North-west – New South Wales.

6

Ports of Entry

New South Wales,[1] the low-lying region next to Hudson Bay, is one of the three regions into which the Northwest is naturally divided, the others being the Great Plains and the Stony Region (see map 2). Stretching diagonally across all three from the northwest to the southeast is the Great Western Forest which gives way to the open Grasslands to the south and to the Barren Grounds to the north. The white residents of the Northwest are familiar with these regions either from discussion or from first-hand experience, but it would be wrong to suppose that this is the manner in which they view the country. Instead, they see it in terms of the wonderful river systems which weave together the several regions. For the convenience of the prospective settler, the traders' view of the Northwest has been adopted here and each of the principal river "countries" will be discussed in some detail. But before doing so, let us look at the main ports of entry into the country: York Factory, Churchill Factory and Fort William, and then at the East Winnipeg, Muskrat and English River countries and the Barren Grounds which lie between these ports and the river countries.

YORK FACTORY

York Factory is not only the oldest port in the Northwest but is, indeed, among the oldest settlements in North America, having been established (as Fort Nelson) in 1682, the same year as Philadelphia, the former capital of the United States. Its situation (see fig. 3) had been chosen for its convenient communication with the Indians of the interior who could journey down to the factory by way of either the Hayes or Nel-

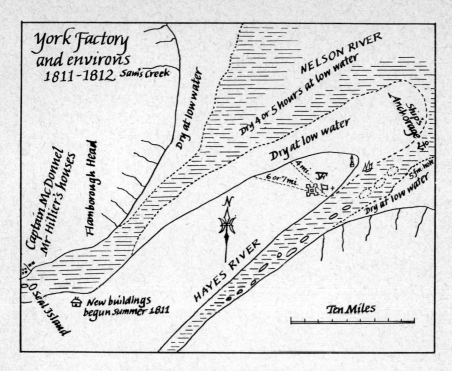

FIGURE 3 York Factory and Environs, 1811-1812

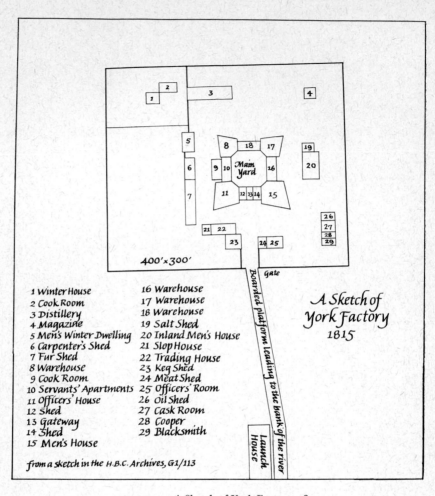

FIGURE 4 A Sketch of York Factory, 1815

son rivers. These rivers follow a northeasterly course across New South
Wales. Throughout most of their passage they flow towards one another
until, about 25 miles from the sea, they are only five miles apart. From
there until they finally merge at Hudson Bay their routes are nearly
parallel. It was on the long point of land between their final ascents that
the Hudson's Bay Company chose to place its main establishment in the
Northwest, York Factory. The buildings (see fig. 4) are situated on the
Hayes at a point where the peninsula is about four miles wide.[2] The
Hayes, rather than the mighty Nelson, was chosen because it was considered by the natives to be much the safer river to travel upon and
consequently they had generally used it in coming down to the bay.
Moreover, it was generally open a month before the Nelson.[3] An added
advantage of the Hayes over the Nelson has been the boulder-strewn
mud-flats at its mouth which provide protection from attack from the
sea, even if they also make it difficult for the supply ship to approach
the factory. The latter can only anchor at Five Fathom Hole, three miles
from the factory, a distance that is nothing but an expanse of glistening
mud between almost every tide.[4]

The factory is built on low miry ground about 100 yards from the
river. During the open season it is always surrounded by stagnant water.
The main building is two storeys high, badly designed and as badly
constructed. From its heaving foundations to its lead roof, it is inconvenient in every respect and indifferent in appearance. The best rooms
have grates similar to those used in England for burning coal. But the
front bars have been removed to enable logs to be used which are burned
standing on end. Most of the heat goes up the chimneys which are
merely deep narrow holes with straight jambs. Canadian or Swedish
stoves would be far more satisfactory but, complains Miles Macdonell,
there are none in use "in all the country."

All of the buildings, except the launch house and the canoe store, are
surrounded by a rectangular stockade some 400 by 300 feet. The pickets
are about 18 feet above the ground and so slender and open that they
could give no protection from an enemy. Outside the stockade, on the
bank of the river close to the wharf, is a store called the launch house.
Each spring, it is in danger of being carried away by the breaking up of
the ice, and the precaution of removing the stores into the factory must
be taken. This year, however, the stores were little safer in the factory
since it, too, was flooded. So grave was the threat at one point, that
manned boats had been kept on the ready at the front gate so that the

inhabitants could save themselves and some of the stores, had the waters continued to rise.[5]

Because the factory is built in a swamp, its cellars are full of water from June to November, and must be pumped out several times a week. During this time, nothing can be kept in them.[6] But even in winter, their use is limited, since anything which might be damaged through freezing can not be stored in them.[7] With the coming of the cold weather and the freezing of the swampy ground, the buildings tend to shift on their foundations, causing the doors and windows to cast. Through the resulting gaps, whip the winter's winds. So cold is the main building, and so inefficient and ineffectual are its fireplaces, that serious consideration is being given to abandoning it in winter. The men would be moved to the woods a few miles off. A responsible person would be left in charge of the factory with one or two others to assist in the care of the gates and other tasks. In this way, five or six fires could be saved while most of the men would enjoy the comfort of a snug winter house. The winter house would be built of "temporary materials" so that after the woods near it had been burned off, it could be either moved to a new site, or readily abandoned since the original cost would have been very low.[8]

Although the factory buildings are still being lived in during the present winter of 1811-12, it should be pointed out that for many years it has been the custom for some of the people to take to log tents in the woods during the severe weather;[9] particularly, the sick who could not be permitted to live in the factory because there are no fireplaces in the men's cabins.[10] These log tents must have been similar to those used by Edward Ellis more than half a century ago. His tents "were made of Trees hewn and cut, about sixteen Feet long, raised close together, their Ends lying one against another at the Top, but extending at the Bottom, in the Form of the Roof of a Country-House. Between these Logs the Vacancies were stuffed with Moss, and that being plaistered over with Clay, made a warm Hutt; the Door was low and small, a Fire-Place in the middle, and a Hole over it, to let out the Smoke."[11] Ellis supposed the "contrivance" to have been borrowed from the Indians although James Isham, his contemporary, said that they "never build any."[12]

In October of this year (1811), an irregular line of log tents were built along the north bank of the Nelson River, about 50 miles from York Factory, to house the group of Irish and Scots settlers. These tents are high in front with a shade roof sloping to the rear, and are covered over with moss and clay nearly a foot thick.[13] They have been placed near a point known as the "Deer Crossing Place," where it was thought there would be a ready supply of food. According to the natives and the tradi-tions of their forefathers, there has never been a year when, at certain seasons, the deer have not passed that way.[14] About two miles of deer fences, with snares concealed in them have been erected on both sides of the river, but by the end of the year, the deer still had not come.[15]

Across the river and a bit down stream, the year-old outpost of York, known as the "New Establishment," has also been disappointed by the failure of the deer. Its success last winter had caused the chief at York to rashly predict that his factory, from then onward, could be virtually independent of English provisions. But now he must be ruefully echoing Hearne's warning, based upon 20 years of experience in the Northwest, that anyone who relies "much on the produce of the different seasons, will frequently be deceived, and occasionally expose himself and men to great want." "In some years," said Hearne, "hundreds of deer may easily be killed within a mile of York Fort; and in others, there is not one to be seen within twenty or thirty miles. One day thousands and tens of thousands of geese are seen, but the next they all raise flight, and go to the North to breed. Salmon ... is so plentiful in some years at Churchill River, that it might be procured in any quantity; at others so scarce as to be thought a great delicacy."[16]

It is to be hoped that the garden laid out at the New Establishment will be more productive than the deer hedge has so far been. The soil about the house appears to be rich and "being from its low situation ex-posed to the inundation of a Creek and the River receives each year tribute of rich manure the finest nature produces."[17] Certainly, any produce from this garden would be extremely welcome at York for, in 1811, there was no garden at the factory itself. (The cabbages served at the factory in October had come from the garden at Churchill Factory.) Miles Macdonell, with the critical eye of the new arrival, claims that a garden formerly cultivated at the old factory at York had produced well, but that the present chief "has no taste that way."[18] Relations between Macdonell and the chief, William Auld, have not been very cordial and it is possible that Macdonell is being unfair. There is, of course, a serious shortage of men and it might well be that Auld has felt he can not spare the hands for a garden.

Macdonell is spending his first winter in the Northwest. When his comments were made he had not yet experienced the full extremes of the climate of New South Wales, where Umfreville reported that "a good Fahrenheit's Thermometer frequently stood at 50 degrees below the cypher in the month of January; whereas in summer, the mercury would very frequently ascend to 90 deg. above the cypher, making a difference of 140 degrees between the extremities of heat and cold." The frost never leaves the ground. Even in summer it remains at a depth of four feet below the surface in open areas and in places where the forest shuts out the sun, to a depth of only two feet. But even if the climate were less extreme, Umfreville felt that the "loose and clayey" nature of the soil at York would have made it very unfit for agriculture. He conceded that "a tolerable quantity of cresses, radishes, lettuces, and cabbages" could have been procured with proper cultivation and, in a favourable season, even peas and beans; but he warned that "these so seldom come to any perfection, that they are esteemed a kind of luxury."[19]

Macdonell admits that the season is too short for growing grain but has observed that good meadows might be made in every part of the country which he has so far seen. Auld would no doubt agree with this, but would also have to point out the difficulties involved in keeping domesticated animals in such a severe climate. Sufficient grass must be cut to last the eight months of winter and, during this period, the cattle as well as the store hogs are fed in the house.[20] At the present time there are three cows and as many horses at York Factory.[21] Hay is procured from islands in the vicinity. Macdonell claims that these could furnish fodder for a considerable stock, were the people expert in making it. Instead of following the present practice of cutting only what is close to the water's edge and bringing it away in boats to the factory to dry, he suggests that it could be cured and stacked on the spot; and since the islands do not flood until spring, that it could easily be brought away in winter.[22]

With so little in the way of agricultural produce and country provisions, York Factory has always relied heavily on European supplies, particularly salted meats.[23] This has resulted in periodic epidemics of scurvy. Those suffering from the disease have always been put into a log tent "for the benefit of having a fire near their bed."[24] York has been the most notorious post for scurvy, although the disease is not unknown at the other bayside factories.[25] By the end of 1811, scurvy has not made its expected appearance, although Macdonell is not very hopeful for the months ahead since, with the failure of the deer-hedge, his men are now living entirely on salted provisions. In an attempt to stave off the disease, he has requested from Auld "a quantity of Essence of Malt, Chrystalized Salts of Lemon, &c."[26] Auld apparently did not have sufficient stocks on hand at York Factory, for when he left for Churchill late in October, he took with him two men with Indians and dogs, who were to return to York with a load of "Essence of Malt and Cranberries."[27]

Auld has gone to Churchill for the winter to help reduce the amount of wood burned at York.[28] During the past summer at Churchill, many of the superfluous servants from the interior had been employed in rafting fire-wood, while awaiting the arrival of the annual ship. The ship, as already seen, had been so late in reaching the Northwest, that it had by-passed Churchill and had gone right on to York. As a result, a huge pile of wood accumulated which, along with the coal from England on hand, should last for three or four years at least.[29] Unlike the Churchill, the Hayes and Nelson rivers do not seem to be used for rafting down fire-wood, although drift-wood is known to collect at Flamborough Head.[30] Instead, horses are employed to haul in fire-wood during the winter months. Late in December 1811, after the deer and other animals had failed to materialize, Auld's replacement at York sardonically wrote, "our fire-wood hunters succeed better, thank God the Trees are not migratory, else no doubt they too would have shunned our now unhallowed and pestilential neighbourhood."[31] Nevertheless, the line of trees over the years has been retreating ever further from York and the other bayside factories, under the relentless demands for fire-wood and timber. This has been particularly true at Churchill where the trees are both further from the factory and smaller in size than at the other factories. There, the country has been ransacked for timber so long that nothing worthy of the name can now be obtained. Back in 1802, when some planks were required to repair the launch, a number of men were sent in search of timber. After several days of hunting, the best they could find was a "patch of middling stout trees" which had to be hauled several miles overland before being sent 26 miles by water to the factory. On this, as on other occasions, the needed timber was finally obtained from Severn, the most southerly factory in New South Wales.[32]

CHURCHILL FACTORY

By the middle of the eighteenth century, the scattered trees along the banks of the Churchill had been cleared to a distance of some 80 miles from its mouth.[33] Most of them undoubtedly had been consumed in the large fire-places at Fort Prince of Wales (fig. 6) where they had brought the inhabitants a mixture of comfort and distress. It had been the custom at the fort to close the tops of the chimneys with an iron cover as soon as the wood had burned down to glowing coals. This had kept the heat in the house, but unfortunately it had also kept in the smoke as well, causing the inmates' heads to ache, particularly during the 18 hours a day when the shutters were kept closed. In four or five hours, the fire would be out and soon the inside walls of the house and the bed places would be covered with two or three inches of ice. This was chopped off each morning with a hatchet. Three or four times a day, 24 pound shot were made red hot and hung in the windows of the apartments. Yet even with these to supplement the fires, it had not been enough to prevent the beer, wine, ink and so forth, from freezing in the rooms.[34]

Probably few men wept when Fort Prince of Wales was destroyed by the French in 1782. But if they had expected it to be replaced with a more comfortable building, they were doomed to disappointment. The new house, sent out the next year "in frame," had apparently been designed for English conditions and, because of the "thinness of the weather boarding," offered meagre protection from the harsh winds of Hudson Bay.[35] During the following year, Thompson had spent his first winter in the Northwest in this building. He vividly describes the experience: "All our movements more, or less, were for self-preservation: All the wood that could be collected for fuel, gave us only one fire in the morning, and another in the evening. The rest of the day, if bad weather, we had to walk in the guard room with our heavy coats of dressed Beaver; but when the weather was tolerable we passed the day in shooting Grouse. The interior of the walls of the House were covered with rime to the thickness of four inches, pieces of which often broke off, to prevent which we wetted the whole extent, and made it a coat of ice, after which it remained firm, and added to the warmth of the House ..."[36]

During his stay at Churchill, Thompson had visited the granite ruins of Prince of Wales and was much impressed with how the fort, from its strategic position upon Eskimo Point, had commanded the narrow entrance to the mighty Churchill. By land the fort could be approached only by a narrow neck of sand, and by sea only at one place because of the shallowness of the water.[37] The new house, where Thompson wintered, was built five miles above the stone fort. It has been suggested that Samuel Hearne, the Governor of Churchill, had deliberately chosen a location for the new post from which Prince of Wales could not be seen, because he did not wish to be ever reminded that it was he who had surrendered it to the French without firing a single shot. This, however, was not the case. The decision to relocate the post was made by Beaver

FIGURE 5   Churchill Factory

FIGURE 6 Fort Prince of Wales

House, the Company's headquarters in London. It had instructed Hearne to choose "the most convenient Situation above Cuckolds point ... 5 miles higher up the River than where the Stone Fort was built."[38] Probably London had thought it expedient to move to the source of fire-wood and lumber, although it must have known that this was a very marshy area. However, Hearne managed to find a rocky point and there he built his fort.

The rocky point has proved to be a very poor choice. In fact, William Auld has gone so far as to say that the factory "could not have been more disadvantageously placed had the highest premium been given for the most diligent search."[39] The situation, he says, is so inconvenient that a very considerable part of the men's "labour and study" has to be expended in merely overcoming the difficulties it produces. The point is too small – just large enough to accommodate the factory and its palisades, but no more. It is also too high and too steep for easy communication with the water, and yet it is too low for safety since "any old drunken women" could set the place ablaze in a moment by throwing down fire-brands from the higher rocks near by. Nor would there be the slightest hope of extinguishing the fire since water can only be got at a great distance and at an even greater inconvenience. During the winter, the palisades have been of no use whatever since they are covered over with drifted snow to a depth of fifteen feet. Fresh water comes from a cask sunk in a swamp about three hundred yards from the factory. Unfortunately, it is on the same level as the high tides so that in the autumn, it is rare when the cask is not overflowed with sea-water. But what really vexes Auld is the knowledge that near at hand is an ideal site for a factory. Not only does it have a large fresh-water pond, but it is well situated for defence and easily accessible from the river. Moreover, part of the site is level and admirably suited for a garden. So eligible has the spot appeared to everyone at the factory that they have often considered putting up a palisade around it to prevent the Canadians from settling there, should they ever come to the Churchill. There is not a single other place on the river suitable for an establishment.[40]

Although Churchill had a garden in 1811, when York did not, it must be pointed out that Churchill is even worse situated for provisions than York. For not only is its climate more severe, because of its more northerly location, but the banks along the lowest ten miles of the river are nothing but loose gravel, bare rocks, or marshes. Each year they are overflowed by the spring tides and never dry before they are flooded once again. William Wales, F.R.S., once explored this area to see if he could discover any ground suitable for growing grain. But "in all that extent." he later wrote, "we did not find one acre, which, in my opinion, was likely to do it." Wales was less pessimistic about the prospects of growing oats in ground near the old stone fort, although he had been "well convinced" that no other grain could be raised. He based his optimism upon a trial he had seen which led him to believe that oats "might be brought to some tolerable degree of perfection in time, with proper culture."[41] This trial, however, is almost certainly the same one referred to by Hearne who was at Churchill when Wales was there. Hearne, who had served with the Navy in Spain before going to Hudson Bay, described the oat field as "nothing but a hot burning sand, like the Spanish lines at Gibralter, the success of the experiment may be easily guessed; which was, that it did not produce a single grain."[42]

The problems involved in keeping livestock at Churchill are similar to those at York. With a great deal of labour, sufficient hay is cut and dried in the marshes to keep a few animals during the long winter.[43] Local provisions are also similar to those found at York. They consist mainly of ducks and geese from the coastal marshes, as deer from the interior woodlands can never be depended upon. In many areas of the Northwest, where game is scarce, fish have played an important supplementary role in the traders' diet. But in New South Wales this has never been the case. For fish are few in both kind and number. Hearne maintained that the black whale, white whale, salmon, and a small fish called "kepling" are the "only species of Sea-fish" found in that part of the country.[44]

York, however, has one great advantage over Churchill Factory in that the Hayes and Nelson lead to Lake Winnipeg and ultimately to the pemmican lands along the Saskatchewan and Red Rivers. The Churchill River, on the other hand, is poor in provisions. Along its banks are few plains and those which do exist are too densely covered with trees for the buffalo to graze. The only exception is the area around its source in the Beaver River.[45]

In the autumn of 1808, a few Chipewyans, who had summered far to the north of Churchill, arrived at the factory with 300 pounds of venison to trade. On their way there, they were way-laid by a considerable number of Eskimos who "laid them under contributions." Guns and ammunitions, of course, changed owners, but fortunately for the Indians, they were allowed to continue to the factory for a fresh stock.[46] Such incidents are all too common between members of the different native groups. But no post is more familiar with them than is Churchill.

For here is the meeting place of three of the four major native groups of the Northwest – the Southern Indian [Algonkian], Northern Indian [Athapaskan] and the Eskimo [Eskimoan] (see fig. map 5). All three groups are extremely jealous of one another, making it essential for the traders at Churchill to be ever on their guard not to show favouritism to any one of them.[47] The Southern Indians are represented by the Crees who form the "Home Guard," not only at Churchill, but at York and at its outpost, Fort Severn, as well. The Home Guard are Indians who live near the factories where they can be called upon to assist in case of attack, to help in the hunt, to carry messages, and to aid in the transport of furs and goods between the bay and the posts in the interior. Apparently, they have not always been the gainers from their long contact with the whites. In fact, it fills Miles Macdonell with melancholy when he reflects "that during their long intercourse with the whites they have not acquired one moral virtue, nor is the faintest idea of the true deity to be found among them." Their morale and loyalty have now slipped so low, he says, that the people who had offered to defend the factories against the French attack in 1782, today would not even come to take part in the goose hunts. There are no chiefs among them and they are "in the utmost state of individual debasement and depravity than can be conceived."[48]

Most of New South Wales is occupied by the Crees except for the Churchill area, which is shared with the Chipewyans of the Northern Indian group, and the coastal strip north of Churchill, which is the domain of the Eskimos. The Chipewyans are somewhat less debauched than the Crees, mostly because their contact with the whites has been less intimate and for a shorter time; while the Eskimos, though long associated with Europeans, have always kept their distance and are comparatively little influenced by them.

About the middle of the second half of the eighteenth century, the Hudson's Bay Company, with the invaluable assistance of Hearne's Matonabbee, was instrumental in bringing about a truce between the Chipewyans and the Crees.[49] It is still in effect today, although quarrels still break out from time to time, particularly where liquor and women are concerned. But another feud, that between the Chipewyans and the Eskimos, still persists into the present. Its origins are lost in history. James Knight, the founder of Churchill nearly a century ago, regarded the Eskimos as the aggressors while Hearne, some fifty years later, placed the blame on the Chipewyans. Whenever an important Chipewyan died, he explained, it was generally believed that they had been conjured to death, either by some of their own countrymen, by some of the Crees, or by some of the Eskimos. Too often the suspicion fell on the latter which was "the grand reason their never being peace with those poor distressed people." An exception during Hearne's time, were the Eskimos of Knapp's Bay, Navel's Bay and Whale Cove. They were not attacked by the Chipewyans because they were under the protection of Churchill Factory which annually sent a sloop up the coast to trade with them.[50] The sloop, complete with an Eskimo interpreter, has enabled the company to trade with Eskimos who are too timid to come to the factory. During the winter, however, when the Chipewyans are absent, the Eskimos sometimes become bolder, in fact, too bold. In 1805, for example, the Governor of Churchill was alarmed to see "the whole of the Esquimaux returned again wanting much to winter at the factory." It was only "with great difficulty" that he "persuaded them to go to their own Country to hunt furs and return early in the spring to kill Whales and Seals which they ... promised to do."[51] The following year they returned, with 61 seals, in time to take part in the whaling.[52]

Traders from the company's sloop now visit the Eskimos' tents with the greatest freedom and safety in areas where not so long ago, they would not have dared to venture unarmed.[53] Fortunately, few of the unhappy incidents which marred the early relations between the whites and Eskimos now occur. Part of the improvement has probably been due to the influence of a number of Eskimo interpreters, trained at Churchill during the last half century. These have not only learned English, but often Cree or Chipewyan as well. In fact, the whites usually communicate with the Eskimos in Cree.[54] There is now an Eskimo youth staying at the factory who arrived only a few months ago but already he promises "much advantage" in the company's "future connection with these people."[55]

It had been intended that Churchill should trade with the Eskimos. But the main reason for establishing it had been to tap the trade of the Chipewyans and other Northern [Athapaskan] Indians, the apex of whose lands reached the bay at Churchill. The somewhat older York Factory had been expected to continue to monopolize the trade with the [Algonkian] Crees and their [Siouan] allies, the Assiniboines. But these tribes, already armed with guns, soon cut the Northern Indians off, and quickly dominated the Churchill trade as well. The fact that they were armed and came to the factories by canoe while the Northern Indians travelled on foot, gave them a tremendous advantage over their enemy-rivals.[56] Since both York and Churchill ended up trading with the same tribes, an unintentional and unwelcome rivalry has developed between the two factories which has been highly damaging to the company's interests.

Most of the Northern Indians who did manage to trade at Churchill Factory were of the Chipewyan tribe. They occupied a large tract between Reindeer Lake and Churchill.[57] It was relatively rich in reindeer but very poor in fur animals. South of them lay reasonably good fur lands but the Chipewyans were prevented from trading or hunting there by the Crees with whom they were then at war. To the northwest were the Yellow-knives and Dogribs whose countries produced excellent furs. From them the Chipewyans obtained by purchase, extortion or theft, most of the peltry they brought to Churchill to trade.

After the truce was arranged by Matonabbee, the Chipewyans began hunting on Cree lands "without giving the least offence to the proper inhabitants," and soon their trade at Churchill increased by many thousands of Made Beaver. Amidst such prosperity, who could have predicted that in a few years the truce would lead to disaster for the Chipewyans. For from their former enemies, during the winter of 1781-2, they caught smallpox which carried off nine-tenths of them and particularly those people who composed the trade at Churchill Factory. The few survivors, following the example of the Crees, began to carry their furs to the Canadians, who had by then settled in the heart of their country. With most of the Chipewyan middlemen gone, the Yellow-knife and Dogrib trade failed which, in turn, led to yet another catastrophe. For the sake of the few remnants of iron-work which remained among the two peoples, a war broke out in which the more numerous Dogribs destroyed nearly all of the Yellow-knives. Soon after the war, the few Yellow knives who remained found their way to a Canadian post to trade and were thus lost to the Hudson's Bay Company as well as to the few surviving Chipewyan middlemen.[58] For many years the trade at Churchill languished and, as will be seen later, only began to recover about five years ago.[59]

FORT WILLIAM

The North West Company has only one port of entry into the Northwest, Fort William (see fig. 7).[60] Easily the largest establishment in the whole of the Northwest, it is situated on the Kaministiquia River about 500 rods from its mouth, near the place where the French had built their

Fort Kaministiquia before the British conquest of Canada. Like York, it was built upon low swampy ground but, unlike York, its inhabitants have succeeded "by incredible labor and perseverance ... in draining the marshes and reducing yielding soil to solidarity."[61]

In many respects Fort William has a more fortunate location than do the bayside factories. Not only does its milder climate enable its gardens to produce more but it is better situated in relation to country provisions as well. Its dense forests have assured an abundant supply of wood for building and for fuel, not to mention materials for boats and canoes. Since most of the Indians belong to the same tribe (Ojibwa), Fort William has not been faced with the tribal squabbles which have plagued Churchill. Moreover, its remote location in the interior of the country has, so far, removed the threat of enemy attack; this may change should relations with the United States deteriorate. Like the bayside factories, Fort William has become increasingly less concerned with local trade and more involved with co-ordinating the company's activities throughout the Northwest. For this purpose, the wintering partners annually meet with those from Montreal in the great hall of the fort to plan the company's activities for the following year.

7

East Winnipeg,
Muskrat and English River Countries,
and the Barren Grounds

Between Fort William and York Factory on the east, and Lake Winnipeg on the west is a vast section of the Stony Region known as the East Winnipeg Country (see map 3). Its inhabitants, Crees and Ojibwas, are not numerous, for the land is incapable of supporting a large population. Though originally rich in animals, the forests are now largely exhausted. Fur animals are very few indeed, and deer are virtually unknown. The natives have come to rely mainly on the fish in the lakes,[1] although some of the Objibwa have turned to agriculture[2] while others have chosen to abandon the country and have migrated to the lands of the Assiniboines and Crees to the westward.[3]

Except for a few small outposts away from the main routes, all of the houses in the East Winnipeg Country are now intended as staging points for canoes and boats going to and from the interior, rather than for trading furs. There is Oxford House and Rock Fort on the Hayes, and Rainy Lake House, Rat Portage House and Fort Bas-de-la-Rivière-Winnipeg on the Fort William route (see map 6). Each is an important supply depot and storehouse.

North of the East Winnipeg Country is the Muskrat Country. It is an area worthy of considerable discussion not so much because of the furs and provisions which it produces (for its production is not great), but because it illustrates so well the complexities of the fur trade in the Northwest, as well as the great difficulties and hardships which face those who are engaged in it.

Strictly speaking, the Muskrat Country comprises only the area east of the Sturgeon-Weir between the Nelson and Churchill rivers,[4] although earlier traders of the region have tended to link it up with the lower valley of the Churchill as far as Reindeer Lake.[5] The term is used here in its wider sense. The maze of rivers and lakes which cover the surface of much of the Muskrat Country are easily accessible from the Nelson, Churchill and Saskatchewan rivers. In the early days of the trade, it was these waterways which enabled the Crees and Chipewyans who inhabited the country to take their furs with comparative ease to the bayside factories to trade. Although the country was never rich in furs, the Hudson's Bay Company enjoyed a steady trade from this area for many years. Then came the Canadians, and the Hudson's Bay Company saw the greater part of the furs go to their rivals for several years. However, in 1793, the English company at last sent people into the Muskrat Country and it soon recaptured much of the trade, which it continues to hold until this day. Because of the short distance its men have to travel and the large quantity of goods it can afford to supply, the English have had little difficulty in underselling their rivals.[6] Moreover, the shorter route has meant that the English traders can arrive earlier and thus commit the natives to trade with them. To assure happy relations between themselves and a wide range of Indian bands, as well as to out-fox their rivals, the English have adopted a policy of establishing themselves for a year or two in one place and then moving to another.[7] Because the posts they build are soon to be abandoned, little care has been taken in their construction. "We built log Huts to pass the winter," wrote Thompson of Bedford House, "the chimneys were of mud and coarse grass, but somehow did not carry off the smoke, and the Huts were wretched with smoke, so that however bad the weather, we were glad to leave the Huts."[8] It had been the practice for the men's house to be built some distance from the store-house and the master's house. But when this came to the attention of the governor of Churchill in 1807, he decided that the posts were too vulnerable and immediately ordered that all detached dwellings be immediately taken down and rebuilt attached to the store-house, with the men's quarters forming one end and the master's appartment, the other. Henceforth, no apology or excuse would be accepted "for deviating from this indispensible precaution."[9]

Because of the general scarcity of game animals in the Muskrat Country, it has been even more necessary than elsewhere for the posts to be located near good fisheries. This was the lesson learned at Fairford House during a hungry winter in 1795-6. The house was built on the bank of the Churchill just a mile below the mouth of the Reindeer

River. It had been an excellent place for trade but, because of the poor fishery, the men could "barely maintain" themselves and the post soon had to be abandoned. The Churchill is poor for fish and so is generally unsuitable for settlement, although some of the deep lakes, "wholly independent" but discharging into it, have very good fisheries indeed.[10] But even on those lakes, the fishery can unpredictably fail, as did the one on Reindeer Lake during the present winter.[11] Considering it is on the Churchill, Nelson House has enjoyed a reasonable fishery for many years. During the winter of 1810-11, however, the English traders were forced by the Canadians to abandon the spot where they had placed their nets for the past eighteen years. Fortunately, however, they were able to find another place before starvation overtook them, for animals in this area are exceedingly scarce. The mosses and willows which cover the ground can support only a few straggling moose; buffalo are unknown, and seldom do reindeer penetrate from the north.[12] Traders on the Nelson have apparently fared no better. At Sipiwesk Lake House, fish are described as being "very Scarce," but at Split Lake the situation is somewhat brighter. There, fish are caught throughout the year "but not in great numbers nor of the best quality."[13] However, since the post is situated on a deer crossing there is always the hope of supplementing the fish with fresh venison between August and November, and again in April, each year.[14]

Although the climate of the Muskrat Country is far more favourable to vegetation than it is at the factories along the coast, it is far from being equal to that of the more southerly districts of the Northwest; or of situations which are more "remote from the chilling influence of the sea."[15] Agriculture is therefore necessarily limited. At Split Lake, for example, the climate will permit potatoes, turnips, and cabbages to be grown but not corn.[16]

Split Lake House provides an interesting example of the competition not only between the English and the Canadian traders but also of the rivalry within the English company itself. Built in response to Canadian competition in 1790, it was the first Hudson's Bay Company post in the Muskrat Country. Although it was intended to draw furs from the Canadians, there were soon complaints from Churchill that the Indians who traded at the new post were Chipewyans "who never in their lives *saw York Factory* but yearly brought the produce of their hunt to Churchill, and were engaged every spring to kill Geese there." In 1791 another settlement was made on the Nelson and trade at Churchill dropped accordingly. The next year, yet another post was founded and there was a further decrease. But in the following year, 1793, Churchill entered the competition with a post up the Churchill River, and soon her trade began to recover.[17]

This rivalry between company posts undoubtedly delighted the Indians. It tended to raise the prices of their furs and provided a wonderful opportunity for them to escape from their debts at one factory by going to an outpost of the other.[18] In this, they were aided and abetted by some of the more unscrupulous inland traders. To increase their own portion of the trade, they were not above diverting furs from their fellow company men. The injured parties frequently took revenge with similar actions. Tempers rose. Accusations followed counter-accusations, and the situation became increasingly confused. In 1803, the exasperated governor of Churchill complained bitterly to his opposite number at York that one of his men was continuing "his practices upon our Northern [Chipewyan] Indians, intercepting them, seducing them, and villainously deceiving them by propagating false and injurious reports, which would scarcely become a Canadian."[19] As early as 1795, the dispute reached the London Committee room where David Thompson's charts were unrolled and an attempt made to work out trading areas for each factory. But it was a difficult situation to arbitrate, for, even if a trader did refuse to trade with the Indians who came to him because they belonged to another post, there was no guarantee that the Indians would not then go to the Canadians rather than to the other company post.[20]

The rivalry continued at least until last year, when the whole of the Northwest was put under the command of a single superintendent. One of his duties was to end the York – Churchill rivalry and to prevent it from developing elsewhere. At the same time, the Muskrat Country was placed under an inland master responsible to York. But by then the country was largely hunted out and its productiveness so diminished that W. Holmes, the first inland master, does not think it will pay the company to remain in the area even supposing they should gain the whole of the trade.

Years of competition between the Canadians and the English, and between the two English factories, has produced a sellers' market which the Indians have known how to exploit. Liquor is virtually the only thing they will now accept for beaver, the only fur presently in demand on the London market. Even if our goods were "embroidered in Gold,"

moans Holmes, the Indians will not trade if we "keep back Liquor."
And so the liquor continues to flow. But even so, seldom do the Indians
repay two-thirds of their credits, small though they usually are.[21] By
now, most of the beaver within easy range of the posts have been exter-
minated. Yet the natives are reluctant to go further afield in search of
other beaver areas because they can no longer bear to be far from the
source of their liquor. As a result, many of the poor debauched wretches
are so reduced in circumstances that during the hard winter of 1810-11
some of them were forced to eat the few furs they did get in order to
survive.[22] However, it must be pointed out that the destruction of the
beaver has not been entirely of their own doing. Much of the damage
has been perpetrated by Indians from Canada who were brought into
the Muskrat Country to hunt for the Canadians. Auld has been extremely bitter about the interlopers and claims that wherever there is
plenty of food for the intruders' support, there the fur animals will soon
be "extirpated" by them.[23] So discouraged are some of the local Indians
becoming that they are beginning to migrate towards Cumberland
House where there are more furs and provisions.[24] If the trend continues, it is likely that very few posts will be retained in the area in the
future. Already, moderately successful posts like the one belonging to
the Hudson's Bay Company at Indian Lake are being closed down. In
this particular case, the English post has been getting more of the trade
than its rival's establishment near by.[25] But apparently the company
does not feel that it is justifying its expenses.

The future of the Muskrat Country looks bleak indeed. Not only is
it becoming less productive in itself but, with the migration of its natives, there will be fewer middlemen to carry the furs and provisions of
richer areas to its trading posts. To the traders, it will seem even more
of a barrier between the fur-lands of the north and west and the Great
Lakes and Hudson Bay.

Above the mouth of the Reindeer River, the Churchill is usually
known as the English River, and the area which it drains as the English
River District or Department. Although also part of the Stony Region,
its climate is more favourable to the "productions of the vegetable and
animal kingdoms" than is that of the Muskrat Country. Furs and provisions are produced in considerable quantity but, like the Muskrat
Country, the English River is important primarily because of its geographical position. For through it runs the main route to the Athabasca
Country, the Eldorado of the fur trade. For several years, the Athabasca

Country has been the exclusive preserve of the North West Company. Now it would seem that the English River District may become so as well. For by the end of 1811, as we have seen, through bullying and even through open violence, the Canadians have succeeded in driving nearly all of their English rivals from the district. They know that the English River District is the geographical key to the Athabasca Country and they have been prepared to go to almost any lengths to keep the Hudson's Bay Company traders out of it.

The North West Company brigades bound for the English River District and the Athabasca Country enter the English River near Portage-de-Traite, after coming from the Saskatchewan by way of Cumberland House, the Sturgeon-Weir River and Beaver Lake. Portage-de-Traite takes its name from an event which took place in 1774-5. Joseph Frobisher, a trader from Canada, after having wintered near by, met in the spring a group of Indians making their annual journey to Churchill to trade. He persuaded them to trade with him instead and soon he had all the furs his canoes could carry. Ever since this coup, the carrying-place has been known as Portage-de-Traite. Before that, it had been called Frog Portage from the Crees having placed a stretched skin of a frog there as a sign of derision to the natives of the country whom they regarded with contempt because, among other things, they were ignorant of how to prepare, stretch and dry the skins of the beaver.[26] As far as the Canadians are concerned, the carrying-place might well be called "Portage Cornucopia" for across it has flowed not only the furs of the Athabasca Country and English River District, but some of those of the Muskrat Country as well. An envious official of the Hudson's Bay Company reported in 1811 that "not less than 1,300 Bundles of furs came over the Frog Portage last year." In 1809, he said 52 canoes with six or seven men in each went north; but in 1810, there were only 34 with five or six men, "which is a very strange difference."[27] Possibly the difference was not quite as great as the Hudson's Bay man believed, for 38 canoes had been assigned to this area at the annual meeting of the North West Company at Fort William in 1810. Of these, 31 had been apportioned to the Athabasca Country and seven to the English River. In the same year, only three canoes were assigned to the Muskrat Country.[28] These figures illustrate well the relative importance of the three districts to the North West Company.

From Portage-de-Traite, the brigades head up the Churchill, pass through several "lakes" in the river and negotiate 36 portages before they come to a well-built fort on the north side of Lac-Ile-à-la-Crosse, the headquarters of the North West Company's English River Department. The post has an excellent garden. From the lake the best of white fish are taken throughout the year, and along its banks moose, deer and other game animals are captured.[29] The only Indians who come to trade are the Chipewyans and Crees. Since the peace arranged by Matonabbee, the Chipewyans have been allowed by the Crees to hunt on their lands south of the Churchill, but not without exacting contributions when they occasionally meet them. Failure to pay can bring punishment with arms. The contributions are often levied when the two tribes meet at the trading posts and are usually in the form of rum, which the Chipewyans readily part with since they seldom drink it themselves.[30] Relations between the two peoples seem to be good on the whole and from the Crees, the Chipewyans are now learning how to build canoes and in other ways how to adapt themselves to the living conditions of their new lands.[31]

About the turn of the century the Hudson's Bay Company had built beside the North West Company at Lac-Ile-à-Crosse,[32] but from the beginning, this distant outpost of the English company met with unusually fierce opposition because of its strategic position in relation to the Athabasca Country. Any further expansion of the English in this area is to be prevented. Last year, for instance, when the Hudson's Bay Company tried to buy a few canoes to go up the Beaver River to settle at Green Lake, the Canadians forbad the Chipewyans to sell them any.[33] Green Lake is situated on the edge of the Stony Region. Beyond it, the Beaver flows through the Great Plains and in one place, near Lac d'Orignal [Moose Lake], approaches the Saskatchewan. From the plains, buffalo can be procured and from the Saskatchewan, dried meat and pemmican, which can be easily carried across to Beaver River by way of Lac d'Orignal and brought down the river to Green Lake. Thus, a post on Green Lake would have given the Hudson's Bay Company the provision depot which it needed if it were to extend its operations into the Athabasca Country. A similar depot has been operated by the North West Company for several years. In fact, it is the provisions from this post which have enabled the canoes each year to speed down the English River with the minimum of delay. During a period of expansion about the turn of the century, the Hudson's Bay Company did manage to build a post on Green Lake called Essex House, but it flourished for only a short time.[34] After the Canadians had prevented the Chipewyans from selling them the canoes they required last year, the English efforts to re-establish themselves upon the lake took on a rather pathetic air as Mr. Sutherland began to saw in two the company's small boat at Ile-à-la-Crosse to lengthen it by four feet.[35] But before the enlarged boat could be used in an advance towards Green Lake, the Canadians had succeeded in driving the English from their base at Ile-à-la-Crosse, and forced them to retreat down the English River towards the Muskrat Country.[36]

From Ile-à-la-Crosse, the annual brigades of the North West Company paddle northwestwardly through Buffalo [Peter Pond] Lake to Methye Lake and finally to the Methye Portage, the most famous portage of them all. This enables the brigades to cross the great divide which separates the rivers draining into Hudson Bay from those flowing northward into the Frozen Ocean. It is a long portage – eight miles and fifteen hundred yards, according to Turnor[37] – but, because the plateau-like divide is level and thinly wooded, the road is good. From a high hill near the western end of the portage, the traders may catch a breath-taking view of the promised land of the fur trade, the Athabaska Country.[38]

A far more arduous route to the Athabasca Country lies across the Barren Grounds. Although used by some of the natives, this route is never travelled by the traders because of its difficult waterways and the scarcity of food. Its rivers and lakes are less useful for transportation than elsewhere in the Northwest because of their arrangement and the fact that they are frozen over much of the year.[39] The vegetation consists largely of mosses and lichens which support the reindeer [caribou] which, in turn, make possible the little human habitation that exists there.[40] These animals travel in vast herds and, because of the sparseness of vegetation, are nearly always in motion. According to Hearne, their direction is usually either from east to west or west to east, depending upon the season, and the prevailing winds. "From November till May," he wrote, "the bucks continue to the Westward, among the woods, when their horns begin to sprout; after which they proceed on to the Eastward, to the barren grounds; and the does that have been on the barren ground all the Winter, are taught by instinct to advance to the Westward to meet them, in order to propagate their species."[41]

The natives of the Land of Little Sticks bordering onto the Barren Grounds are all of the same [Athapaskan] group. The most important of them are the Chipewyans who, as already seen, occupy the strategic area north of the Churchill between the fur lands of the west and Hudson Bay. To the north and west of them are the tribes from whom they obtain many of the furs which they trade to the Europeans. These are Yellow-knives, Hares, Dogribs and Slaves. Like the Chipewyans, the Yellow-knives and Hares follow the reindeer out onto the Barren Grounds during the summer. The Dogribs, however, make only quick sorties onto the Barren Grounds, while the timid Slaves prefer to remain under the cover of the trees.[42] All of these tribes of the northern Stony Region travel on foot and use their tiny canoes only for crossing rivers and narrow lakes, or for hunting reindeer. The reindeer provide their main subsistence, as well as their clothing and many other useful articles. But sometimes the reindeer suddenly and inexplicably disappear. On these occasions the Indians can often fall back, for food at least, upon the rich fisheries of the lakes and rivers and, if they are very lucky, capture a few water-birds as well. Some of the marshes produce several kinds of grass which grow very rapidly but are "dealt out with so sparing a hand as to be barely sufficient to serve the geese, swans, and other birds of passage, during their migrations in the Spring and Fall, while they remain in a moulting state." Alpine hares are also "pretty plentiful" in some parts of the Barren Grounds as well as some herds of musk-oxen. To the westward among the woods, there are rabbits and partridges. But should these, as well as the birds and fish, fail as well, there is always the black, hard crumply moss growing upon the rocks. It is far from appetizing in appearance but, when boiled to a gummy consistency, is actually quite palatable. In fact, Hearne said that most people grow fond of it. It is "remarkably good and pleasing when used to thicken any kind of broth," he wrote, but it is "generally most esteemed when boiled in fish-liquor."

Yet in spite of this apparent abundance of food on the Barren Grounds, Hearne found that half of the inhabitants, and perhaps the other half as well, are frequently in danger of starving to death, partly, as he observed, "owing to their want of economy." Scenes of distress, he wrote, have been particularly common during the long dangerous journeys to Churchill when, presumably, the Indians have been more intent upon reaching their goal than following the reindeer, or in seeking out the best fishing areas along the way. For the more distant tribes there is, as already discussed, the additional hazard of falling prey to the depredations of their kinsmen, the Chipewyans, who are always ready to relieve them of their furs, goods, and women, and, sometimes, even of their lives.[43] In this way, the Chipewyans have ruthlessly guarded their one big asset in the trade, *their geographical position.* During recent years, however, now that they have largely turned their attention to the fur lands of the Crees to the south of them, they seem to have missed, or even to have ignored, the small bands of Indians from the Northwest who are again coming to Churchill to trade.

In a similar way, the Eskimos immediately north of Churchill assume the position of middlemen in the trade with their relations living further to the north. When the more northerly tribes travel to the factory to trade, they must pass through the lands of their southern relations. While doing so they are filled with all sorts of malicious rumours about the white traders and generally discouraged from going any further. At the same time, the southerners offer to take their furs off their hands for a mere trifle. This having been done, the southerners proceed to the factory where they exchange them for trading goods and are then ready to journey to the northward to go into business for themselves. For many years, the Hudson's Bay Company has tried to persuade the nearer tribes to come to the factory to hunt whales, and to leave the fur trade to the more distant Eskimos. But as late as 1811, these efforts had met with little success.[44] It is to enable the northern Eskimos to avoid their grasping neighbours, as well as the depredations of the Chipewyans, which has caused the company annually to send a boat northward to trade with the Eskimos along the west coast of the bay. As far as is known, the Eskimos live only near the sea-coast.[45] They apparently never venture inland and, unlike the Indians, remain on the Barren Grounds throughout the year.

There are no trading posts on the Barren Grounds: its limited trade is conducted from posts along its periphery. There is Churchill in the east and a number of North West Company posts in the west. Among the latter are Fort Chipewyan, Slave Fort, Fort Providence, Great Bear Lake House, Fort Norman and Fort Good Hope. All of them are approached by way of the Great Plains, and from the plains come much of the provisions which enables the posts to exist.

8

The Red River, Saskatchewan
and Athabasca Countries

The Athabasca Country is the most remote and least known of the three great river "countries" which occupy the Great Plains between the Stony Region and the Rockies (see map 3). These are the Red River Country, drained by the Upper (Assiniboine) and Lower Red Rivers; the Saskatchewan Country, by the Saskatchewan and its two Branches; and the Athabasca Country, by the rivers of the Mackenzie basin. In sharp contrast to the broken streams of the East Winnipeg, Muskrat and English River countries of the Stony Region, with their innumerable rapids and lakes, these rivers have few rapids and, according to Thompson, do not form a single lake.[1] This, of course, means that few portages are necessary. There are, however, many places where a great deal of difficult poling and tracking is required.

Since the principal route to the Athabasca Country is by way of the Saskatchewan and because both the Saskatchewan and Red River Countries provide the pemmican necessary for journeys into the Athabasca Country, they will be described first. From the fur traders' point of view, the Red and Saskatchewan river systems are remarkably alike. Both are composed of two large branches which merge a comparatively short distance from their mouths. In each case, the smaller northern branch is by far the more important of the two. This is because they pass through a wide variety of vegetation, ranging from open grasslands to fairly dense forests, and consequently are able to produce both furs and provisions, not to mention the raw materials for houses, boats, canoes and clothing. The southern branches, on the other hand, flow most of their lengths through open plains. Only on their uppermost reaches are there significant forests and furs. As a result, they can produce little other than provisions and wolf and bear pelts; even this production of these inferior furs has been greatly handicapped, as will be shown later, by the presence of hostile tribes and by the absence of building materials and fuel.

The two main rivers and their branches are joined by innumerable smaller streams. Some of these originate in the foothills of the Rockies, or in the hills along the Assiniboine, while others have their sources on the plains. But whatever their origin, many of the tributaries, in common with the main rivers themselves, flow through a variety of vegetation and, like them, are capable of producing either furs or provisions, and often both. Generally speaking, trading posts are placed at, or near, the mouths of one of these tributaries. A number of factors have to be considered before the actual site is chosen. First of all, there are the general considerations: what furs or provisions does the river produce; are they required at the present time; would operations here interfere with another post of the same company; are the natives well disposed towards the company; is it on an Indian travel route, or near one of their gathering places; would the site be between the lands of two mutually hostile tribes; if so, perhaps, two posts, one in the lands of each tribe, would be less dangerous and more profitable to the company than one post catering to two hostile tribes? Once the general area for the post has been chosen, there are still a number of local factors to be considered in choosing the precise situation for the house: would there be sufficient wood for building and for fuel; would there be easy access to the river; do the buffalo seek shelter in the area in winter; is there a deer run or a good fishery; is the land suitable for a garden; could the position be easily defended; are there meadows for the horses? Seldom, however, has it been possible for the traders to make an ideal choice. Nearly always, trade rivalry being what it is, there has been an opposition present which has prevented them from doing so; and consequently posts have frequently been located as a result of a desire to achieve some short term advantage over an opponent.

The first trader to arrive in a new area has considerable latitude in choosing a place for his house. But rivals who come after him usually feel obliged either to build beside him, in the hope of attracting the Indians from his gate, or above him, in order to intercept the Indians on their way down stream to the older house. If the latter course is followed, the first trader will almost certainly then either have to move his post to a position beside the new house, or, at least, establish an outpost there, or he may choose to build a post above it. If the last alternative is followed, another round of moves will likely result, provided that the traders have the necessary resources and men. This type of competition has particularly favoured the large and powerful North West Company which has been able to meet opposition by establishing as many small posts as it has clerks and men to operate them, knowing full well that its smaller rivals would not be able to match them at every place. To harass their rivals, some of the North West Company posts have been established and abandoned several times.[2] This technique was used to good effect against the xy Company and was largely responsible for its absorption by the larger company in 1804. Since the union, the enlarged North West Company has directed its energies into new activities in the Athabasca Country and, beyond the Rockies, in New Caledonia. Many of its posts in the Red River and Saskatchewan countries, as well as most of those which had belonged to the xy Company, have recently been closed down in accordance with the new company policy of consolidation, to result, it is hoped, in a relatively small number of larger posts. Many of these are located near the houses of the smaller and weaker Hudson's Bay Company.

Most of the abandoned houses scattered throughout the Saskatchewan and Red River countries date from the days of the xy Company. The majority had been hastily built during one of the chaotic autumns of that time. Usually, with winter rapidly closing in, little thought could be given to either site or situation. However, the months which followed soon showed the traders whether or not they had been fortunate in their choice. A poor fishery, or a failure in provisions or in furs, meant that they had been unlucky and that the post would soon have to be abandoned. But some of those which did manage to pass the test of winter failed miserably in the spring, when it was discovered, after the frost had left the iron-hard ground, that they had been built in the middle of a swamp. Today there often remains only a pile of stones where the chimney had stood and a few charred or rotten logs to show where not long ago a group of white men had struggled to live. Each pile of stones has its own story to tell. They speak of areas where the fur animals have been hunted out or are no longer in demand in London: they tell of Indian troubles particularly on the open plains where several posts have had to be abandoned because of hostile natives, and where some have actually been destroyed by them; or they tell the less romantic story of buildings which were abandoned because they were old, and rotten, and full of lice.

The large number of ruins along the Red below the junction of the Upper (Assiniboine) and Lower Red, and below the forks of the Saskatchewan, remind the traveller of the dramatic rivalry of a few years ago. By now, however, relations between the two surviving companies have largely stabilized themselves in this part of the Northwest and active posts remain at only one place on each river – at Cumberland Lake on the Saskatchewan, where both companies have posts, and immediately below the mouth of the Assiniboine on the Red, where the North West Company has its Fort Gibraltar. Although Fort Gibraltar, like Cumberland, is primarily a depot for storing the provisions gathered along the two branches of its river, it can hardly be compared with the much more important Saskatchewan post. Far more valid would be a comparison between the posts at the mouth of the Winnipeg River – Fort Bas-de-la-Rivière-Winnipeg and Fort Alexander – with Cumberland. For these posts, although not actually on the Red, nevertheless receive most of their provisions from the Upper and Lower Red and, like Cumberland, supply the brigades on their way to and from the interior. The North West Company's Bas-de-la-Rivière is by far the more important of the two, since it supplies all of the northern brigades. Until recently, the Hudson's Bay Company's Fort Alexander had played a similar role, although on a much more modest scale, by supplying the brigades from Albany (at the bottom of the bay) on their way to and from the interior by way of the Winnipeg River. These brigades were discontinued in 1810, and the posts which they had served have been assigned to York Factory.[3] This does not mark the end of the Hudson's Bay Company's activities in this area, however. For some of the men now wintering at Nelson encampment are scheduled to be sent in the spring of 1812 to the mouth of the Winnipeg to build "near the Canadian provision-store." The proposed post is intended to develop trade on the eastern side of Lake Winnipeg and is to be known as the East Winnipeg Factory.[4]

Cumberland House (see fig. 9) is the oldest and most important inland post of the Hudson's Bay Company. It was built in 1774 by Samuel Hearne after much care in selecting the site. Before finally settling at Pine Island [Cumberland] Lake, Hearne had surveyed in detail the area between this lake and Basquiau [The Pas], looking for the most suitable

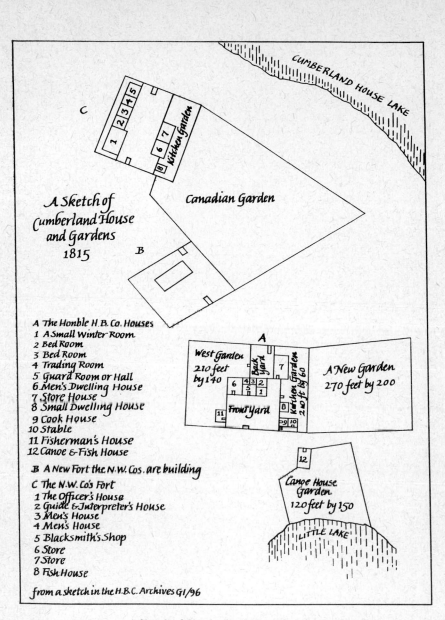

CUMBERLAND HOUSE LAKE

C

Kitchen Garden

Canadian Garden

A Sketch of
Cumberland House
and Gardens
1815

B

A The Honble H.B.Co. Houses
1 A Small Winter Room
2 Bed Room
3 Bed Room
4 Trading Room
5 Guard Room or Hall
6 Men's Dwelling House
7 Store House
8 Small Dwelling House
9 Cook House
10 Stable
11 Fisherman's House
12 Canoe & Fish House

B A New Fort the N.W. Cos. are building

C The N.W. Co's Fort
1 The Officer's House
2 Guide & Interpreter's House
3 Men's House
4 Men's House
5 Blacksmith's Shop
6 Store
7 Store
8 Fish House

from a sketch in the H.B.C. Archives G1/96

A

West Garden
210 feet
by 140

Back Yard

Kitchen Garden
20 ft by 60

A New Garden
270 feet by 200

Front Yard

Canoe House
Garden
120 feet by 150

LITTLE LAKE

FIGURE 9   A Sketch of Cumberland House and Gardens, 1815

situation and seeking the advice of the local Indians. Near The Pas, he had "met 22 Canoes of Basquiau Indians who seem'd very Courtious, ask'd me how I lik'd their Country and said they approv'd of my settleing in their Quarter, and offer'd their assistance in Procureing Provisions &c."[5]

In many ways, The Pas would have been an ideal situation for Hearne's purposes. A long distance below and above it, the Saskatchewan flows through a vast reedy marsh. But at The Pas, there is an extensive gravel plain, an island of dry ground in a watery wilderness. From it, passable trails lead to the higher lands of the Muskrat Country to the north, and to the Great Plains to the south. From time out of mind, the Indians have used these trails to come to The Pas to trade. On occasion, they have proved troublesome to the traders passing up and down the river, although since the smallpox epidemic of 1781-2, when their numbers were greatly reduced, they have not been much of a problem.[6]

The French had a settlement at The Pas (called Fort Pascoyac) but, when Hearne visited the site, the only sign of the place having been occupied was the absence of trees, and the remains of a fire-place in which many of the missing trees must have been consumed. This lack of wood for fuel and for building seems to have discouraged Hearne and, after discussions with the leading Indians, he decided that it would be better to build at Cumberland Lake, it being "the general opinion of those Indians that that Part will be more comodious both for Drawing the Indians to Trade as well as for Provisions than Basquiau [The Pas], it laying in the Middle between three Tribes."[7]

Today, the Hudson's Bay Company's buildings at Cumberland are in a good state of preservation, considering that they were built fifteen or twenty years ago. Both the dwelling house and store are made of squared pine logs and covered with boards.[8] Beside the English post the North West Company built its own "Cumberland House" in 1793.[9]

Both posts now function primarily as provision depots, although in the past they carried on a considerable local trade in furs as well. Most of the limited returns now made are in martens or muskrats. There are also a few beaver skins but these usually originate a great distance from Cumberland.[10] The North West Company, according to Alexander Henry, now regards this part of the trade as being "of no great advantage to us" and has allowed it to be monopolized by the Hudson's Bay Company. However, without greatly inconveniencing themselves, it is difficult to see how the Canadians could have prevented the English from doing so. For, as Henry himself has pointed out, the Hudson's Bay Company, unlike its rival, has no great northern brigades to provision with the large supplies of pemmican which it receives from the Saskatchewan. This means that it has been able to afford to feed the local Indians "whose country is wretchedly destitute of game animals" throughout the year in return for their furs. The natives consist of a band of Crees and a few straggling Ojibwas.[11] The latter have undoubtedly migrated from their over-hunted lands east of Lake Winnipeg. At the moment, they are being joined by some of the Indians of the Muskrat Country and New South Wales, whose lands are also being rapidly hunted out.[12]

Hearne's decision to locate at Cumberland was probably far wiser than he knew. Thirty-seven years later, its lake is still producing sufficient fish throughout the year to sustain both the men and the dogs. During May, and again in September and October, flocks of geese supplement the fish. There are also some reindeer and moose, as well as pemmican from the Saskatchewan Country.[13]

In spite of the severe climate, which is said to consist of six months of winter and six months of summer,[14] agriculture has been remarkably successful. The soil is reasonably good for the latitude although a great deal of hard work is required to remove the stones covering it before gardens can be planted. Potatoes and all kinds of garden stuff have been raised and barley grows "to perfection".[15]

As is to be expected in a land with six months of winter, the rivers and lakes are frozen over for much of the year. The ice in Cumberland Lake does not usually break up until the 15th or 20th of May, although it leaves the river fifteen or twenty days earlier. Water communication is therefore limited to about five and a half months of the year.[16] During the early part of the open season, large pemmican brigades can be seen, paddling rapidly along with the spring current, as they come out of the buffalo country bound for the warehouses at Cumberland. Alexander Henry reported in 1808, that the North West Company usually brings down from 300 to 500 bags of pemmican, and upwards of 200 kegs of grease each spring. Part of the grease is taken to Fort William, he said, but the whole of the pemmican is "required for our people going out in the spring and coming back in the fall." Some of the pemmican comes from further up the main stream where the plains approach the river and where the tree-covered hummocks along its banks provide shelter

FIGURE 7   Fort William, 1811

FIGURE 8   A Winter View of Great Slave Lake, 1771

and grass for the buffalo during the winter.[17] More pemmican comes from similar country along the north branch, while still more comes from the open plains of the south branch.

The South Saskatchewan, like the Lower Red, flows mostly through open plains. Both rivers, as a result, produced provisions but few furs, and so had held comparatively little attraction for the fur traders until the trade had expanded into the far northwest and created a huge demand for the products of these rivers. This is well illustrated by the returns of the Lower Red River Department of the North West Company from 1800 to 1808. During this period, the production of furs declined while that of provisions showed a large increase.[18]

Both rivers drain countries which were more forested in the past. For here, as elsewhere along the margins of the open plains, the forest is being forced to give up territory to the advancing grasslands by the annual prairie fires. A number of years ago, Thompson reported that the south branch of the Saskatchewan was "for the most part ... bare of Woods, and those that remain are fast diminishing by fire."[19] More recently, when travelling along the western bank of the Red, he saw the charred stumps of many trees and concluded that "it was evident this side of the river was once a Pine Forest."[20] This, of course, is the area in which Lord Selkirk plans to place his settlement. In the past, the general absence of wood has meant that trading posts could be built only in the occasional spots where there were trees lining the river. Such places are to be found here and there along the middle section of the Lower Red, but since the trees do not extend any distance away from the river, it will likely become necessary to carry wood for building and for fuel from some distance. However, it is unlikely that the shortage of wood can prevent the fulfilling of Thompson's prediction that the area will become "a pastoral or agricultural country," for the soil of the river is rich and deep and "everywhere fit for cutivation."[21] Possibly the best place for Selkirk's settlement would be the country about the junction of the Upper and Lower Red, which has been glowingly described by Harmon as appearing "to have a richer soil than at any other place I have observed in this part of the World – and is covered with Oak, Basswood, Elm, Poplar and Burch &c. also are here Red Plumbs & Grapes &c."[22] However, it must also be pointed out that the area was subjected to an "extraordinary inundation" this spring when the Lower Red overflowed its banks for four miles on either side. The flood is believed to have been caused by the melting of an unusually large amount of snow which had fallen near the river's source during the past winter. But since nothing similar has taken place in the memory of the oldest Indian, it may be hoped that it will not happen again. Interestingly enough, the Upper Red was not affected by the flood, being "no more swollen than usual."[23]

For many years it was believed that trees grew along the lowest part of the south branch of the Saskatchewan, and that the remainder of the river flowed through open plains, entirely devoid of wood and consequently unproductive of furs; and, without wood for fuel, it would be impossible to settle. Because of this belief, the river had remained unexplored throughout most of its length as late as 1800, when, so far as is definitely known, it was descended for the first time by a group of Nor'westers who had entered its headwaters from the headwaters of the North Saskatchewan. Later in the same year, it was again explored by Peter Fidler and several men of the Hudson's Bay Company.[24] The reason for this sudden interest in a river so long passed by was probably the realization about this time, that towards its upper reaches "where the plains terminate toward the rocky mountain, there is a space of hilly country clothed with wood, and inhabited also by animals of the fur kind."[25] Exploration has not, however, been followed by any large scale exploitation and the small trade of this new area is now carried on from Rocky Mountain House on the north branch. A post had been established by the North West Company on the Bow, an upper tributary of the South Saskatchewan, in 1802.[26] About the same time, the Hudson's Bay Company, North West Company and XY Company all built posts further to the east. These were near the place where the south branch was joined by the Red Deer. They had been intended to draw the Blackfeet and Piegans southward and the Indians of the Missouri northward (see map 5); but the natives proved to be very troublesome and by 1805 all three posts had been abandoned.[27]

The natives had also been troublesome at "South Branch House," the name given to several posts operated by both the North West Company and Hudson's Bay Company along a stretch of the South Saskatchewan extending from 70 to 100 miles from its mouth. In fact, in 1784, the Gros Ventre went so far as to destroy the Hudson's Bay Company post and killed all but one of its inhabitants. On the same occasion they also turned their fury upon the North West Company's post immediately after burning the English house. But the Nor'westers, seeing what was happening to their neighbours, had time to prepare for the attack which followed, and managed to come through it safely. The Gros Ventre had resented the traders for selling arms to several neighbouring tribes with whom they were at war.

Like the south branch of the Saskatchewan, some of the upper tributaries of the Lower Red, particularly the Red Lake River, drain lands which are covered with trees and which, in the past, had been comparatively rich in furs. These are mostly along the western margin of the Stony Region. Until recently, beaver were quite plentiful here, but, because of the peculiar soil and relatively mild climate of the area, they tend to build less strong houses than elsewhere, and so have been an easier prey for the hunters than elsewhere in the Northwest. As a result, few of them now remain. Game animals, too, are relatively scarce and both the traders and natives have, on occasions, been forced to live on a diet of wild rice and maple sugar. Both are gathered locally.[28] The natives are mostly Ojibwa. On occasion they leave the woods of their homeland to journey up the Lower Red in search of their inveterate enemy, the Sioux. This is in spite of the fact that the Ojibwa are generally inferior in number to the Sioux[29] and, since they have no horses, they must meet the mounted Sioux on foot.[30] Not surprisingly, reports Mackenzie, the Ojibwa are getting the worst of these skirmishes. If they continue to venture out of the woods, "which form their only protection", he says, they will probably soon be "extirpated."[31] Thompson, however, implies that the Ojibwas have been quite successful in their forays. For when he met Sheshepaskut, their principal chief in 1798, he described him as the man who had repressed the incursions of the Sioux, and who had driven the "Village Indians" to the Missouri.[32]

Thompson's "Village Indians" are, of course, the Mandans who have already been seen selling the produce of their fields to the fur traders who formerly journeyed to their country to trade. Now that the Mandans are out of their reach, the younger Ojibwa complain that they no longer have any means for distinguishing themselves in battle.[33] This, however, would seem to be an empty complaint for, as long as the feud with the Sioux continues, there should be opportunity enough.

The intending colonist would be well advised not to attempt to settle or even to travel along the more southern parts of the Red River. For many years, it has been a no-man's land between the territories of the Ojibwa and Sioux. For this reason, it has been little frequented by other than war parties and is therefore generally a poor place for trade. Moreover, the Sioux have come to dislike heartily the traders because they

have been supplying arms to their Ojibwa enemies; and it can be assumed that they will do all in their power to make this a dangerous area
for white habitation. There is ample reason to believe that the attack
on William Henry's House on the lower Red River, recently mentioned
by Harmon,[34] is only one of many such incidents.

At the present time, the Hudson's Bay Company would seem to have
only one post on the Lower Red. This is Fort Pembina, situated near
the mouth of the river of the same name. Like the neighbouring North
West Company post, its main function is to gather provisions. Further
up river, the Nor'westers also have three fur trading posts. These are
only temporary, however, since the general scarcity of furs in the area
does not make it worthwhile for a given place to be hunted upon a
second winter.[35]

The native situation on the Upper Red, or Assiniboine, is somewhat
more peaceful than it is on the Lower Red. This is in spite of the fact
that the two principal tribes living there, the [Siouan] Assiniboine and
the [Algonkian] Cree, speak two totally different languages. An uneasy
friendship prevails between them which has partly grown out of the
Assiniboines need for an ally against their estranged kinsmen, the Sioux,
and partly as a result of the fact that the two tribes do not compete economically. The lack of competition is well illustrated along the Upper
Red, where the Assiniboine Indians, a plains people, occupy the country
along its middle section, and trade pemmican, wolves and bears. They
have little interest in the wooded countries along the upper and lower
reaches of the river, which they leave to the woodland Crees and their
near relatives, the Ojibwa, who are now moving into the area from east
of Lake Winnipeg. These tribes are expert in hunting beaver and other
fur animals and, of course, provide most of the peltry collected in this
part of the country. There is a similar division of territory along the
North Saskatchewan, with the Crees generally occupying the wooded
areas and the Assiniboine the open plains but, as will be seen later, there
are other tribes as well. During recent years, some of the Crees have given
up their forest life to adopt the ways of their Assiniboine allies of the
grasslands. However, they are still not as proficient as the Assiniboine
on horseback and, like all woods tribes, prefer to use firearms for killing
game. The Assiniboine, on the other hand, still kill buffalo with bows
and arrows which they find just as convenient as guns.[36]

Besides the Sioux, the Crees and Assiniboines also have a common
enemy in the Gros Ventre, whom they are now in the process of driving
from the Northwest. Some of the Gros Ventre have recently taken up

residence beside the Mandans on the Missouri and from their new neighbours are learning how to dwell in villages and to live from agriculture.[37]

The Gros Ventre once occupied the point of land between the two branches of the Saskatchewan. But trouble with their neighbours forced them south of the south branch. This is a poor country and produces only buffalo robes (which the Gros Ventre dress in a superior manner) and some foxes, bears, wolves and dried provisions. Only the latter have been much in demand during recent years and, as a result, the Gros Ventre have fared badly at the trading posts. This has meant that their enemies, whose richer lands have provided a more abundant trade, have been better supplied in arms than they. Consequently, the Gros Ventre have blamed the traders for their troubles and whenever the opportunity has arisen, they have not hesitated to commit "depredation, pillage, and murder" at the white settlements. To date, they have succeeded in plundering at least two Hudson's Bay Company posts and in murdering the occupants of them. In both cases, the neighbouring North West Company posts were successful in repulsing similar attacks.[38]

It has already been seen how the Sioux resent the whites for arming the Ojibwa. They have, of course, been further angered by the trading of guns and ammunition to the Crees and Assiniboines – not to mention the Mandans. For the parties of traders who had journeyed to the Missouri to procure the products of the Mandans' gardens, had usually taken a supply of firearms with them which the Mandans had been glad to buy in order to be able to protect themselves from the Sioux who live all around them.

During their visits to the Mandans, the traders had often tried to persuade these gentle people to trap beaver and to bring them to the Upper Red to trade. But the Mandans, who are economically self-sufficient, could see little reason for leaving their fortified villages and thus exposing themselves to attack by their enemies.[39] From their country to the Souris River, the nearest tributary of the Upper Red, is a winter journey of ten or twelve days on horse-back. And since it is almost entirely through open country, they would have been in danger not only of attack by the Sioux or Ojibwa, but of freezing to death for want of fuel and shelter.[40] Nevertheless, to encourage them to come, the North West Company in 1795, built Ash House for them on the Souris. But the post soon had to be abandoned "from it's [sic] being too open to the incursions of the Sioux Indians." From then onward, the Sioux have made it increasingly dangerous for the whites to go to the Missouri[41] and in 1807, the Mandan trade was abandoned altogether.[42]

With the end of the Mandan trade, Fort Souris has apparently been abandoned also. There remain active trading posts of any importance at only seven places on the Upper Red and its tributaries, although there are undoubtedly a number of small temporary outposts as well. The first post to be reached in travelling up the river from its mouth is Portage-la-Prairie, "so called by the Indians from time out of mind," because it is at the beginning of the portage to Lake Manitoba, some twelve miles away. The French had followed the Indians over this route and made good use of the portage for sending in their goods for Fort Dauphin.[43] At present, both the Hudson's Bay Company and North West Company maintain posts at the beginning of the portage.

From Portage-la-Prairie, the river continues to follow its devious course to Brandon House. So frequent are its innumerable bends, that an Indian has compared its route to that of a spy "who went here and there, and everywhere, to see what was going on in the country."[44] One Nor'wester estimated that a man on foot could go as far in three hours as the canoes could in a day. Consequently, there is ample time for those who go up by land to hunt buffalo, moose and fish, in order to keep the canoes supplied with fresh provisions.[45]

From Brandon to Aspen River, trees are very scarce along the Upper Red. In fact, except for a few favoured places, such as Montagne-à-la-Bosse, where the North West Company has a post, there is not sufficient wood either for building or for fuel.[46] Six days by canoe above Montagne-à-la-Bosse, the Upper Red is joined by the Qu'Appelle. From this important tributary, which flows from the open plains, comes most of the provisions of the Upper Red River country, and both companies maintain large depots there.[47] From the Qu'Appelle, the Upper Red continues through open plains to the mouth of the Shell River where the two companies are established. The Shell River drains the forested Dauphin [Duck and Riding Mountains] Hills and consequently its trade includes furs, as well as provisions, from the neighbouring plains. In a sense it is a transitional post, for those below it produce mainly provisions while those above it are engaged mainly in collecting furs.

Above the Shell River, the Upper Red receives many small rivers and brooks. Most of these originate in a small range of hills to the northeast of the river. Seen from the plains, the west side of these hills [Manitoba Escarpment] has a gentle elevation of about 200 feet. But when observed from the east, they present an elevation of from 500 to 800 feet above the surrounding country. The forests of large trees which cover these hills provide shelter for the animals which contribute most of the furs gathered along this river. For many years, this district was among the most productive in the whole of the Northwest. But by now it has been largely hunted out. That this should have happened was almost inevitable, for the area is not only relatively restricted, but also readily accessible. It can be entered not only from the Upper Red, but from Lake Winnipeg via the Dauphin River, and from Cedar Lake by way of Lake Winnipegosis and Swan River as well. It was recently the centre of some of the keenest competition in the history of the trade, and has been hunted upon by its native Indians, by Ojibwas from east of Lake Winnipeg, and by the Nipissings, Algonquins and Iroquois from Canada.[48]

The Swan River route provides a short-cut to the Upper Red for the traders from York Factory, and has enabled them to reach the district a month before the Canadians from the Grand Portage can put in an appearance.[49] This, of course, has given the English a considerable advantage over their rivals. The area through which they come, between Lake Winnipeg and the Assiniboine, the so-called Swan River Country, was also once rich in furs, and particularly in beaver. When Thompson visited the district in 1797, he reported that "these sagacious animals were in full possession of the country, but their destruction had already begun, and was now in full operation."[50] The relentless activities of the large companies, which have operated competing posts at several places on both the Swan and Red Deer rivers, have now greatly reduced the beaver population.

Travel among the posts on the Swan and Red Deer, and between them and those on the upper Upper Red, is relatively easy on horseback, in spite of the presence of numerous small streams and ponds.[51] For example, it requires only three days for the Hudson's Bay Company to carry its merchandise from the Swan to the Assiniboine River.[52] Horses can also be used to go from the Assiniboine to the North West Company post at Dauphin Lake, south of Lake Winnipegosis. This journey takes only four days on horseback but about two months via the round about canoe route.[53]

The North West Company's Fort Dauphin, in common with its posts on the Red Deer and Swan Rivers, receives its supplies from the depot at Bas-de-la-Rivière-Winnipeg. Three small brigades from that depot set out across Lake Winnipeg for the mouth of the Dauphin River. They then travel up the Dauphin and pass through Lake Saint Martin to Lake Manitoba which they cross to its northwestern end. Here, Meadow

Portage leads them into Lake Winnipegosis where the three brigades separate. One goes southward to Fort Dauphin and the other two northward to Swan River and Red Deer River, respectively.[54]

Both companies enter the North Saskatchewan at the forks, and conduct their trade along its banks in very similar ways. In fact, in one place, at Fort White Earth River, the two competing posts are actually built within the same stockade.[55] This strange departure from the normal cut-throat rivalry between the two companies is a recent development which has grown out of a need for mutual protection against the increasing hostility of the natives in this area. The problem is basically the same as on the Assiniboine. There is an out-group, the Blackfoot nation, whose lands do not produce much in the way of valuable furs, and there is an in-group, the Crees and their Assiniboine allies, who do have access to fur countries. The Blackfoot nation, which consists of three [Algonkian] tribes, the Blackfoot, Bloods and Piegans, is at war with the Crees and Assiniboines. Consequently, they have resented the fact that their enemies have had the means for providing themselves with more arms than they could obtain themselves. For a number of years before 1809, the Hudson's Bay Company (but not the North West Company) had conducted a trade in wolf-skins with the Blackfoot, but in that year, orders arrived from England to the effect that no more wolves were to be traded. It was impossible for the English traders to explain to the Blackfoot that the change in policy had been due to the continental blockade in Europe and it has "exasperated those savage brutes to the last degree."[56]

The new Hudson's Bay Company policy led to a tense situation along the Saskatchewan which was greatly complicated by the events of the summer of 1808 which ended with the murder of several Piegans by the Crees. This had put the whole Blackfoot nation in a vengeful mood and they resolved to go on the war-path, either against the Crees or against the whites who had armed them.[57] Meanwhile, the Crees, fearing that the Blackfoot would themselves obtain arms from the traders, gathered on the north branch at the mouth of the Battle River in the autumn of 1808, and probably would have attacked the traders on their way up with supplies had they not fallen into disagreement among themselves.[58] During the following winter, the tense situation continued. Summer came and with it the news that the English would no longer take wolves which resulted in an uproar among the Blackfoot nation. This was followed later in the summer by intelligence that the Crees and Assiniboines had declared war against the Europeans and were determined to "sweep the river clear of Whites, and steal every horse." Thus the traders found themselves at variance with nearly every Indian on the river.

Both companies decided that only a radical operation could reduce the danger of an attack by one or other or both of these hostile groups. The first step was to separate the two Indian alliances in order to prevent them from engaging in any further conflicts which might end by being turned against the whites. To help bring about this separation, both companies decided to reduce the number of posts on the river to three. These would be widely separated and large enough to withstand attack. Each would deal with only one group of natives. To implement the new plan, a post was hurriedly built in 1810 at White Earth River on the upper reaches of the north branch. It replaced Fort Vermilion, where both companies had had posts, and the North West Company's Fort Augustus and Hudson's Bay Company's Fort Edmonton which had been only a musket shot apart.[59] It is hoped that the new post will draw the tribes of the Blackfoot nation. An outpost will be established up river, from time to time, to trade with the woodland Assiniboines and Crees.

The plains Crees are expected to go down the river to trade at The Montée where the Hudson's Bay Company is to have its Fort Carlton and the North West Company, its Fort La Montée. Whether or not these posts are yet in operation is not clear, but their function will be to provide for the Assiniboines, plains Crees, woodland Crees and Ojibwas of that part of the country.

Because they are roughly half-way between Cumberland and White Earth River, the posts at The Montée are expected to function as provision depots as well as collecting places for Cumberland. As provision depots, they will be especially useful during the downward journey of the canoes and boats in the spring, because it is doubtful if White Earth River, with its large population to support, will ever be able to supply the canoes with much in the way of food; and as already pointed out, there would not be time for hunting and fishing during the trip down. Both posts at White Earth River have an unusually large number of mouths to feed. A count of heads at the North West Company post on 3 June 1810, showed 28 men, 35 women and 72 children, or a total of 135. On the same date, there were 85 people at the Hudson's Bay Post. This is a large population to be supported "off the country" and perhaps it is not to be wondered that the inhabitants "suffered much with hunger"[60] during last winter, which was a particularly severe one. Fortunately, however, they did not suffer unduly from the cold. For their houses, although hastily built, are snugly constructed of pine logs and covered with mud and pine bark, and "white-washed" with local clay which is as white as lime.[61] In their haste to establish the new post and to solve the Indian problem, apparently the traders gave little thought to the agricultural potential of the new site. For it was soon discovered that its climate was too harsh for a successful garden. It would be tempting to blame the failure of the first summer upon an "unusual year" had the garden at the abandoned Fort Augustus also failed. But, indeed, it produced well.[62] Alexander Henry believes the difference in climate between the two posts to be due to Fort White Earth River being slightly further north than Fort Augustus and points out that only a few miles north or south on the Saskatchewan "makes a material alternation in the face of the country, especially in depth of snow."[63]

Above Fort White Earth River, at the head of navigation on the North Saskatchewan, about a mile and a half beyond the entrance to the Clearwater River, are two more active trading posts, the Hudson's Bay Company's Acton House and the North West Company's Rocky Mountain House.[64] The latter was built back in 1799[65] and by now "its rotten old buildings" are falling to pieces. During the autumn of 1810 repairs were carried out, particularly to the gates and bastions but they are still "wretched buildings for defense." With better buildings, however, the position would be comparatively easy to hold, for the post is situated upon a high bank on the north side of the river. Most of the Indians who come to trade live south of the river and therefore would find it difficult to ambush the post without being discovered. Now that many of the trees have been cut down for use at the house, there is "a grand view of the Rocky mountains" although, for some traders, its enjoyment is lessened by the sound of a nearby waterfall "whose perpetual roaring makes it a dismal neighbour in this solitary spot." This waterfall, or rapid, is the first of any importance to be encountered in ascending the Saskatchewan. True, there are many small rapids below it where the water runs over sloping beds of rocks and gravel, but this is the first real break in navigation.[66] Above it, and especially as the higher mountains are approached, the rapids become ever more frequent and the water increasingly shallow. Before long, there is not enough water for the canoes to pass with more than half cargo, and finally, as the great divide is reached, they must be taken from the water and carried across to the headwaters of the Columbia in New Caledonia.

Rocky Mountain House is one of the three bases from which the North West Company is developing its trade in New Caledonia. The others are Henry's House on the Athabasca and a post on the upper Peace, also called Rocky Mountain House. The latter is easily the most important of the three, partly because it is not bedeviled by the serious Indian problems which plague the other two, particularly Rocky Mountain House on the Saskatchewan. The natives who trade at the Saskatchewan post are anxious to prevent their enemies across the mountains from obtaining arms and so are taking every means within their power to stop the traders from going there. They are mostly Piegans, Blackfoot and Bloods, although there are also a few Gros Ventres, (who are now living in friendship with the Blackfoot nation), as well as the whole of the Sarcees. The Sarcees are a small [Athapaskan] tribe who have recently crossed the Saskatchewan to live with their Blackfoot allies. When they lived north of the Saskatchewan, the Sarcees were excellent beaver hunters and had brought in large quantities of furs, "and were accordingly much indulged by the traders."[67] But contact with the Blackfoot has led them to become "fully as lazy and indolent" as the Blackfoot themselves[68] and by 1809, their hunt had fallen to very little, although they still expect the traders "to treat them as before."[69] At the moment, the Sarcees are occupying a position closer to the Rockies than usual in order to be out of reach of the Assiniboine with whom they quarrelled in the summer of 1810.[70] Normally this area is inhabited by the Piegans, the largest tribe of the Blackfoot nation. This is good beaver country and the Piegans, unlike the other tribes of the nation, are reasonable beaver hunters, which probably explains why they have got along better with the whites than did the other two.[71]

Little is known about the neighbouring Acton House, but since the Hudson's Bay Company has not yet entered the New Caledonia trade, it is probably not as important as Rocky Mountain House. That a high degree of co-operation exists between the two houses may be taken for granted, for both face the future in fear. During the summer of 1811, many of the Fall Indians, who trade there, made a raid upon some American traders and Crow Indians on the Yellowstone River. As they were leaving the scene of the skirmish, they were told that in future they would be spared the trouble of coming to war for next summer the Crows, in company with some Americans, would go to war on the

Saskatchewan. This struck terror in the Fall Indians who, having no friends and little to trade with the whites for arms, hatched a plan to enter the fort in one body, pick a quarrel, kill every white man and loot the place. They sought support of the Piegans but the plan did not suit a majority of them, who argued that such an attack would eliminate permanently their source of arms, ammunition, tobacco and liquor. Instead, they persuaded the Fall Indians to make buffalo robes with which to buy ammunition to defend themselves. This the Fall Indians agreed to do but only after the Piegans threatened to fight them if they attacked the post. The traders are well aware of the bad intentions of the Fall Indians and so as the year comes to a close, are living in dread that the chain of events unleashed last summer will end in the destruction of their posts and even in their deaths.[72]

THE ATHABASCA COUNTRY

The trader crossing the Rockies for the first time must view the Columbia with the same sense of achievement he would experience in first glimpsing the Athabasca Country from the high hill on the far side of the Methye Portage. It is not so much the satisfaction of having conquered a difficult portage as of having at last reached a fabulous land. A land about which so much had been heard during the short summer evenings by the camp-fire and the long winter nights at the trading post. Perhaps in some ways, the Athabasca Country is a disappointment when it is finally reached. But certainly not so for its size: for it comprises the whole of the area east of the Rockies drained by the Mackenzie. Much of this country is an extension of the Great Plains but it also includes a wide western margin of the Stony Region. The southern part is generally covered by the Great Western Forest but north of Lake Athabasca and Great Slave Lake, the forest fades into the Land of Little Sticks.

On a rocky point on the north shore of Lake Athabasca near the entrance to Slave River is Fort Chipewyan, the North West Company's headquarters for the Athabasca Country.[73] Before 1804, it had been on the south shore of the lake as shown by Arrowsmith's map of 1811. Like most of the other important posts of the Northwest, Fort Chipewyan is surrounded by marshes which are much flooded in the spring and autumn. During those seasons, as at the other posts, the marshes are filled with ducks and geese. These are shot and preserved for winter use in salt which is "very plenty at this place" and which can be traded "at a very easy rate" from the Indians.[74] Near the post is the usual garden which during part of the year relieves the endless monotony of the trader's diet.[75] Here, as elsewhere, the diet consists largely of fish from the lake,[76] although whenever possible, this is supplemented with moose, reindeer and buffalo meat.

During the winter of 1791-2, the Hudson's Bay Company had also established a post at Fort Chipewyan.[77] But it was only of an exploratory nature and was withdrawn immediately afterwards, leaving the Canadians completely in control of the Athabasca Country, an area larger than any country in Europe. For a time, the Canadians were divided into rival factions but, after 1804, virtually all of them came under the control of the North West Company. With no opposition, the North West Company found the Athabasca Country an easy empire to rule. For apart from some Crees, who had pushed their way in from the south with the aid of the white man's guns, and a few Eskimos at the mouth of the Mackenzie, all of the natives speak similar [Athapaskan] languages. As has been seen, these woodland tribes are generally far more peaceful than the Indians of the plains and, although they occasionally go to war against one another, they seldom involve the traders in their disputes.

There is an excellent transportation system, consisting of a well-arranged network of navigable rivers and lakes, radiating from the "capital" to all parts of the country. One of the main routes, of course, is the Athabasca River. It provides the only important link with the outside world. From it, by way of the Clearwater River and the Methye Portage, the Athabasca Country receives all of its supplies and trading goods. In 1810, 31 canoes loaded with goods and supplies went in,[78] and 33 came out, carrying 783 packs of furs. Each pack weighed 85 pounds and was composed almost entirely of beaver since there were not sufficient men available to carry out the less valuable skins. These consisted mainly of wolves and wolverines, and were left behind in the country.[79]

When the canoes enter the Athabasca River from the Clearwater, most of them go down river to Lake Athabasca and Fort Chipewyan. But a few (there were five in 1810) go up river to supply the posts on Lesser Slave Lake and Lac-la-Biche, as well as those on the headwaters of the Athabasca in the Rocky Mountains. The other canoes deposit their cargoes at Fort Chipewyan where the outfits for all of the trading posts in the remainder of the Athabasca Country are made up. During the autumn, most of the men in charge of those posts come to Chipewyan to receive their goods.[80] Because the outfits for the Athabasca River are not made up at Fort Chipewyan, the area is not, for administrative purposes, usually regarded as part of the Athabasca Department but is considered a separate entity, the Athabasca River District.

Because the North West Company has no competition in the Athabasca Country, it is able to fix its prices as high as the market will bear. From Chipewyan, operations of the various districts can be co-ordinated to produce a high degree of efficiency for the district as a whole. For example, the Peace River is given the task of supplying most of the pemmican for the Fort Chipewyan depot, although the Slave River has extensive buffalo plains,[81] as well as the Peace.[82] Undoubtedly the company has considered it more economic to bring the pemmican by canoes or boats down the Peace, where only two or three men are required, than up the Slave where a full crew would be necessary.

In many ways the Peace could be described as the North Saskatchewan of the Athabasca Country. For like that region, it produces mostly furs in its upper reaches, and mostly provisions along its lower limits. Dunvegan, and the posts below it, function mostly as pemmican gathering stations, while those above it are largely concerned with collecting furs.[83] The uppermost post, again as on the Saskatchewan, is Rocky Mountain House, a base for conducting the New Caledonia trade. However, unlike the North Saskatchewan, the native situation on the Peace is fairly stable at present. It has not always been so. For when the Crees first received fire-arms from the traders, they ruthlessly attacked the inhabitants of the lower Peace, who had not yet obtained arms, and drove them up the river. These defenceless people were Beaver Indians. In 1783, they too received arms and with them were able to patch up a peace with the Crees at Peace Point on the lower Peace. From this event, the river derived its name. Since the time the peace was established, the Beaver have adopted many of the manners and customs of their former enemies[84] and together they have pushed back the Sekani Indians, who had occupied the upper river. The Sekani are very similar to the Beaver in dialect, manners and customs. So much so, in fact, that Harmon suspects that "at no distant period" they all belonged to the same tribe, and that some misunderstanding between the Sekani and the rest of the tribe caused them to be driven "from place to place, up the Peace River, until they were, at length, obliged to cross the Rocky Mountain."[85] In 1805, the North West Company established a post at McLeod's Lake, on the other side of the mountains, for the harassed Sekani. Since then, it has been rewarded with a large trade in beaver.[86]

Like the post at McLeod Lake, most of the houses in the Athabasca

Country have been carefully situated in order to trade with specific tribes. Most of the posts are located along the western edge of the Stony Region, although they are supplied from the navigable rivers of the Great Plains. In this way, the North West Company is able to bring their goods into the Indians' own countries and so spare them the long dangerous journey across the Stony Region to trade at the English factories on Hudson Bay. For the Chipewyans, there is Fort Chipewyan, Fond-du-Lac, and Slave Fort; for the Yellowknives, Fort Providence; for the Slaves, Fort Forks of the Mackenzie and Fort Rivière-au-Liard; for the Dogribs, Great Bear Lake House; and for the Hares, Fort Norman. Of course, none of these posts trades only with one tribe. But as far as possible it is the company's policy to provide at least one outlet for each tribe. In doing so, it hopes to keep conflicts from developing among the tribes, and to prevent any of them from becoming "middle-men."

The Canadian attempt to monopolize the Athabasca Country has not been completely successful. Immediately after the absorption of the XY Company in 1804, the enlarged North West Company raised its prices and soon there were complaints of harsh treatment from the Indians as well.[87] The Hudson's Bay Company was quick to exploit this growing dissatisfaction and before long, Indians from as far away as Lake Athabasca and Great Slave Lake (see fig. 8) were travelling to Churchill to trade.[88] In spite of the fact that it was usually necessary to expend the powder, shot and so forth, which had been the object of the trip, on the homeward lap,[89] these Indians apparently considered the journey worthwhile if it meant avoiding the Canadians. This has been especially fortunate for Churchill which, like York, has been plagued by a shortage of men during the past few years; at the present time more than two-thirds of its furs are carried to its gates from great distances by the disgruntled Indians.[90] In other words, the recent increase in trade at Churchill has been largely fortuitous and apparently it has been recognized as such by the London Committee because, in 1810, it decided that most of the inland trade, including Athabasca, would be in future conducted from York. In fact, it would now seem that even Churchill itself is destined to be reduced to a mere outpost of York. It has recently been proposed that the posts on the Churchill should be supplied from York – those on the lower river by schooner, while those on the upper river by means of boats and canoes via the Burntwood River and portage.[91] The schooner would be the one now used to supply Severn Factory from York. Undoubtedly these changes are in preparation for the company's long projected drive into the Athabasca Country. York, rather than

Churchill, has been chosen as the base largely because of its superior situation for supplies. However, any attempt by York to tap the furs of the Athabasca Country is bound to lead to a major skirmish with the North West Company. At the present time, more than one-third of the boats and canoes allocated to the various departments by the Canadian company are assigned to the Athabasca Country.[92] The furs from this cold region are among the richest produced in the whole of the Northwest and yet, because it has no competition, the North West Company has been able to procure them more cheaply than possible anywhere else. It is clear that the Canadians will not give up their monopoly without a struggle – a struggle which might well involve the settlers in Selkirk's colony.

The intending settler may well query the wisdom of proceeding to such a distant colony which not only presents the normal hardships of a first settlement but the additional hazards which may result from the rivalry between the two companies. Indeed, it is possible that he has already been frightened by the hostile remarks made in London by merchants connected with the North West Company and by Sir Alexander Mackenzie who is said to have pledged himself in a most "unequivocal & decise" manner to oppose the settlement with all the means in his power. In fact, he had now gone as far as to threaten the colony with the Assiniboine Indians who are represented as the most warlike in North America.[93] The prospective settler, however, should take heart in the knowledge that these statements have in no way dinted the courage of Miles Macdonell, who is determined to press on with the establishment of the colony. He is convinced that once the project has gained sufficient strength in Ireland and the Highlands of Scotland, no individual opposition can have much effect unless the government should also decide against it. This last, he feels to be a rather remote possibility since the government is aware that a British settlement in the Northwest would serve as a check to the expansion of the Americans who are beginning to extend themselves in that quarter, and, should a rupture occur with the United States (and at the time of writing this would seem to be a distinct possibility), the settlement would enable the British to cause some annoyance on their back frontier.[94]

What are the prospects for agriculture in the Northwest? Those who know the country intimately vary in their assessments. Daniel Harmon, for example, feels that even the more northerly part, between 52 and 70 degrees north latitude contains many fertile plains and valleys and that a quarter (if not a third) of the whole could be cultivated to advantage.[95]

Sir Alexander Mackenzie, on the other hand, believes that the proportion of the Northwest fit for cultivation is very small and that as long as any land remains uncultivated to the south of it, there will be no temptation to settle it. He is convinced that not only will it long continue to be in the possession of its present inhabitants but it will increasingly become a refuge for Indians from further south who prefer the life of their forefathers to the improvements of civilization.[96] David Thompson is in substantial agreement with Mackenzie and feels that the great plains "appear to have been given by Providence to the Red Men for ever, as the wilds and sands of Africa are given to the Arabians."[97]

The Red River Valley, however, appears to be much richer than other parts of the Northwest, and there is every reason to believe that a colony would flourish there. Not only is the soil rich and deep but there are vast herds of buffalo, which should guarantee provisions during the first difficult years.[98] Those useful animals were glowingly described by Edward Umfreville who, a few decades ago, wrote that should this country ever be "established and manufacturers settled therein, every part of this animal would be turned to account: as for tallow, hides, horns and hoofs." He even thought they might be easily tamed to the plough by taking them young in the month of April and May which he claimed could be easily accomplished by "a man who is swift of foot ... without assistance of a horse."[99] Possibly Umfreville was a bit overly optimistic when he suggested hitching the buffalo to a plough but he did not exaggerate when he spoke of the value of this animal. Not only will it provide the new settlement with food and other useful articles but it will also enable it to supply some of the provisions which the colony is meant to provide for the Hudson's Bay Company.

In the years to come, it is expected that the settlers from the Highlands of Scotland and from Ireland will be joined by many Hudson's Bay Company traders who will find in the new colony an "asylum for themselves & their numerous offspring." Those who have taken Indian wives are expected to find the settlement especially attractive, since it will provide them with an opportunity of remaining in the Northwest after their retirement from the company's service. Many servants of the Canadian company also have families by Indian women and it is to be supposed that they, too, will welcome an opportunity of joining the colony as soon as they see it begun on a permanent footing.[100] Thus the settlement along the Red River will be remarkable for being composed not only of persons of British extraction but of French Canadians, Indians and halfbreeds as well.

Bibliography

MANUSCRIPT SOURCES

Hudson's Bay Company Archives, London

The bulk of the material has been classified under two sections: A and B. Section A relates to the company as a whole; section B to the affairs of individual trading posts.

Section A includes: minute books, extracts of the minutes of the committee, London agenda books, grand ledgers, grand journals, officers' and servants' ledgers, account books, servants' commissions, cash books, bills payable books, invoice book of shipments, fur sale book, London correspondence outward, London correspondence inward.

Section B has been further subdivided according to the different types of records, a lower case letter having been allocated for each sub-division:

a   post journals
b   correspondence books (outward and inward entries)
c   correspondence (inward)
d   account books
e   reports on districts
f   lists of servants
z   miscellaneous items

The remainder of the material is classified under sections C, D, E, F and G and includes the ships' logs, private journals of some of the traders, North West Company correspondence and maps.

National Library of Scotland, Edinburgh. The Edward Ellice papers.

Public Archives of Canada, Ottawa.

"Q" Series. These are copies of the Public Record Office papers contained in c.o.42. The "Q" Series has been calendared in the Canadian Archives Reports.

Selkirk Papers. These are copies of Selkirk's papers. The originals were later accidentally burned in Great Britain.

Public Record Office, London. c.o. 42 series.

Royal Commonwealth Society, London. Several documents relating to the North West Company.

BOOKS, ARTICLES AND THESES

Adair, James. *History of the American Indians.* London, 1775.

Adam, Graeme Mercer. *The Canadian Northwest.* Whitby, 1885.

Alcock, F. J. "Past and Present Trade Routes to the Canadian Northwest," *Geographical Review,* x, 2 (1920), pp. 57-83.

Anburey, Thomas. *Travels Through the Interior Parts of America,* 2 vols. London, 1789.

Armstrong, G. H. *The Origin and Meaning of Place Names in Canada.* Toronto, 1930.

Arrowsmith, Aaron. *A Companion to a Map of the World.* London, 1794.

Atlas of Canada, Geographical Branch, Mines and Technical Surveys. Ottawa, 1957.

Atwood, W. W. *The Physiographic Provinces of North America.* Boston, 1940.

Back, Sir George. *Narrative of the Arctic Land Expedition to the Mouth of the Great Fish River, and Along the Shores of the Arctic Ocean, in the Years 1833, 1834, and 1835.* London, 1836.

Baker, Edna. *Prairie Place Names.* Toronto, 1934.

Baker, J. N. L. *A History of Geographical Discovery and Exploration.* London, 1937.

Bancroft, H. H. *History of the Northwest Coast, 1543-1846.* 2 vols. San Francisco, 1884.

Barbeau, Marius. *Indian Days in the Canadian Rockies.* Toronto, 1923.

Barrington, Daines. *Observations on the Floating Ice which is Found in High Northern and Southern Latitudes.* London, 1776.

Barrow, John, ed. *Geography of Hudson's Bay, 1727 to 1751.* London, 1852.

Barry, George. *History of the Orkney Islands.* 2nd ed. London, 1808.

Barton, Benjamin Smith. *New Views of the Origin of the Tribes and Nations of America.* Philadelphia, 1797.

Bond, James H. *From out of the Yukon.* Portland, Ore., 1948.

Boucherville, Thomas Verchères de. "Journal ... dans ses voyages aux pays d'en haut, et durant la dernière guerre avec les Américains," *Canadian Antiquarian and Numismatic Journal,* 3rd series, III, pp. 1-167.

Bowan, Emanuel. *Complete System of Geography.* London, 1747.

Bradbury, John. *Travels in the Interior of America in the Years 1809, 1810 and 1811.* London, 1817.

Brebner, J. B. *The Explorers of North America 1492-1806.* New York, 1933.

Brissot de Warville, Jean Pierre. *New Travels in the United States of America.* 2nd ed. London, 1794.

Brouillette, B. *La pénétration du continent Américain par les Canadiens français 1763-1846.* Montréal, 1939.

Brown, Ralph Hall. "Materials Bearing upon the Geography of the Atlantic Seaboard, 1790 to 1810," *Annals Association of American Geographers,* XXVIII, 1938, pp. 201-31; *Mirror for Americans, likeness of the Eastern Seaboard 1810.* New York, 1943.

Bryce, G. "The Assiniboine River and Its Forts," *Transactions,* Royal Society of Canada, X, s. 2 (1892), pp. 69-78; "Five Forts of Winnipeg," *Transactions,* Royal Society of Canada, III, s. 2 (1885), pp. 135-45; *The Remarkable History of the Hudson's Bay Co.* Toronto, 1910.

Buchanan, Angus. *Wild Life in Canada.* London, 1920.

Burpee, L. J., ed. *An Adventurer from Hudson Bay.* Journal of Matthew Cocking, from York Factory to the Blackfoot country 1772-3. *Transactions,* Royal Society of Canada, 3rd series, II, s. 2, 1908; "Highways of the Fur Trade," *Transactions,* Royal Society of Canada, 3rd series, VIII, s. 2 (1914), pp. 183-92; *A Historical Atlas of Canada.* Toronto, 1927; *On the Old Athabasca Trail.* Toronto, 1926; *The Search for the Western Sea: The Story of the Exploration of North-Western America.* Toronto, 1908.

Cameron, Austin W. *Canadian Mammals.* Ottawa, 1958.

Campbell, M. W. *The North West Company,* Toronto, 1957; *The Saskatchewan.* New York, 1950.

Carver, Jonathan. *Three Years Travels through the Interior Parts of North America.* Philadelphia, 1796.

Catlin, George. *Letters and Notes on the North American Indians.* 2 vols. London, 1851.

Clouston, J. Storer, ed. *The Orkney Parishes.* Reprint of the accounts of the Orkney Parishes in Sir John Sinclair's *Statistical Account of Scotland (1795-8).* Kirkwall, 1927; *A History of Orkney. Kirkwall,* 1932.

Cluny, Alexander. *The American Traveller; or, Observations on the Present State, Culture and Commerce of the British Colonies in America,&c.* London, 1769.

Coats, W. *The Geography of Hudson's Bay: Being the Remarks of Captain W. Coats, in Many Voyages to that Locality, between the Years 1727 and 1751,* ed. John Barrow. London, 1852.

Cook, James. *A Voyage to the Pacific Ocean undertaken by the Command of His Majesty for Making Discoveries in the Northern Hemisphere.* London, 1785.

Coues, Elliott, ed. *New Light on the Early History of the Greater Northwest: The Manuscript Journals of Alexander Henry and of David Thompson, 1799-1814.* New York, 1897.

Cowie, Isaac. *The Company of Adventurers.* Toronto, 1913.

Craig, Gerald. *Early Travellers in Canada.* Toronto, 1955.

Crone, G. R. *Maps and their Makers.* London, 1953.

Crone, G. R. and R. A. Skelton. *English Collections of Voyages & Travels 1625-1848.* In E. Lynam, ed., *Richard Hakluyt and His Successors.* London, 1946, pp. 63-140.

Crouse, N. M. "The Location of Fort Maurepas," *Canadian Historical Review,* IX, 3 (Sept. 1928), pp. 206-22.

Currie, A. W. *Economics of Canadian Transportation.* Toronto, 1954.

Dalrymple, Alexander. *Memoir of a Map of the Lands around the North Pole.* London, 1789.

Davidson, Gordon Charles. *The North West Company.* Berkeley, 1918.

Delaute, Frank. *The Voyageurs: Canoe Trip Diary, Hayes River, 1956.* Ottawa, 1957.

DeSmet, Pierre-Jean. *Life, Letters and Travels,* ed. H. M. Chittenden and A. T. Richardson. New York, 1905.

Dobbs, Arthur. *An Account of the Countries Adjoining to Hudson's Bay, in Northwest Part of America.* London, 1744.

Douglas, David. *Journal kept by David Douglas during his Travels in North America, 1823-27.* London, 1914.

Douglas, R., ed. *Nipigon to Winnipeg. A Canoe Voyage through Western Ontario by Edward Umfreville in 1784 with Extracts from the*

Writings of Other Early Travellers through the Regions. Ottawa, 1929.

Downes, P. G. *Sleeping Island: The Story of One Man's Travels in the Great Barren Lands of the Canadian North.* New York, 1943.

Dugas, G. *L'ouest canadien: sa découverte par le Sieur de la Vérendrye; son exploitation par les compagnies de traiteurs jusqu'à l'année 1822.* Montréal, 1896.

Dymond, J. R. "Fluctuations in Animal Populations with Special Reference to those of Canada," *Transactions,* Royal Society of Canada, XLI, s. 5 (1947), p. 1.

Dymond, Joseph and William Wales. "Observations on the State of the Air, Winds, Weather &c., made at Prince of Wales Fort, on the North-West Coast of Hudson's Bay, in the Years 1768 and 1769," *Phil. Trans.,* LX (1770). London, 1771, pp. 137-78.

Easterbrook, W. T. and H. G. J. Aitken. *Canadian Economic History.* Toronto, 1956.

[Ellice, Edward]. *The Communications of Mercator upon the Contest between the Earl of Selkirk and the Hudson's Bay Company on one Side, and the North West Company on the Other.* Montreal, 1817.

Ewers, J. C. "Were the Blackfoot Rich in Horses?" *American Anthropologist,* XLV (1943), pp. 602-10.

Finch, Vernon C., et al. *Elements of Geography, Physical and Cultural.* 4th ed. New York, 1957.

Fleming, R. Harvey. "McTavish, Frobisher and Company of Montreal," *Canadian Historical Review,* X (June 1929), pp. 136-52; "Phyn, Ellice and Company of Schenectady," *Contributions to Canadian Economics,* IV (1932), pp. 7-41; "The Origin of Sir Alexander McKenzie and Co.," *Canadian Historical Review,* IX (June 1928), pp. 137-55.

Forde, Cyril Daryll. *Habitat, Economy and Society: A Geographical Introduction to Ethnology.* 6th ed. London, 1948.

Forester, John Reinhold. "A Letter from Mr. John Reinhold Forester, F.R.S. to William Watson, M.D. Giving Some Account of the Roots Used by the Indians, in the Neighbourhood of Hudson's Bay, to Dye Porcupine Quills," *Phil. Trans.,* LXII, pp. 54-9; "An Account of the Birds Sent from Hudson's Bay with Observations Relative to their Natural History; and Latin Descriptions of Some of the Most Uncommon." *Phil. Trans.,* LXII, pp. 382-433.

Franchère, Gabriel. *Narrative of a Voyage to the Northwest Coast of America in the Years 1811, 1812, 1813, and 1814; or, the First*

American Settlement on the Pacific. Trans. and ed., J. V. Huntington. Vol. VI, *Early Western Travels*, ed. R. G. Thwaites. Cleveland, 1904.

Franklin, J. *Narrative of a Journey to the Shores of the Polar Sea.* London, 1823.

Fraser, Simon. *First Journal ... from April 12th to July 18th, 1806.* Canadian Archives Report for 1929. Ottawa, 1930.

Fraser, Simon. *Letters and Journals, 1806-1808,* ed. W. Kaye Lamb. Toronto, 1960.

Freuchen, Peter and Finn Salomonsen. *The Arctic Year.* New York, 1958.

Furniss, O. C. "Some Notes on Newly Discovered Fur Posts on the Saskatchewan River," *Canadian Historical Review*, XXIV, 3 (Sept. 1943), pp. 266-72.

Galbraith, John S. *The Hudson's Bay Company as an Imperial Factor, 1821-1869.* Berkeley, 1957.

Gale, Samuel. *Notices on the Claims of the Hudson's Bay Co. and the Conduct of its Adversaries.* London, 1819.

Garry, Francis, N. A., ed. "Diary of Nicholas Garry, Deputy-Governor of the Hudson's Bay Company from 1822-35; A Detailed Narrative of his Travels in the North West Territories of North America In 1821," *Transactions*, Royal Society of Canada, 2nd series, VI, s. 2 (1900), pp. 73-204.

Gass, Patrick. *A Journal of the Voyages and Travels of a Corps of Discovery, under the Command of Capt. Lewis and Capt. Clark of the Army of the United States.* Pittsburgh, 1807.

Gates, Charles, ed. *Five Fur-Traders of the Northwest. Being the narrative of Peter Pond and the diaries of John Macdonell, Archibald N. McLeod, Hugh Faries and Thomas Connor.* Minneapolis, 1933.

Gibbon, John Murray. "The Orkneyman in Canada," *Transactions*, Royal Society of Canada, 3rd series, XLIV, s. 2 (1950), pp. 47-59.

Gilbert, E. W. *The Exploration of Western America.* Cambridge, 1933.

Glazebrook, G. de T. *A History of Transportation in Canada.* Toronto, 1938.

Glover, R. "The Difficulties of the Hudson's Bay Company's Penetration of the West," *Canadian Historical Review*, XXIX, 3 (Sept. 1948), pp. 240-54; ed., *A Journey from Prince of Wales's Fort.* By Samuel Hearne. Toronto, 1958; ed., *David Thompson's Narrative.* Toronto, 1962.

Golder, F. A. *Russian Expansion on the Pacific 1641-1850*. Cleveland, 1914.

Graham, Henry G. *Social Life of Scotland in the Eighteenth Century*. London, 1937.

Gray, Hugh. *Letters from Canada. Written During a Residence there in the Years 1806, 1807 and 1808. Showing the Present State of Canada*. London, 1809.

Great Britain, Parliament, House of Commons. *Report from the Select Committee on the Hudson's Bay Company; Together with the Proceedings of the Committee, Minutes of Evidence, Appendix and Index ... 1857*. London, 1858.

Grierson, P. J. H. *The Silent Trade*. Edinburgh, 1903.

Grinnell, George Bird. "Horses," *Handbook of American Indians North of Mexico*, I, pp. 569-71.

Guthrie, William. *A System of Modern Geography*. London, 1811.

Haines, Francis D. "How Did the Indians Get Their Horses?" *American Anthropologist*, XL (1938), pp. 112-17; "The Northward Spread of Horses among the Plains Indians," *American Anthropologist*, XL (1938), pp. 429-37.

Harmon, Daniel William. *Sixteen Years in the Indian Country*, ed. W. Kaye Lamb. Toronto, 1957.

Heagerty, J. J. *Four Centuries of Medical History in Canada*. Toronto, 1928.

Hearne, Samuel. *A Journey from Prince of Wales's Fort in Hudson's Bay to the Northern Ocean, 1769, 1770, 1771, 1772*, ed. Richard Glover. Toronto, 1958; *A Journey from Prince of Wales's Fort in Hudson's Bay to the Northern Ocean*, ed. J. B. Tyrrell. Toronto, 1911.

Hendry, Anthony. *The Journal of York Factory to the Blackfoot Country, 1754-55*, ed. L. J. Burpee, *Transactions*, Royal Society of Canada, 3rd series, I, s. 2 (1907).

Hennepin, Father Louis. *A New Discovery of a Vast Country in America*, ed. Reuben Gold Thwaites. 2 vols. Chicago, 1903.

Henry, Alexander, the younger. *New Light on the Early History of the Great Northwest*, ed. Elliot Coues. New York, 1897.

Henry, Alexander, the elder. *Travels and Adventures in Canada and the Indian Territories between the Years 1760 and 1776*, ed. James Bain. Toronto, 1901; *Travels and Adventures in Canada and the Indian Territories between the Years 1760 and 1776*. New York, 1809.

[Henry, John]. *On the Origin and Progress of the North-West Company of Canada*. London, 1811.

Heriot, George. *Travels through the Canadas*. London, 1807.

Hewson, J. B. *A History of the Practice of Navigation*. Glasgow, 1951.

Hind, Henry Youle. *Report on the Assiniboine and Saskatchewan Exploring Expedition of 1858*. Toronto, 1859.

Historical, Geographical, Political and Natural History of North America, An. By "a gentleman immediately returned from a tour of that continent." 2 vols. London, 1805.

Hodge, Frederick Webb, ed. *Handbook of American Indians North of Mexico*. Bureau of American Ethnology, Bulletin 30, 2 vols. Washington, 1910.

Hudson's Bay House. *Hudson's Bay Company: A Brief History*. London, 1934.

Hunter, John D. *Memoirs of a Captivity among the Indians of North America*. London, 1823.

Huntington, Ellsworth. *The Red Man's Continent: A Chronicle of Aboriginal America*. New Haven, 1919.

Hutton, James. "Theory of the Earth; or an Investigation of the Laws Observable in the Composition, Dissolution and Restoration of Land upon the Globe," *Transactions*, Royal Society of Edinburgh, I, p. 209.

Imley, Gilbert. *A Topographical Description of the Western Territory of North America*. 3rd ed. London, 1797.

Innis, Harold A. *Essays in Canadian Economic History*, ed. Mary Q. Innis. Toronto, 1956; *The Fur Trade in Canada: An Introduction to Canadian Economic History*. Toronto, 1956; "The North West Company," *Canadian Historical Review*, VIII (Dec. 1927), pp. 308-21; *Peter Pond, Fur-Trader and Adventurer*. Toronto, 1830; "Peter Pond and the Influence of Capt. James Cook on Exploration in the Interior of North America," *Transactions*, Royal Society of Canada, 3rd series, XXII, s. 2 (1928), pp. 131-41.

Innis, Harold A. and A. R. M. Lower, eds. *Select Documents in Canadian Economic History, 1497-1783*. Toronto, 1929; *Select Documents in Canadian Economic History, 1783-1885*. Toronto, 1933.

Jackson, Marjorie, Gordon. "The Beginnings of British Trade at Michilimackinac," *Minnesota History* (Sept. 1930), pp. 231-70.

Jeffreys, Thomas. *The American Atlas: or, A Geographical Description of the Whole Continent of America*. London, 1776.

Jenness, Diamond, ed. *The American Aborigines: Their Origin and Antiquity.* Toronto, 1933; *The Indians of Canada.* 3rd ed. Ottawa, 1955.

Jérémie. *Twenty Years of York Factory, 1694-1714. Jérémie's Account of Hudson Strait and Bay,* trans. R. Douglas and J. N. Wallace. Ottawa, 1926.

Jewitt, John R. *The Adventures and Suffering of John R. Jewitt.* Edinburgh, 1824.

Jones, L. R. and P. W. Bryan. *North America: An Historical Economic and Regional Geography.* London, 1954.

Kelsey, Henry. *The Kelsey Papers.* Public Archives. Ottawa, 1929.

Kendrew, W. G. *The Climates of the Continents.* 5th ed. London, 1961.

Kenney, J. F., ed. *The Founding of Churchill. Being the Journal of Captain James Knight, Governor-in-Chief in Hudson Bay, from the 14th of July to the 13th of September 1717.* London, 1932.

Kerr, D. G. G., ed. *A Historical Atlas of Canada.* Toronto, 1960.

Kidd, Kenneth E. *Canadian of Long Ago: The Story of the Canadian Indian.* Toronto, 1951.

Kimble, George H. T. *Our American Weather.* New York, 1955; *Geography of the Northlands,* ed. George H. T. Kimble and Dorothy Good. New York, 1955.

Kirwan, Richard. *An Estimate of the Temperature of Different Latitudes.* London, 1787.

Knight, James. *The Founding of Churchill,* ed. James F. Kenney. London, 1932.

Lamb, H. H. "The World's Changing Climate," *The Listener,* 7 April 1960.

Lambert, John. *Travels through Lower Canada and the United States of America in 1806-7-8.* 3 vols. London, 1810.

Landmann, George. *Adventures and Recollections of Colonel Landmann, Late of the Corps of Royal Engineers.* 2 vols. London, 1852.

La Pérouse, Comte de. "Expédition de la Baie d'Hudson: Extrait du journal de Pierre-Bruno-Jean de la Mouneraye," *Bull. de la Société de Géographie.* ser. 7, T.G. 1888; *A Voyage Around the World Performed in the Years 1785, 1786, 1787 and 1788.* London, 1799.

La Place, P. S. *The Systems of the World,* trans. J. Pond. 2 vols. London, 1809.

La Rochefoucault-Liancourt, François Alexandre Frédéric, Duc de. *Travels in Canada, 1795.* Ontario, Sessional Papers, XLIX, part 10. Toronto, 1917.

Laut, Agnes C. *The Adventurers of England. Chronicles of Canada*, XVIII. Toronto, 1916; *The Conquest of the Great North-West*. Toronto [1908].

La Vérendrye, Pierre Gaultier de Varennes. *Journals and Letters of Pierre Gaultier de Varennes de La Vérendrye and His Sons*, ed. L. J. Burpee. Toronto, 1927.

Lind, James. *A Treatise of Scurvy*. Edinburgh, 1753.

Long, John. *John Long's Voyages and Travels in the Years 1768-88*, ed. Milo Milton Quaife. Chicago, 1922.

Low, G. *Fauna Orcadensis*, Edinburgh, 1813.

Lower, A. R. M. *Canada: Nation and Neighbour*. Toronto, 1952.

Macdonell, Captain Miles. *Selkirk Settlement. Letter Book of Captain Miles Macdonell, 1811 and 1812*. P.A.C. *Report*, 1886, pp. 187-826.

McGillivray, Duncan. *The Journal of Duncan McGillivray of the North West Company at Fort George on the Saskatchewan, 1794-5*, ed. Arthur S. Morton. Toronto, 1929.

[McGillivray, Duncan]. *Some Account of the Trade Carried by the North West Company*. P.A.C. *Report*, 1928. (Ottawa, 1929), Appendix E, pp. 56-73. This document was the basis of John Henry's *On the Origin and Progress of the North West Company of Canada*. London, 1811.

McGuire, Joseph D. "Trails and Trade Routes," in *Handbook of American Indians North of Mexico*, ed. Frederick Webb Hodge. Bureau of American Ethnology, Bulletin 30, 2 vols. Washington, 1910.

MacKay, Douglas. *The Honourable Company: A History of the Hudson's Bay Company*. Indianapolis [1936].

McKeevor, Thomas. *A Voyage to Hudson's Bay, During the Summer of 1812*. London, 1819.

Mackenzie, Sir Alexander. *Voyages from Montreal, on the River St. Lawrence, through the Continent of North America, to the Frozen and Pacific Oceans; in the Years 1789 and 1793. With a Preliminary Account of the Rise, Progress and Present State of the Fur-Trade of that Country*. London, 1801.

Mackenzie, Murdoch. *Orcades: or a Geographic and Hydrographic Survey of the Orkney and Lewis Islands, in Eight Maps*. London, 1750.

Malthus, T. R. *An Essay on the Principle of Population*. 3rd ed. 2 vols. London, 1806.

Martin, Archer. *The Hudson's Bay Company's Land Tenures and the Occupation of Assiniboia by Lord Selkirk's Settlers; with a List of*

Grantees under the Earl and the Company. London, 1898.

Martin, Chester. *Lord Selkirk's Work in Canada.* Oxford Historical and Literary Studies, VII. Oxford, 1916; *Red River Settlement Papers.* Archives Branch. Ottawa, 1910.

Marwick, Hugh. *The Orkney Norn.* Oxford, 1929.

Mason, Michael, H. *The Arctic Forests.* London, 1924.

Masson, L.-F.: *Les Bourgeois de le Compagnie du Nord-Ouest,* 2 vols. Québec, 1889-90.

Merk, Frederic. *Fur Trade and Empire: George Simpson's Journal, 1824-5.* Harvard Historical Studies, XXXI Cambridge, Mass., 1931.

Merrill, Gordon Clark. "The Human Geography of the Lesser Slave Lake Area of Central Alberta." Unpublished MA thesis, McGill University, 1951.

Middleton, Christopher. "The Effects of Cold," *The Geography of Hudson's Bay,* ed. John Barrow. London, 1852.

Milet-Moreau, M. L. A. *Voyage de la Pérouse.* Paris, 1798.

Moll, Herman. *A System of Geography; or a New and Accurate Description of the Earth.* London, 1701.

Mooney, J. "Aboriginal Population of America," *Smith. Misc. Coll.,* LXXX, 7. Washington, 1928.

Morse, Jedidiah. *The American Gazetteer.* Boston, 1810; *The American Geography.* 5th ed. Boston, 1812.

Morton, A. S. "Five Fur Trade Posts on the Lower Qu'Appelle River 1787-1819," *Transactions,* Royal Society of Canada. 3rd series, XXXV, s. 2 (May 1941), pp. 81-93; *The History of the Canadian West to 1870-71; Being a History of Rupert's Land (the Hudson's Bay Company's Territory) and of the North-West Territory.* London [1939]; *Journal of Duncan McGillivray of the Northwest Company at Fort George on the Saskatchewan 1794-5.* Toronto, 1929; "Nipawi on the Saskatchewan River and Historic Sites," *Transactions,* Royal Society of Canada, 3rd series, XXXVIII, s. 2, (1944), pp. 117-35; "The Posts of the Fur-Traders on the Upper Assiniboine River," *Transaction,* Royal Society of Canada, 3rd series, XXXVI, s. 2 (1942), pp. 101-14.

Morton, W. L. *Manitoba: A History.* Toronto, 1957.

Murray, Hugh. *Historical Account of Discoveries and Travels in North America.* London, 1829.

Nute, Grace Lee. *Lake Superior.* Indianapolis & Toronto, 1944; *Rainy River Country. Minnesota Historical Society.* St. Paul, 1950; *The*

Voyageurs' Highway. Minnesota Historical Society. St. Paul, 1941.

Ogden, Peter Skene. *Traits of American-Indian Life and Character by a Fur Trader*. London, 1853.

Oliver, Edmund H. "The Beginnings of Agriculture in Saskatchewan," *Transactions, Royal Society of Canada*, 3rd series, XXIX, s. 2 (1935), pp. 1-32.

Oliver, Edmund H., ed. *The Canadian North-West*. Pubs. of the Canadian Archives, No. 9. 2 vols. Ottawa, 1914, 1915; "The Settlement of Saskatchewan to 1914," *Transactions*, Royal Society of Canada, 3rd series, XX, s. 2 (1926), pp. 63-87.

Palliser, John. *1860-63 Exploration – British North America*. London, 1863.

Palliser, John et al. *Journals, Detailed Reports and Observations, Relative to Palliser's Exploration of British North America, 1857, 1858, 1859, 1860*. London, 1863.

Parliamentary Committee on the Hudson's Bay Company, 1857. Blue Book, HBC, pp. 322-44 for Ellice on H.B.C., X.Y.C. and N.W.C.

Paullin, Charles O. *Atlas of the Historical Geography of the United States*, ed. John K. Wright. Washington & New York, 1932.

Pennant, Thomas. *Arctic Zoology*. London, 1784-7.

Perrault, Jean Baptiste. *Narrative of the Travels and Adventures of a Merchant Voyageur in the Savage Countries of Northern America, Leaving Montreal the 20th of May 1783* [1820], ed. John Sharpless Fox. Michigan Pioneer and Historical Collections, XXXVII (1909-10), pp. 508-619.

Pike, Warburton. *The Barren Ground of Northern Canada*. London, 1917.

Pond, Peter. *Journal of "Sir" Peter Pond*. [Hartford, Conn., n.d.]

Purchas, Samuel. *Purchas His Pilgrimes*. 20 vols. Glasgow, 1905-7.

Putman, Donald F. and Donald P. Kerr. *A Regional Geography of Canada*. Toronto, 1956.

Rand, A. L. *Mammals of the Eastern Rockies and Western Plains of Canada*. National Museum of Canada, Bulletin No. 108. Ottawa, 1948.

Rich, E. E., ed. *Cumberland and Hudson House Journals*. 1st series, 1775-9. London, 1951; *Cumberland House Journals and Inland Journals*. 2nd series 1779-82. London, 1952; *The History of the Hudson's Bay Company*. 2 vols. London, 1959; *Isham's Observations and Notes 1743-49*. Toronto, 1949.

Richardson, Sir John. *Arctic Searching Expedition.* London, 1851; *Account of the Quadrupeds and Birds.* London, 1825; *Fauna Boreali-Americana.* Part I, *The Quadrupeds.* London, 1829; *Fauna Boreali-Americana.* Part III, *The Fish.* London, 1836; Appendix, zoological remarks, in *Narrative of the Arctic Land Expedition to the Mouth of the Great Fish River and Along the Shores of the Arctic Ocean, in the Years 1833, 1834 and 1835, by Captain Back,* R.N. London, 1836; "Remarks on the Climate and Vegetable Productions of the Hudson's Bay Countries," *Edinburgh Philosophical Journal,* XII, no. 24 (1825), pp. 197-234.

Richardson, Sir John and William Swainson. *Fauna Boreali-Americana.* Part II, *The Birds.* London, 1831.

Roberts, Leslie. *The Mackenzie.* New York, 1949.

Robson, Joseph. *An Account of Six Years Residence in Hudson's Bay from 1733 to 1736, and 1744 to 1747.* London, 1752.

Rodrick, David. "An Assiniboine Horse-Raiding Expedition," *American Anthropologist,* XLI (1939), pp. 611-16.

Roe, Frank Gilbert. "The Extermination of the Buffalo in Western Canada," *Canadian Historical Review,* XV (1934), pp. 1-23; "From Dogs to Horses among the Western Indian Tribes," *Transactions,* Royal Society of Canada, 3rd series, XXXIII, s. 2, (1939), pp. 209-75; *The Indian and the Horse.* Norman, Okla. and Toronto, 1957; *The North American Buffalo.* Toronto, 1951.

Ross, Alexander. *Adventures of First Settlers on the Oregon or Columbia River.* London, 1849; *Fur Hunters of the Far Northwest.* London, 1855.

Ruggles, Richard I. "The Historical Geography and Cartography of the Canadian West." Unpublished PH.D. thesis, London University, 1958.

Sabine, Joseph. Zoological appendix in *A Journey to the Polar Sea,* by John Franklin. London, 1823.

Scharff, Robert Francis. *Distribution and Origin of Life in America.* London, 1911.

Schooling, Sir William. *The Hudson's Bay Company, 1670-1920.* London, 1920.

Selkirk, Thomas Douglas, 5th Earl of. *Sketch of the British Fur-trade in North America, with Observations Relative to the North West Company of Montreal.* London, 1816.

Seton, Ernest Thompson. *The Arctic Prairies.* New York, 1911; *Life*

Histories of Northern Animals. 2 vols. New York, 1910; *Lives of Game Animals.* 4 vols. New York, 1929.

Simpson, Sir George. *Fur Trade and Empire*, ed. Frederick Merk. Cambridge, Mass., 1931; *Narrative of a Journey Round the World during the Years 1841 and 1842.* London, 1857; *Simpson's Athabaska Journal, 1820-21*, ed. by E. E. Rich. Toronto, 1938.

Skinner, Alanson. "The Culture of the Plains Cree," *American Anthropologist*, XVI (1914), pp. 68-87, 314-18; "Notes on the Eastern Cree and Northern Saulteau," *Anthropological Papers of the American Museum of Natural History*, IX (1911), pp. 1-177.

Smith, Marian W. "The War Complex of the Plains Indians," *Proceedings*, American Philosophical Society, LXXVIII (1938), pp. 425-64.

Smith, Samuel Stanhope. *An Essay on the Causes of the Variety of Complexion and Figure in the Human Species.* New Brunswick, 1810.

Spinden, H. J. "Population of Ancient America," *Geographical Review*, XVIII (1928), pp. 641-60.

Stamp, L. Dudley and F. Kenneth Hare. *Physical Geography for Canada.* Toronto, 1953.

Stanwell-Fletcher, Theodora C. *The Tundra World.* Boston, 1952.

Stevens, Wayne Edson. *The Northwest Fur-Trade, 1763-1800.* University of Illinois Studies in the Social Sciences, XIV, 1703. Urbana, 1928.

Stewart, David A. "Early Assiniboine Trading Posts of the Souris-mouth Group 1785-1832," *Transactions*, Historical and Scientific Society of Manitoba, v new series (July 1930).

Swainson, William and John Richardson. *Fauna Boreali-Americana.* Part II, *The Birds.* 1831.

Thompson, David. *David Thompson's Narrative*, ed. J. B. Tyrrell, Toronto, 1916; *David Thompson's Narrative*, ed. R. Glover, Toronto, 1962.

Thwaites, Reuben Gold, ed. *Early Western Travels, 1748-1846.* 32 vols. Cleveland, 1904-7; *The Jesuit Relations and Allied Documents. Travels and Explorations of Jesuit Missionaries in New France, 1610-1791.* Cleveland, 1896-1901; *Original Journals of the Lewis-Clark Expedition (1804-1806).* 7 vols. and atlas. New York, 1904.

Travener, P. A. *The Birds of Canada.* Toronto, 1943.

Tyrrell, J. B., ed. *David Thompson's Narrative of his Explorations in Western America, 1784-1812.* Toronto, 1916; *Documents Relating to the Early History of Hudson Bay.* Toronto, 1931; *Journals of*

Samuel Hearne and Philip Turnor. Toronto, 1934; "Report on the Country between Athabasca Lake and Churchill River," *Summary Report,* Part I, Geological Survey of Canada, 1895; "Report on the Doobaunt, Kazan and Ferguson Rivers and the North-West Coast of Hudson Bay," *Annual Report,* Geological Survey of Canada, new series, IX, (1896); *Across the Sub-Arctic of Canada. A Journey of 3,200 Miles by Canoe and Snow-shoe through the Barren Lands.* Toronto, 1897.

Tytler, Patrick Fraser. *The Northern Coasts of America and the Hudson's Bay Territories.* London, 1854.

Umfreville, Edward. *The Present State of Hudson's Bay, Containing a Full Description of that Settlement, and the Adjacent Country; and Likewise of the Fur Trade with Hints for its Improvement,* ed. W. Stewart Wallace. Toronto, 1954.

Vancouver, George. *A Voyage of Discovery to the North Pacific Ocean, and Round the World: in which the Coast of North-West America has been Carefully Examined and Accurately Surveyed.* 3 vols. and atlas. London, 1798.

Vandiveer, C. A. *The Fur-Trade and Early Western Explorations.* Cleveland, 1929.

Voorhis, E. *Historic Forts and Trading Posts of the French Regime and of the English Fur Trading Companies.* Ottawa, 1930.

Wales, William. "Journal of a Voyage Made by Order of the Royal Society to Churchill River, on the North-west Coast of Hudson's Bay; of Thirteen Months Residence in that Country, and of the Voyage Back to England in 1768, 1769. *Phil. Trans.,* LX, pp. 100-36.

Walker, John. *Elements of Geography and Natural and Civil History.* 3rd ed. London, 1800.

Wallace, J. N. *The Wintering Partners of Peace River from the Earliest Records to the Union in 1821.* Ottawa, 1929.

Wallace, W. Stewart, ed. *Documents Relating to the North West Company.* Toronto, 1934; *The Pedlars from Quebec and Other Papers on the Nor'Westers.* Toronto, 1954.

Watson, J. Wreford. *General Geography.* Vancouver, 1957.

Waugh, F. W. "Canadian Aboriginal Canoes," *The Canadian Field-Naturalist,* XXXIII, No. 2 (May 1919).

Williams, Glyndwr. "The British Search by Sea for the Northwest Passage, 1719-1794." Unpublished PH.D. thesis, University of London, 1959.

Williams, Meade C. *Early Mackinac. A Sketch Historical and Descriptive.* New York, 1912.

Williamson, Hugh. *Observations on the Climate in Different Parts of America, Compared with the Climate in Corresponding Parts of the Other Continent.* New York, 1811.

Wilson, Beckles. *The Great Company: Being a History of the Honourable Company of Merchants-Adventurers Trading into Hudson's Bay.* 2 vols. London, 1900.

Wissler, Clark. "Ethnological Diversity in America and its Significance," in *The American Aborigines*, ed. D. Jenness (Toronto, 1933), pp. 167-216.

Wright, J. F. C. *Saskatchewan, the History of a Province.* Toronto, 1955.

BIBLIOGRAPHIES AND CHECKLISTS

Andrews, Charles M. and Frances G. Davenport. *Guide to the Manuscript Materials for the History of the United States to 1783*, British Museum, Minor London Archives, and the libraries of Oxford and Cambridge. Carnegie Institution of Washington, Publication No. 90. Washington, 1908.

Andrews, Charles M. *Guide to the Materials for American History, to 1783*, Public Record Office of Great Britain. Carnegie Institution of Washington, Publication No. 90A. 2 vols. Washington, 1912.

Arctic Institute of North America. *Arctic Bibliography*, prepared for and in co-operation with the Department of Defense. Washington, 1953.

Arctic Institute of North America. *List of Books on the north available at the Arctic Institute of North America.* Montreal, 1946.

Besterman, Theodore, ed. *British Sources of Reference and Information, A Guide to Societies, Works of Reference and Information.* London, 1947.

Canada. *Canadian Graduate Theses in the Humanities and Social Sciences, 1921-1946.* Ottawa, 1951.

Canada, Geographic Board. *Catalogue of the Maps in the Collection of the Geographic Board. List of the Maps Corrected to 1st January 1922.*

Canada, Mines and Technical Surveys Dept., Geographical Branch. *Bibliography on the Climate of the Prairie Provinces and the Northwest Territories and Yukon.*

Canada, Mines and Technical Surveys Department, Geographical Branch. *Twenty-five Year Bibliography of Canadian Geography (1930-55) Western Canada.*

Canada, National Film Board. *List of Photographs of Value to the Geographical Bureau Depicting Types of Country, Peoples, Industries, Transportation and Settlements.* Ottawa, 1948.

Canada, Public Archives. *Annual Report.* Ottawa, 1881 to 1954.

Canada, Public Archives. *Catalogue of Maps, Plans and Charts in the Map Room of the Dominion Archives.* Ottawa, 1912.

Canada, Reconstruction and Supply Dept. Resources and Development Branch. *Catalogues including Dominion and Provincial Government Maps, Plans and Publications.* Ottawa, 1946.

Comas, Juan. *Bibliografia selectiva des las culturas indigenas de America.* Mexico, Institute Panamericano de Geografia e Historia, 1953.

Crick, B. R. and M. Alman. *A Guide to Manuscripts Relating to America in Great Britain and Ireland.* Oxford, 1961.

Dutilly, Artheme. *Bibliography of Bibliographies on the Arctic.* Appendix ii: "Prominent Names in Arctic Explorations." Washington, 1945.

Goodman, Marie Cleckner. *Map Collections in the United States. A Directory.* New York, 1954.

MacDonald, Christine. *Publications of the Governments of the North-West Territories and the Province of Saskatchewan, 1877-1947. Preliminary Check List.* Regina, 1948.

McGill University, Library School. *A Bibliography of Canadian Bibliographies.* Montreal, 1930.

Matthews, William. *Canadian Diaries and Autobiographies.* Berkley & Los Angeles, 1950.

Peel, B. B. *A Bibliography of the Prairie Provinces to 1953.* Toronto, 1956.

Royal Geographical Society. *New Geographical Literature and Maps,* No. 1, *n.s.* (June 1951).

Sealock, Richard B. and Pauline A. Seely. *Bibliography of Place Name Literature, United States, Canada, Alaska and Newfoundland.* Chicago, 1948.

Story, Norah. *The Oxford Companion to Canadian History and Literature.* Toronto, 1967.

Tod, Dorothea D. and Audrey Cordingley. *A Check List of Canadian Imprints, 1900-1925.* Ottawa, 1950.

Toronto [Public Libraries]. *The Canadian Catalogue of Books Published in Canada, about Canada, as well as those Written by Canadians.* Toronto, 1923?-1950.

Toronto Public Library. *Books and Pamphlets Published in Canada up to the Year 1837, Copies of which are in the Public Library, Toronto.* Toronto, 1916.

Toronto Public Libraries. *Contributions to Canadian Bibliography, The Canadian North West.* Toronto, 1931.

Wright, J. K. and E. T. Platt. *Aids to Geographical Research – Bibliographies, Periodicals, Atlases, Gazeteers, Other Reference Works.* American Geographical Society. New York, 1947.

Appendix

Report of the Northwest Population in 1805

Departments	Whites			Indians		
	Men	Women	Children	Men	Women	Children
Athabasca	208	48	84		(Not given)	
Athabasca River	37	12	15	55	38	66
English River	78	40	63	211	380	1,100
Rat River	25	7	10	70	90	150
Fort-des-Prairies	136	59	103	4,823	13,632	45,906
Fort Dauphin	45	22	18	19	17	31
Upper Red River	56	52	82	1,170	1,200	2,500
Lower Red River	75	40	60	160	190	250
Lake Winnipic	88	11	15	90	111	194
Las-la-Pluie	46	10	10	103	141	195
Fond-du-Lac	128	29	50	499	784	1,944
Nepigon	90	20	20	238	283	299
Kamanistiquia, Mille-Lacs and Lac-des-Chiens	62	16	36	70	84	178
Le Pic	16	2	3	44	45	58
	1,090	368	569	7,502	16,995	52,871
AMKCo. Men & Co.	520	37	31			
	1,610	405	600	7,502	16,995	52,871

The above table was compiled by Alexander Henry, the younger, as given in Elliot Coues, ed., *New Light on the Early History of the Greater Northwest*, I, 282.

Henry's estimates for the native population totals 77,368. This is probably too high, since it is more than double the total of 38,000 given in 1809 by a fellow employee of the North West Company, Duncan McGillivray. (Duncan McGillivray, *Some Account of the Trade Carried on by the North-West Company*, pp. 65-8.) The bulk of the discrepancy comes from the wide difference in their estimates of the number of plains Indians: Henry's figures for Fort des Prairies (which presumably includes the whole of the Upper Saskatchewan) and the Upper Red [Assiniboine] River total 69,231 against McGillivray's 30,000 for the same area. Possibly Henry made an error in copying his figures for Fort des Prairies, for they do not seem to agree with one another: it is most unlikely that there would be nearly three times as many women as men. Neither Henry nor McGillivray appear to have included the Indians around Hudson Bay, and McGillivray omits the Indians in the territory ceded to the United States as well. However, both include the Indians north of Lake Superior. Henry does not attempt to estimate the number of natives in the Athabasca Department, but McGillivray, while admitting that their numbers could not "be easily ascertained on account of their wandering mode of life," believes there must have been at least 10,000 souls. Both men ignore the Eskimo population altogether.

McGillivray also gives estimates of the population by tribe. These are expressed in three ways: by individuals, by families, and by tents. Unfortunately he does not always give the number of persons per family or per tent. The following table is based on his estimates:

POPULATION OF THE NORTHWEST BY TRIBE (1809)   (a)

ALGONKIAN:

Ojibwa	5,100 to 5,300	(b)
Cree	3,800	(c)
Cree and Ojibwa (undifferentiated)	600	(d)
Blackfoot, Blood and Piegan	5,700	(e)
Gros Ventre	1,150	(f)

ATHAPASKAN:

Sarcee	350	(g)
Other	11,000	(h)

SIOUAN:

Assiniboine	2,900	(i)
Total	30,600	(j)

(a) Tribes have been grouped under linguistic families.

(b) Figure includes 2,800 Ojibwas inhabiting the north shore of Lake Superior.

(c) The number of Crees on the Missinippi [Churchill] River was given as 350 families or 2,000 souls. This ratio of persons per family was used in calculating the population of the other Algonkian tribes.

(d) No differentiation was made between the 600 Crees and Ojibwa who traded at Fort Dauphin.

(e) McGillivray grouped these closely related tribes together and estimated that there were 700 tents or 1,000 families.

(f) "The Fall Indians [Gros Ventre] consist of about 200 tents of families ... "

(g) "The Cercies [Sarcee] are but a few in number of about 60 families ... " This number is low compared with Thompson's estimate of 650 persons or 90 tents; *Narrative*, p. 327. Henry also stated that there were 90 tents; Coues, *New Light*, p. 532.

(h) The population of the Athabasca Department (consisting almost exclusively of Athapaskans) was given as more than 10,000. Another 150 Athapaskan families (Chipewyans) lived outside the department along the banks of the Saskatchewan.

(i) McGillivray said that about 1,500 Assiniboines inhabited the plains north and west of the Mississippi. Another 230 families lived in the Saskatchewan country, making a total of about 2,900 persons. This agrees with Thompson's estimate of 3,200 (*Thompson's Narrative*, p. 327), but is much lower than Henry's 880 tents (Coues, *New Light*, p. 523). Probably Henry included many Indians south of the border as well.

(j) McGillivray does not explain why his estimates by tribes totalled considerably less than his estimates by area.

Notes

CHAPTER 1

1/J. B. Tyrrell, ed., *David Thompson's Narrative*, p. lix. This is the edition used throughout for references to the narrative.

2/*Encyclopedia Canadiana*, x, p. 71. J. B. Tyrrell called him "the greatest practical land geographer that the world has produced" (*Thompson's Narrative*, p. xxxii). Tyrrell spoke from a position of authority for he, himself, from 1883 to 1898, had carried on similar explorations (also by canoe, horseback and on foot) over many of the same routes which Thompson had surveyed and explored a century earlier; *David Thompson's Narrative*, pp. xviii-xix. See also Richard Glover, *David Thompson's Narrative*, Champlain Society, 1962, pp. xi-lxii.

3/Alexander Mackenzie, *Voyages from Montreal through the continent of North America*, p. v (preface).

4/*Journals of Samuel Hearne and Philip Turnor*, ed. J. B. Tyrrell, p. 317.

5/Mackenzie, *Voyages*, pp. vi-vii (preface).

6/J. B. Tyrrell in *David Thompson's Narrative*, p. lx.

7/HBC Archives, A. 11/52, f 1, London Inward, Peter Fidler at Oxford House, 10 July 1802.

8/P. G. Downes, *Sleeping Island*, p. 74.

9/G. R. Crone, *Maps and Their Makers*, p. 149.

10/Thompson's great map of the Northwest, one of the most heroic efforts in the history of cartography, was not finished until 1814. For many years, it hung on the wall of the boardroom of the North West Company at Fort William. It was not published until 1916, although the information contained in it had been sent to Arrowsmith who used it (without credit to Thompson) in later editions of his map of North America (J. B. Tyrrell in *Thompson's Narrative*, p. lxiii).

11/*Journals of Hearne and Turnor*, pp. 91-3.

12/HBC Archives, B. 89/a/2, Peter Fidler's Ile-à-la-Crosse Journal (1810-11).

13/J. B. Tyrrell in *Thompson's Narrative*, pp. lxxxvi-xciv.

14/HBC Archives, A. 11/16, f 15, London Inward, William Auld at Churchill to London Committee, 24 August 1811.

15/Mackenzie, *Voyages*, pp. 405-6.

16/*Ibid.*, p. lxviii.

17/Elliott Coues, *New Light on the Early History of the Great Northwest*, II, pp. 456-7.

18/HBC Archives, A. 11/18, f 28d, London Inward, reply to public letter by William Auld, York Factory, 26 September 1811.

19/Mackenzie, *Voyages*, pp. 405-6.

20/Richard Kirwen, *An Estimate of the Temperature of Different Latitudes*, p. 39.

21/Mackenzie, *Voyages*, p. 405.

22/Samuel Hearne, *A Journey from Prince of Wales's Fort in Hudson's Bay to the Northern Ocean*, p. 65, ed. by R. Glover. This is the edition used throughout for citations from Hearne's narrative.

23/*David Thompson's Narrative*, p. 137.

24/*Cumberland and Hudson House Journals*, ed. E. E. Rich, I, p. xxxiii.

25/L.-R. Masson, *Les Bourgeois de la Compagnie du Nord-Ouest*, I, p. 269. Masson uses "flets de bois" for "Ilets de bois." It is likely that he transcribed the word incorrectly from Macdonell's manuscript.

26/*Thompson's Narrative*, p. 323.

27/*Ibid*, p. 110.

28/Pennant, *Arctic Zoology*, Advertisement [preface].

29/*Philosophical Transactions of the Royal Society*, LXII, pp. 382-433.

CHAPTER 2

1/Clark Wissler, *Ethnological Diversity in America and its Significance*, p. 168.

2/Benjamin Smith Barton, *New Views of the Origin of the Tribes and Nations of America*, p. iv.

3/Wissler, *Ethnological Diversity*, p. 169.

4/James Adair, *History of the American Indians*.

5/Wissler, *Ethnological Diversity*, p. 169.

6/B. S. Barton, *New Views*, p. cvi.

7/Wissler, *Ethnological Diversity*, p. 168.

8/B. S. Barton, *New Views*, p. cvi.

9/Thomas Pennant, *Arctic Zoology*, pp. clx-clxi.

10/Mackenzie, *Voyages*, pp. 406, 407.

11/W. Coats, *Geography of Hudson's Bay*, ed. John Barrow, pp. 74-5.

12/*Thompson's Narrative*, p. 22.

13/Mackenzie, *Voyages*, p. 407.

14/*Thompson's Narrative*, p. 559.

15/Harmon, *Sixteen Years*, p. 237.

16/*Thompson's Narrative*, pp. 311, 312, 457.

17/*Ibid.*, p. 205.

18/Milnes to Hobart, Quebec, 30 October 1802, *Annual Report on the Canadian Archives* (hereafter P.A.C. *Report*), 1892, p. 142.

19/HBC Archives, A. 30/11: *Names of the Company's Servants at Hudson's Bay 1812* lists 21 servants as being born "In Hudson's Bay."

20/C. N. Bell, quoted by E. Coues, *New Light*, I, pp. 426-7.

21/HBC Archives, E. 3/3, f 58d, Peter Fidler's Journal, 24 May 1808.

22/*Ibid*.

23/Coues, *New Light*, I, p. 426.

24/HBC Archives, B. 42/b/57, f 5, Churchill Correspondence Book, 1811-12.

25/*Ibid*.

26/The number of North West Company men in the Northwest in 1811 can only be estimated. According to Henry (see table above) there were 1,090 in 1805. But he includes a somewhat larger area than the Hudson's Bay Company's Northern Department with which, for the purposes of this study, the boundaries of the Northwest are taken to coincide. By excluding the men employed outside the limits of the Northern Department, his total is reduced to about 850 men. By "AMK Co. Men & Co.," Henry must have meant the XY Company, a sharp competitor of the North West Company until late in 1804, when it was absorbed by the North West Company. (Henry evidently compiled his list before news of the union reached him.) Since the policy of the XY Company had been to oppose the North West Company at as many places as possible, it is safe to assume that the distribution of its employees was similar to that of the company it opposed. The approximate number of XY Company men employed in the area of the Northern Department can, therefore, be arrived at by reducing the total number in proportion to the reduction in the total for the North West Company, i.e., from 520 to 400 men. Together, then, the two companies would have had about 1,250 men in 1805.

Henry's figures seem reasonable when compared with those issued in 1802 by Mc-Tavish, Frobisher & Co., Montreal agents for the North West Company. Like Henry, they gave the population by departments of the North West Company. For the area of the Hudson's Bay Company's Northern Department, their figures come to about 770 men. To this, they said, must be added another third to arrive at the total number of traders from Canada. That is, 260 must be added to 770, making a total of 1,030 "Canadians." An increase of 220 men in five years was not unreasonable in this period of keen competition and expansion. After freeing itself of its Canadian competitor by absorbing it, the greatly enlarged North West Company was more than a match for its remaining rival, the Hudson's Bay Company, which was then seriously handicapped by a manpower shortage caused by the Napoleonic wars. From the union until after 1811, the North West Company had little difficulty in keeping the English Company at bay, and with their greatly augmented numbers, were able to extend their activities not only in the North West but beyond the mountains and into New Caledonia as well. It is doubtful if a further increase in manpower was found necessary before 1811 and, with the expansion beyond the Rockies, it is possible that the number of men used in the Northwest itself actually decreased.

27/See Masson, *Les Bouregois*, I, pp. 395-413, for a partial list of the employees of the North West Company after the union in 1804.

28/*The Orkney Parishes*, ed. J. S. Clouston, p. 13.

29/William Auld from Miles Macdonell, Hudson's Bay Encampment, 25 December 1811, P.A.C. *Report*, 1886, pp. cc-cci.

30/George Barry, *History of the Orkney Islands*, pp. 342-3.

31/Murdoch Mackenzie, *Orcades: or a Georgraphic and Hydrographic Survey of the Orkney and Lewis Islands in Eight Maps*, p. 2.

32/*Thompson's Narrative*, pp. 6-7.

33/Barry, *History of Orkney Islands*, p. vi.

34/*Thompson's Narrative*, p. 134.

35/*Orkney Parishes*, ed. Clouston, p. 75.

36/*Thompson's Narrative*, p. 135.

37/*Orkney Parishes*, ed. Clouston, p. 75.

38/*Ibid.*, p. 122.

39/*Ibid.*, p. 75.

40/Rev. William Clouston in *ibid.*, p. 122.

41/Rev. Francis Liddell in *ibid.*, p. 75.

42/*Ibid.*, p. 121.

43/Hugh Marwick, *The Orkney Norn*, pp. xxvi-xxvii.

44/Miles Macdonell to William Auld, Hudson's Bay Encampment, 25 December 1811, P.A.C. *Report*, 1886, pp. cc-cci.

45/HBC Archives, A. 6/17, f 63d, London Outward, to George Charles at Churchill, 31 May 1805.

46/Miles Macdonell to Lord Selkirk, *Report on the Canadian Archives*, 1886, p. ccxvii.

47/HBC Archives, A. 1/50, f 11, Minute Book (1810-14).

48/HBC Archives, A. 1/50, f 57, Report of Committee of Servants (1810), Minute Book (1810-14).

49/HBC Archives, A. 11/18, f 24d, London Inward, reply to public letter by William Auld, York Factory, 26 September 1811.

50/HBC Archives, C. 1/323, *Edward and Ann*, Ship's Log (1811), *Eddystone*, Ship's Log (1811).

51/Miles Macdonell to William Auld, Nelson Encampment, 25 December 1811, P.A.C. *Report*, 1886, pp. cc-cci.

52/*Ibid.*, p. cci.

53/HBC Archives, C. 1/323, *Edward and Ann*, Ship's Log (1811), *Eddystone*, Ship's Log (1811).

54/HBC Archives, A. 11/18, f 24d, London Inward, reply to public letter by William Auld, York Factory, 26 September 1811.

55/Daniel Harmon wrote in 1805 at Fort Assiniboine that "it is now upwards of fifty years since a French Missionary left this area, who had resided here a number of years to instruct the Natives in the Christian Religion. He taught them some short Prayers, the whole of which some of them have not yet forgotten" (*Sixteen Years* p. 90).

56/HBC Archives, A. 11/18, f 24d, London Inward, reply to public letter by William Auld, York Factory, 26 September 1811.

57/Harmon, *Sixteen Years*, pp. 198, 37-8.

58/*Thompson's Narrative*, p. 235.

59/Harmon, *Sixteen Years*, p. 198.

60/*Thompson's Narrative*, p. 92.

61/HBC Archives, A. 11/18, f 22, London Inward, reply to public letter by William Auld, York Factory, 26 September 1811.

62/Mackenzie, *Orcades*, p. 2.

63/HBC Achives, A. 11/18, f 24d, London Inward, reply to public letter by William Auld, York Factory, 26 September 1811.

64/*Ibid.*, f 22.

65/On 29 August 1811, a comet appeared which had not been predicted by the astronomers. It was still visible in December, although "much diminished in splendour" (*Scots Magazine*, 1812, p. 14). In London, a field preacher, well known in the neighbourhood of Paddington, viewed the nightly appearance of the comet far more gravely than did Auld. In his opinion, it was "a manifest indication of the wrath of Heaven" and that the destruction of the world by fire was at hand; *The Observer*, 22 September 1811, number 1025.

66/HBC Archives, B. 42/a/136a, f 18d, William Auld's Memorandum Book (1810-11).

67/HBC Archives, A. 11/18, f 23, London Inward, reply to public letter by William Auld, York Factory, 26 September 1811.

68/Edward Umfreville, *The Present State of Hudson's Bay*, p. 109.

69/HBC Archives, A. 11/18, f 23, London Inward, reply to public letter by William Auld, York Factory, 26 September 1811.

70/HBC Archives, B. 42a/136a, f 18d, William Auld's Memorandum Book (1810-11).

71/HBC Archives, A. 11/18, f 23, London Inward, reply to public letter by William Auld, York Factory, 26 September 1811.

72/Umfreville, *Present State*, pp. 108-10.

73/Masson, *Les Bourgeois*, I, pp. 394-413.

74/Harmon, *Sixteen Years*, p. 55.

75/*Thompson's Narrative*, p. 209.

76/John Lambert in *Early Travellers in Canada*, ed. Gerald M. Craig, p. 35-6.

77/La Rochefoucauld-Liancourt, F.A.F. Duc de, *Travels in Canada*, p. 104.

78/Harmon, *Sixteen Years*, p. 198.

79/*Thompson's Narrative*, p. 107.

80/Harmon, *Sixteen Years*, p. 185.

81/*Ibid.*, p. 29.

82/*Ibid.*, pp. 62-3.

83/*Ibid.*, p. 98.

84/Harmon did live in harmony with his wife, and far from abandoning her, was legally married (Harmon, *Sixteen Years*, p. xv) when the opportunity arose. When the time came for him to leave the Northwest, he took her with him to his home in Vermont and later to Canada. David Thompson's "marriage" to a halfbreed was also very successful and he, too, eventually retired to Canada with his wife.

85/Alexander Henry, the elder, *Travels and Adventures in Canada and the Indian Territories*, ed. James Bain, pp. 248, 333-4.

86/Mackenzie, *Voyages*, p. xcv.

87/Hearne, *A Journey from Prince of Wales's Fort*, p. 57.

88/Harmon, *Sixteen Years*, p. 40.

89/*Journal of Norman McLeod* (1800); HBC Archives 81 (b), f 9, from a photostat copy of the original in the McGill University Library, Montreal.

90/HBC Archives, B. 239/b/82, York Factory Correspondence Book, (1811-12), Swain from Cook, York Factory, 17 December 1811.

91/Miles Macdonell to Lord Selkirk, Nelson Encampment, 29 May 1812, P.A.C. *Report*, 1886, p. ccxvii.

92/HBC Archives, A. 6/17, f 269d, London Outward, to William Auld and Council, 31 May 1808.

93/*Ibid.*, f 119.

94/*Ibid.*, f 112.

95/*Ibid.*, f 269.

96/HBC Archives, B. 42/b/51, f 15, Churchill Factory Correspondence Book (1807-8).

97/HBC Archives, A. 6/17, f 119, London Outward, circular of school instructions sent to various posts in 1807.

98/*Ibid.*, f 170d.

99/*Ibid.*, f 119.

100/*Ibid.*, f 119-119d.

101/Hearne, *A Journey to the Northern Ocean*, p. 82.

102/In April 1811 Harmon sent his three-year-old son George from New Caledonia to Vermont so "that he may be in time instructed in the Christian Religion" (*Sixteen Years*, p. 138).

103/*Ibid.*, p. 50.

104/HBC Archives, E. 3/4, f 7d, Peter Fidler's Journal, Split Lake House (1809).

105/HBC Archives, A. 6/17, f 119-119d, London Outward, circular of school instructions sent to various posts in 1807.

106/Harmon, *Sixteen Years*, p. 123.

107/*Thompson's Narrative*, pp. 108-9.

108/Harmon, *Sixteen Years*, p. 65.

110/*Ibid.*, pp. 21, 22, 30, 31, 40, 41, 52, 53, 65, 88, 89.

111/*Ibid.*, p. 22.

112/*Ibid.*, pp. 89-90.
113/*Thompson's Narrative*, pp. 10-11.
114/Coues, *New Light*, pp. 10-11.
115/Harmon, *Sixteen Years*, pp. 21, 37-8.

CHAPTER 3

1/Arthur S. Morton, *A History of the Canadian West to 1870-71*, pp. 59, 84, 96, 99-102, 103, 218, 300, 333, 384.

2/E. E. Rich, *Hudson's Bay Company 1670-1870*, II, p. 222.

3/Hearne, *Journey to the Northern Ocean*, p. 224.

4/*Ibid.*, pp. 114-15.

5/The St. Lawrence route cost the North West Company at least £10,000 a year more than the Hudson Bay route would have done (G. de T. Glazebrook, *A History of Transportation in Canada*, p. 57). Moreover, by shipping through Canada, the Nor'-westers had to pay out an average of £20,000 a year in export duties (Harold Innis, *The Fur Trade in Canada*, p. 181). Thus the use of the St. Lawrence added about £30,000 a year to the expenses of the Canadian company, which their English rivals did not have to find.

6/Morton, *History of the Canadian West*, pp. 419-20.

7/Mackenzie, *Voyages*, pp. 407-12, 408-9.

8/E. E. Rich, *Hudson's Bay Company*, p. 222. Fearing that the rights of its charter were about to be challenged, the Hudson's Bay Company sought legal advice in 1804. From its lawyers, it learned that the validity of the charter did not rest on an act of Parliament but merely upon the royal prerogative and, in their opinion, the grant of a sole right to trade was beyond the power of the crown, though it had the right to grant land (Rich, *Hudson's Bay Company*, pp. 258-9). On the basis of this advice, the London Committee did not consider it expedient to resort to legal proceedings against the North West Company for defying its charter. The North West Company, for its own part, considered itself justified in trading in the Northwest on the grounds that it derived its rights from the formal cession of Canada by the French (Davidson, *North West Company*, p. 247).

9/Rich, *Hudson's Bay Company*, pp. 231, 258, 263, 302.

10/A copy of the proposal, which was dated Montreal, 7 November 1810, is in the Selkirk Papers, P.A.C., M.G. 19, E 1, Vol. (1), pp. 188-93.

11/Davidson, *North West Company*, pp. 124-6.

12/Rich, *Hudson's Bay Company*, p. 267.

13/HBC Archives, A. 1/49, f 123-123d, Minute Book (1805-10).

14/HBC Archives, B. 239/b/79, f 9d-10, York Factory Correspondence Book (1794-1809), Colen & Council at York to London Committee, dated York Factory, 16 September 1795. B. 239/b/68, f 24d-25, York Factory Correspondence Book (1802-3), from W. Auld, Chief at Churchill to Chief at York.

15/HBC Archives, A. 1/49, f 115d, Minute Book (1805-10), Resolutions of the Committee, 7 March 1810.

16/*Journals of Hearne and Turnor*, p. 474.

17/HBC Archives, B. 89/a/2, f 36d, Peter Fidler's Ile-à-la-Crosse Journal (1810-11).

18/Harmon, *Sixteen Years*, p. 103.

19/Masson, *Les Bourgeois*, II, p. 94.

20/Davidson, *North West Company*, p. 232.

21/HBC Archives, B. 198/c/1, f 9d, Severn Correspondence Inward (1805-25), Gov. and Committee to Thomas and Council at Severn, London, May 1809.

22/HBC Archives, A. 11/18, f 29d, London Inward, reply to public letter by William Auld, York Factory, 26 September 1811.

23/Much of the manpower of the XY Company had been made up of men from the Southwest who had been displaced as a result of the implementation of Jay's Treaty.

24/Duncan McGillivray, *Some Account of the Trade Carried on by the North West Company*, p. 60.

25/J. B. Tyrrell in David *Thompson's Narrative*, pp. xxiii –xxvi.

26/*Thompson's Narrative*, pp. 105-6.

27/*Journals of Hearne and Turnor*, p. 555.

28/E. E. Rich, ed., *Cumberland House Journals*, I, pp. 109-10.

29/*Journals of Hearne and Turnor*, p. 535.

30/Harmon, *Sixteen Years*, p. 55.

31/HBC Archives, A. 6/17, f 114, London Outward, to William Auld and Council at Churchill, 31 May 1807.

32/HBC Archives, A. 6/17, f 119-119d, London Outward, circular of school instructions sent to various posts in 1807.

33/McGillivray, *Some Account of the Trade*, p. 69.

34/*Thompson's Narrative*, p. 113.

35/*Ibid.*, pp. 205-6.

36/Referring to the Chipewyans, who treated their women more harshly than most Indians, Mackenzie wrote: "Though the women are as much in the power of men, as other articles of their property, they are always consulted, and possess a very considerable influence in the traffic with Europeans, and other important concerns" (Mackenzie, *Voyages*, pp. cxxii-cxxiii).

37/William Guthrie, *A System of Modern Geography*, p. 872.

38/W. Coats, *The Geography of Hudson's Bay*, ed. John Barrow, p. 33.

39/Edward Umfreville, *Present State of Hudson's Bay*, pp. 31-2.

40/Hearne, *Journey to the Northern Ocean*, p. 36; *Journals of Hearne and Turnor*, pp. 258, 375.

41/Hearne, *Journey to the Northern Ocean*, p. 36.

42/*Cumberland and Hudson House Journals*, II, pp. 67, 72; *Journals of Hearne and Turnor*, p. 359.

43/*Cumberland and Hudson House Journals*, II, p. 85.

44/HBC Archives, B. 198/c/1, f 3d, Severn Inward (1808-25), Governor and Committee to Thomas Thomas and Council at Severn, London, 20 May 1808.

45/HBC Archives, B. 42/b/52, f 14, Churchill River, Country Correspondence (1808-9), William Auld at Churchill to the officers inland, 1 September 1809.

46/Hearne, *Journey to the Northern Ocean*, pp. 114-15.

47/HBC Archives, B. 141a/4, f 3, Nelson House Journal (1810-11).

48/Hearne, *Journey to the Northern Ocean*, p. 114.

49/*Ibid.*, p. 51.

50/*Ibid.*, p. 186; Umfreville, *Present State*, pp. 28-9.

51/Hearne, *Journey to the Northern Ocean*, p. 187.

52/*Ibid.*, p. 199, 213.

53/*Journals of Hearne and Turnor*, pp. 553-4.

54/*Cumberland and Hudson House Journals*, II, pp. 71, 77-8.

55/McGillivray, *The Journal of Duncan McGillivray*, p. 30.

56/La Rochefoucauld-Liancourt, *Travels in Canada*, p. 113.

57/Mackenzie, *Voyages*, p. vi.

58/La Rochefoucauld-Liancourt, *Travels in Canada*, p. 113.

59/McGillivray, *The Journal of Duncan McGillivray*, p. 47.

60/HBC Archives, E. 2/8, Andrew Graham's "Observations on Hudson's Bay," ff 13d-14.

61/W. Stewart Wallace, ed., *Documents Relating to the North West Company*, pp. 268-9.

62/Coues, *New Light*, pp. 209, 723.

63/*Journals of Hearne and Turnor*, p. 223.

64/*Ibid.*, p. 159; *Cumberland and Hudson House Journals*, I, pp. 5, 80; *Journey to the Northern Ocean*, p. 175.

65/Davidson, *North West Company*, p. 224.

6/Coues, *New Light*, p. 542.

67/*Thompson's Narrative*, p. 365.

68/Duncan McGillivray, *The Journal of Duncan McGillivray*, p. 47.

CHAPTER 4

1/Miles Macdonell to Lord Selkirk, York Factory, 1 October 1811, P.A.C. *Report*, 1886, p. cxciii.

2/According to Edward Umfreville, La Pérouse (1782) attacked Fort Prince of Wales [Churchill] before going on to York Fort "on account of its Northern situation, and the general prevalency of winds from that quarter, thinking to take advantage of them in going to the Southward ... " (Edward Umfreville, *The Present State of Hudson's Bay*, p. 69).

3/HBC Archives, B. 42a/132, f 18d, Churchill Factory Journal (1806-7).

4/Macdonell to Selkirk, York Fort, 1 October 1811, P.A.C. *Report*, 1886, p. cxcii.

5/HBC Archives, C. 1/295, *Eddystone* log, f 46.

6/HBC Archives, mss., "Ships on HBC Business Sailing Between England and York Fort 1670-1900," f 35.

7/HBC Archives, C. 1/295, *Eddystone* log, ff 46-46d, 47.

8/Macdonell to Selkirk, York Factory, 5 October 1811, P.A.C. *Report*, 1886, p. cxcvii.

9/HBC Archives, C. 1/295, *Eddystone* log, f 47.

10/HBC Archives, A. 11/118, f 33, William Auld, York Factory, 4 October 1811, to A. Lean, Esq., Secretary, Hudson's Bay House.

11/HBC Archives, C. 1/295, *Eddystone* log, ff 46-7.

12/HBC Archives, mss., "Ships on HBC Business Between England and York Fort 1670-1900," f 35.

13/This essay into the timber industry was an attempt by the company to bolster its financial position at a time when the fur markets were depressed. It was also the harbinger of a trading pattern which became firmly established during the nineteenth century – immigrants on the outward journey, lumber on the return.

14/HBC Archives, mss., "Ships on HBC Business Sailing between England and York Fort 1670-1900," f 35, f 21, f 20.

15/Hearne, *Journey to the Northern Ocean*, pp. 217-18.

16/Wayne Edson Stevens, *The Northwest Fur-Trade, 1763-1800*, p. 151.

17/La Rochefoucauld-Liancourt, *Travels in Canada*, pp. 112-13.

18/George Thomas Landmann, *Adventures and Recollections*, p. 303.

19/Masson, *Les Bourgeois*, II, p. 312.

20/Landmann, *Adventures and Recollections*, p. 304.

21/Mackenzie, *Voyages*, p. xxvii.

22/Landmann, *Adventures and Recollections*, p. 306. Crooked knife. "A woodworking knife usually having a crooked handle and, often, a hook on one end of the blade, used widely in the north, especially by the Indians, for making snowshoes, fur stretchers, canoes, and all woodwork" [*A Dictionary of Canadianisms*, Toronto, 1967].

23/John Long, *John Long's Voyages and Travels in the Years 1768-1788*, ed. M. M. Quaife, p. 50.

24/Mackenzie, *Voyages*, p. xxix.

25/Alexander Henry, the elder, *Travels and Adventures*, 1809 edition, pp. 15-16.

26/One English visitor, John Lambert, who was in Canada from 1806 to 1808, speculated on the origin of the custom. "I have observed," he wrote, "that in the winter season the driver frequently jumps out of the cariole on the right side, in order to prevent it from upsetting in places where the road is narrow and the snow uneven; this may possibly have given rise to their driving on the right side of the road, though I think the same thing might be accomplished as easily on the left." Lambert added that the custom had by then been made law (John Lambert in *Early Travellers*, ed. G. M. Craig, p. 33).

27/Henry, the elder, *Travels and Adventures*, 1809 ed., pp. 14-16; Harmon, *Sixteen Years*, p. 11.

28/Henry, the elder, *Travels and Adventures*, 1809 ed., pp. 16-22; Harmon, *Sixteen Years*, pp. 11-16.

29/La Rochefoucauld-Liancourt, *Travels in Canada*, p. 112.

30/Harmon, *Sixteen Years*, p. 18.

31/*Ibid.*, pp. 11-16; Henry, the elder, *Travels and Adventures*, 1809 ed., pp. 16-22; Mackenzie, Voyages, pp. xxx-xxxvi.

32/Harmon, *Sixteen Years*, p. 18.

33/Mackenzie, *Voyages*, pp. xxxvii, xxxix.

34/*Documents Relating to the North West Company*, ed. W. S. Wallace, p. 263.

35/Mackenzie, *Voyages*, p. xxxix.

36/John Macdonnell in *Five Fur-Traders of the Northwest*, ed. Charles M. Gates, p. 94.

37/Masson, *Les Bourgeois*, II, p. 312.

38/*Thompson's Narrative*, p. 298.

39/Harmon, *Sixteen Years*, p. 18.

40/La Rochefoucauld-Liancourt, *Travels in Canada*, p. 112.

41/Mackenzie, *Voyages*, p. xxxvii.

42/Masson, *Les Bourgeois*, II, p. 145.

43/*The Beaver*, December 1934, p. 29.

44/Harmon, *Sixteen Years*, p. 19.

45/*The Beaver*, December 1934, p. 29.

46/Gabriel Franchère, *Narrative of a Voyage to the Northwest Coast of America in the Years 1811, 1812, 1813 and 1814*, ed. R. G. Thwaites, pp. 387-8.

47/Davidson, *North West Company*, p. 213.

48/Masson, *Les Bourgeois*, II, p. 307.

49/Public Record Office (hereafter P.R.O.), C.O. 42, Vol. 122, a paper drawn up by the directors of the North West Company, sent to Lieut-Gov. Robert Milnes, dated Montreal, 1 September 1803, signed: McTavish, Frobisher and Co. Directors of the North West Company.

50/Mackenzie, *Voyages*, pp. xlvii-lvi.

51/*Journals of Hearne and Turnor*, p. 222.

52/Masson, *Les Bourgeois*, II, p. 313.

53/Davidson, *The North West Company*, p. 230; Mackenzie, *Voyages*, pp. xxvii-xxviii.

54/Mackenzie, *Voyages*, p. lvi.

55/Harmon, *Sixteen Years*, p. 92.

56/*Documents Relating to the North West Company*, p. 251; *Journals of Hearne and Turnor*, p. 452.

57/ Harmon, *Sixteen Years*, p. 120.

58/ Coues, *New Light*, p. 181.

59/ *Thompson's Narrative*, p. 106.

60/ Masson, *Les Bourgeois*, II, p. 313.

61/ *Ibid.*, p. 314.

62/ *Ibid.*

63/ Mackenzie, *Voyages*, p. lxviii.

64/ HBC Archives, A. 6/17, f 158, London Outward, to Thomas Thomas and Council, Moose Factory, 31 May 1809.

65/ *Cumberland and Hudson House Journals*, I, p. 345.

66/ Masson, *Les Bourgeois*, II, p. 312.

67/ *Cumberland and Hudson House Journals*, I, p. 68.

68/ *Journals of Hearne and Turnor*, pp. 150, 189.

69/ *Cumberland and Hudson House Journals*, I, pp. 87, 345.

70/ Umfreville, *Present State of Hudson's Bay*, p. 36.

71/ *Cumberland and Hudson House Journals*, I, p. 162.

72/ *Journals of Hearne and Turnor*, p. 222.

73/ Miles Macdonell to William Auld, Nelson Encampment, 25 December 1811, P.A.C. *Report*, 1886.

74/ HBC Archives, B. 42/b/57, f 9d, Churchill Correspondence Book [*sic*] (1811-12), Macdonell from W. Auld, York Factory, 16 October 1811.

75/ HBC Archives, B. 239/b/66, f 66, York Factory Correspondence Book (1796-1801).

76/ HBC Archives, B. 42/b/57, f 3, Churchill Correspondence Book [*sic*] (1811-12); Macdonell from W. Auld, York Factory, 16 October 1811.

77/ Coues, *New Light*, p. 463.

78/ *Journals of Hearne and Turnor*, p. 576.

79/ HBC Archives, B. 42/b/57, f 3, Churchill Correspondence Book [*sic*] (1811-12), Macdonell from W. Auld, York Factory, 16 October 1811.

80/ HBC Archives, B. 239/b/79, f 26, York Factory Correspondence Book (1794-1809), Colen and Council at York to London Committee, York Factory, 21 September 1798.

81/ *Journals of Hearne and Turnor*, p. 576.

82/ *Ibid.*, pp. 222-3.

83/ Coues, *New Light*, p. 451.

84/ Miles Macdonell to Lord Selkirk, 1 October 1811, P.A.C. *Report*, 1886, p. cxcvi.

85/ HBC Archives, B. 42/b/55, f 17, Churchill Correspondence Book (1811), Auld to Thomas at Albany, Churchill, 16 August 1811.

86/ Coues, *New Light*, p. 600.

87/ *Thompson's Narrative*, pp. 209, 443.

88/ Coues, *New Light*, p. 539.

89/ *Ibid.*, p. 213.

90/ *Journals of Hearne and Turnor*, p. 452.

91/ Coues, *New Light*, p. 539.

92/ Masson, *Les Bourgeois*, II, p. 22.

93/ Coues, *New Light*, p. 539.

94/ *Ibid.*, p. 509.

95/ Landmann, *Adventures and Recollections*, p. 309.

96/ Davidson, *North West Company*, pp. 218-19.

97/ Coues, *New Light*, pp. 558-9.

98/ Harmon, *Sixteen Years*, pp. 41-2.

99/ Masson, *Les Bourgeois*, II, p. 387, fn.

100/ *Thompson's Narrative*, pp. 30-1.

101/ Hearne, *Journey to the Northern Ocean*, p. 63.

102/*Ibid.*, pp. 26, 62-3.
103/Thomas McKeevor, *A Voyage to Hudson's Bay, during the Summer of 1812*, pp. 33-4.
104/W. Coats, *The Geography of Hudson's Bay*, ed. John Barrow, p. 74.
105/McKeevor, *A Voyage to Hudson's Bay*, p. 34.
106/Harmon, *Sixteen Years*, p. 99.
107/Coues, *New Light*, pp. 490-1.
108/Harmon, *Sixteen Years*, p. 78.
109/*Ibid.*, p. 74.
110/Henry, the elder, *Travels and Adventures*, p. 303.
111/*Ibid.*, p. 286.
112/Pennant, *Arctic Zoology*, p. 39.
113/Harmon, *Sixteen Years*, p. 261.
114/Pennant, *Arctic Zoology*, p. 39.
115/Harmon, *Sixteen Years*, pp. 212, 261.
116/Francis D. Haines, *The Northward Spread of Horses among the Plains Indians*, pp. 433-6.
117/*Ibid.*, also Anthony Hendry, *The Journal of York Fort to the Blackfeet Country, 1754-1755*, ed. L. J. Burpee, p. 351.
118/Coues, *New Light*, p. 535.
119/*Ibid*, p. 518.
120/*Thompson's Narrative*, p. 367.
121/In the north, where the ground was generally wet and swampy, horses were of little use except for dragging fire wood in winter (HBC Archives, E. 3/2, p. 93).
122/Hearne, *Journey to the Northern Ocean*, pp. 207-8.
123/*Ibid.*, p. 35.
124/*Ibid.*, pp. 207-8.
125/Harmon, *Sixteen Years*, pp. 71, 212-13. "Went to the hills with a horse and carriole, low and surrounded with parchment buffalo skin; it weighed only twenty pounds, but was large enough for one person and his bedding." Coues, *New Light*, p. 192.
126/*Thompson's Narrative*, p. 214.
127/James Knight, *The Founding of Churchill*, ed. J. F. Kenney, pp. 94-5.
128/Coues, *New Light*, pp. 191, 205, 210.

CHAPTER 5

1/There were also four or five families of Ottawa Indians from Canada, settled about six miles up the Dead River from its junction with the Red, who raised Indian corn, potatoes and other garden stuff (HBC Archives, E. 3/3 f 58d; Coues, *New Light*, p. 280).
2/Harmon, *Sixteen Years*, p. 211.
3/*Ibid.*, pp. 91, 92.
4/*Thompson's Narrative*, pp. 296, 297.
5/*Cumberland and Hudson House Journals*, II, p. 295.
6/Harmon, *Sixteen Years*, p. 211.
7/Hearne, *Journey to the Northern Ocean*, p. 192.
8/*Thompson's Narrative*, pp. 434, 435.
9/HBC Archives, B. 42/b/50, f 23d, Churchill Correspondence Book (1806-7), circular letter from W. Auld to the officers and traders inland from Churchill Factory, fall of 1807.
10/HBC Archives, B. 42/b/55, f 4d, W. Auld's (Churchill) Correspondence Book, W. Sinclair at Winnipeg from W. Auld, Churchill, 3 March 1811.

11/These included bacon, barley (English, Scottish), beef fat, biscuit (brown, white), French brandy, butter, cheese, chocolate, coffee, crystallized lemon juice, currants, figs, fish salt, flour, hams, herbs, hops, lard, malt, molasses, mustard, oats, groats & meal, oil genoa, peas (grey, hag, split, white) pickles, salt pork, porter, raisins, rice, rum, salt (common, petre), sauce (fish, ketchup), spices (cinnamon, cloves, ginger, mace, nutmeg, pepper), suet, sugar, tea, vinegar, wine (port, sherry) (HBC Archives, B. 239/d/156).

12/HBC Archives, A. 6/17 f 111-111d, London Outward, to William Auld and Council, Churchill, 31 May 1807.

13/HBC Archives, A. 6/18, London Outward, to W. Auld, York Factory, 31 May 1810.

14/Coues, *New Light*, p. 517.

15/*Thompson's Narrative*, p. 367.

16/Coues, *New Light*, pp. 517-20.

17/McGillivray, *The Journal of Duncan McGillivray*, p. 67.

18/*Ibid.*, p. 33.

19/Hearne, *Journey to the Northern Ocean*, pp. 49-51.

20/*Thompson's Narrative*, p. 98.

21/Hearne, *Journey to the Northern Ocean*, pp. 14-15, 177, 265.

22/*Thompson's Narrative*, p. 34.

23/Umfreville, *Present State*, pp. 20-1.

24/*Thompson's Narrative*, pp. 34-5.

25/*Ibid.*

26/Umfreville, *Present State*, p. 20.

27/Hearne, *Journey to the Northern Ocean*, p. 283.

28/Umfreville, *Present State*, pp. 20-1. (The feathers of the geese were sent to London where they commanded a ready sale; *Thompson's Narrative*, p. 35.)

29/Coues, *New Light*, p. 46.

30/*Ibid.*, p. 54.

31/Hearne, *Journey to the Northern Ocean*, p. 294.

32/Harmon, *Sixteen Years*, pp. 46, 99.

33/Hearne, *Journey to the Northern Ocean*, pp. 26, 289-91.

34/HBC Archives, B. 42/b/50, f 23d, Churchill Correspondence Book (1806-7), circular letter from W. Auld to officers and traders inland from Churchill Factory, fall of 1807.

35/Hearne, *Journey to the Northern Ocean*, pp. 137-43.

36/*Thompson's Narrative*, pp. 129, 157-8.

37/Hearne, *Journey to the Northern Ocean*, pp. 11-12, 167-70.

38/Harmon, *Sixteen Years*, pp. 122-3.

39/Franchère, *Narrative*, p. 379.

40/*Thompson's Narrative*, p. 559.

41/Hearne, *Journey to the Northern Ocean*, p. 134.

42/*Thompson's Narrative*, p. 559.

43/Umfreville, *Present State*, pp. 13-14; HBC Archives, B. 42a/133, f 2, Churchill Journal (1807-8).

44/HBC Archives, B. 239/e/1, f 4, York Factory Report 1815, W. H. Cook to Thomas Thomas, dated York Factory, 1 September 1815.

45/*Ibid.*, f 5.

46/Hearne, *Journey to the Northern Ocean*, p. 207.

47/HBC Archives, B. 42a/133, f 4d, Churchill Journal (1808).

48/Francis D. Haines, *The Northward Spread of Horses*, pp. 433-6.

49/La Vérendrye, *Journals and Letters*, ed. L. J. Burpee, p. 387.

50/*Thompson's Narrative*, pp. 370-1.

51/Henry, the elder, ed. Bain, *Travels and Adventures*, p. 316.

52/Harmon, *Sixteen Years*, p. 50.

53/Umfreville, *Present State*, p. 78.

54/McGillivray, *Journal*, pp. 28-9.

55/Coues, *New Light*, p. 523.

56/Harmon, *Sixteen Years*, pp. 57, 213.

57/*Thompson's Narrative*, pp. 367-8.

58/Coues, *New Light*, p. 523.

59/*Ibid.*, *Thompson's Narrative*, p. 367.

60/*Ibid.*

61/"The ships *Hannah* and *Mary* with Norton came to Churchill and brought masons and other artisans, labourers, equipment, and apparently, a horse which died two days after arrival" (James Kenney in James Knight, *The Founding of Churchill*).

62/Coues, *New Light*, p. 600.

63/James Kenney, *The Founding of Churchill*, ed. James Knight, pp. 94-5.

64/Hearne, *Journey to the Northern Ocean*, p. 267.

65/William Wales, *Journal of a voyage made by order of the Royal Society to Churchill River* ... p. 118.

66/HBC Archives, B. 42/b/55, f 17, W. Auld's (Churchill) Correspondence Book (1811), W. Auld to T. Thomas at Albany, dated Churchill, 16 August 1811.

67/*Thompson's Narrative*, p. 69.

68/Coues, *New Light*, p. 579.

69/Hearne, *Journey to the Northern Ocean*, p. 270.

70/The natives often tamed young bears, as well (*Thompson's Narrative*, p. 113).

71/Hearne, *Journey to the Northern Ocean*, p. 242.

72/*Ibid.*, p. 166.

73/*Thompson's Narrative*, p. 63.

74/Hearne, *Journey to the Northern Ocean*, pp. 234, 243, 263, 281-2.

75/HBC Archives, A. 10/1, ff 94-95d, London Inward, Correspondence-general, letter from Frank Oakey to London Committee, dated Hudson's Bay House 12 February 1806.

76/HBC Archives, A. 6/17, ff 89d-90, London Outward, to W. Auld at Churchill, 31 May 1806.

77/HBC Archives, B. 239/b/79, ff 51-51d, York Correspondence (1794-1809), General Letter of York Council to London Committee, 30 August 1806.

78/Hearne, *Journey to the Northern Ocean*, pp. 167-8.

79/*Ibid.*, pp. 127-8.

80/*Thompson's Narrative*, p. 20.

81/Umfreville, *Present State*, p. 19; Harmon, *Sixteen Years*, p. 200; Mackenzie, *Voyages*, p. xcv.

82/Umfreville, *Present State*, p. 19.

83/Mackenzie, *Voyages*, p. xcv.

84/Umfreville, *Present State*, p. 19.

85/Mackenzie, *Voyages*, pp. cxxiv-cxxv.

86/Umfreville, *Present State*, p. 19.

87/Harmon, *Sixteen Years*, p. 200.

88/*Ibid.*

89/*James Isham's Observations on Hudson's Bay*, ed. E. E. Rich, pp. 96-7.

90/Harmon, *Sixteen Years*, p. 199.

91/Mackenzie, *Voyages*, p. cvi.

92/Harmon, *Sixteen Years*, pp. 199-200.

93/*Ibid.*, p. 199. But if the Indians were capable of perpetrating drug frauds, they were also equal to being the dupes of one. Referring to the Chipewyans, Alexander Henry, the elder, wrote in 1776: "Their solicitude and credulity, as to drugs and nostrums, had exposed them to gross deceptions, on the part of the agents of the Hudson's Bay Company. One of the chiefs informed me, that he had been at the Bay the year before, and there purchased a quantity of medicines, which he would allow me to inspect. Accordingly, he brought a bag, containing numerous small papers, in which I found lumps of white sugar, grains of coffee, pepper, allspice, cloves, tea, nutmegs, ginger and other things of this kind, sold as specifics against evil spirits, and against the dangers of battle; as giving power over enemies, and particularly the white bear, of which the Indians in these latitudes are much afraid: – others were infallible against barrenness in women; against difficult labours; and against a variety of other afflictions. In a second parcel, I found small prints; the identical ones, which, in England, are commonly sold in sheets to children, but each of which was here transformed into a talisman, for the cure of some evil, or obtention of some delight; – No. 1, 'A sailor kissing his mistress, on his return from "sea" '; – this worn about the person of a gallant, attracted, though concealed, the affections of the opposite sex! No. 2, 'A soldier in arms'; – this poured a sentiment of valour into the possessor, and gave him the strength of a giant!

By means of these commodities, many customers were secured to the company; and even those Indians, who shortened their voyage by dealing with us, sent forward one canoe, laden with beaver-skins, to purchase articles of this kind, at Cumberland House." (Henry, the elder, *Travels and Adventures*, 1809 ed., pp. 326-7).

94/ Mackenzie, *Voyages*, p. xcviii.
95/ *Ibid.*, p. cvi.
96/ *Cumberland and Hudson House Journals*, I, p. 145; II, p. 246.
97/ *Isham's Observations*, pp. 97-8.
98/ Mackenzie, *Voyages*, p. cxxv.
99/ *Journals of Hearne and Turnor*, p. 139.
100/ *Thompson's Narrative*, p. 52.
101/ Also "Wee suc a pucke," "Labrador tea," or "Ledum groenlandium Oeder."
102/ Umfreville, *Present State*, p. 15.
103/ Hearne, *Journey to the Northern Ocean*, p. 293.
104/ *Thompson's Narrative*, p. 152.
105/ HBC Archives, A. 11/18, f 29b, London Inward, reply to public letter by W. Auld, dated York Factory, 26 September 1811.
106/ Macdonell to Selkirk, Nelson Encampment, 29 May 1812, P.A.C. *Report*, 1886, p. ccxvi.
107/ HBC Archives, B. 42/b/57, f 4d, Churchill Correspondence Book [*sic*] (1811-12), M. Macdonell from W. Auld, York Factory, 16 October 1811.
108/ Macdonell to Selkirk, Nelson Encampment, 29 May 1812, P.A.C. *Report*, 1886, p. ccxvii.
109/ *Thompson's Narrative*, pp. 322-3.
110/ *Ibid.*, p. 337.
111/ *Cumberland and Hudson House Journals*, II, pp. 262-98.
112/ *Ibid.*, II, p. 226.
113/ *Thompson's Narrative*, p. 323.
114/ *Ibid.*, p. 339.
115/ Umfreville, *Present State*, p. 97.
116/ Hearne, *Journey to the Northern Ocean*, p. 171.
117/ *Thompson's Narrative*, pp. 238-9.
118/ *Journals of Hearne and Turnor*, p. 35.
119/ *Documents Relating to the North West Company*, p. 262.

120/HBC Archives, B. 239/b/79, f 40d, York Factory Correspondence Book (1794-1809), Ballenden and Council at York Factory to London Committee, September 1802.

121/*Thompson's Narrative*, pp. 115-16.

122/*Journals of Hearne and Turnor*, p. 318.

123/Mackenzie, *Voyages*, p. 403.

124/Harmon, *Sixteen Years*, p. 113.

125/Coues, *New Light*, pp. 470-1.

126/*Ibid.*, pp. 702, 742, 743.

127/Mackenzie, *Voyages*, p. 96.

128/Coues, *New Light*, p. 702.

129/Mackenzie, *Voyages*, p. 96.

130/*Ibid.*, p. 402.

131/*Ibid.*, p. lxxxvii.

132/*Ibid.*, p. 95.

133/Henry, the elder, *Travels and Adventures*, ed. James Bain, pp. 186, 187, 195, 196: *Thompson's Narrative*, p. 291.

134/Henry, the elder, *Travels and Adventures*, ed. James Bain, p. 187.

135/Mackenzie, *Voyages*, p. cxxvii.

136/Hearne, *Journey to the Northern Ocean*, p. 31.

137/John Reinhold Forster, "A Letter from Mr. John Reinhold Forster, F.R.S. to William Watson, M.D. giving some Account of the Roots used by the Indians, in the Neighbourhood of Hudson's Bay, to dye Porcupine Quills," *Phil. Trans. of the Royal Society*, LXII, pp. 56-7.

138/Coats, *Geography of Hudson's Bay*, p. 75.

139/Wales, *Journal of a Voyage ... to Churchill River*, p. 110.

140/HBC Archives, B. 42a/136a, ff 11d, 12. W. Auld's Memorandum Book (1810-11). In defence of the whales' intelligence, it might be pointed out that during the time of year (June) they frequented this area, the waters were very muddy as the rivers, expanded by the melting snows, dumped large quantities of clay, sand and other debris into the bay (Peter Freuchen, *The Arctic Year*, p. 220).

141/*Thompson's Narrative*, pp. 23-4.

142/HBC Archives, B. 42a/136a, f 11, W. Auld's Memorandum Book (1810-11).

143/*Thompson's Narrative*, p. 23.

144/HBC Archives, B. 42a/136a, f 11, W. Auld's Memorandum Book (1810-11)

145/Hearne, *Journey to the Northern Ocean*, p. 253.

146/Mackenzie, *Voyages*, p. 64.

CHAPTER 6

1/"Wales, New South, a country of vast extent, but little known, lying round the southern part of Hudson Bay." So read the entry in Jedidiah Morse's (1810) *American Gazetteer*. Morse made no attempt to define the limits of New South Wales, but under "Wales, New North," he set its southern boundary at Seal River. However, from this and from contemporary maps, it may be assumed that New South Wales comprised the extensive coastal plain which bordered the southwestern part of Hudson Bay. North of Seal River, the "granitic rocks" of the Stony Region extended to the shores of the bay, but from Seal River southward to Churchill River, a narrow marsh, apparently the alluvial of Seal River, intruded between the rocks and the bay. South of Churchill, the rocks formed a retiring line from the coast to meet the Nelson River some 135 miles from its mouth (*Thompson's Narrative*, p. 8). From there to Severn River, the line seemed to parallel the bay since the first granite was encountered approximately the same distance up that river. From the Severn, it was only a short distance to the eastern boundary of the Northwest. Enclosed between the line of rocks and the bay was the coastal plain of New South Wales. According to Thompson, it was "wholly alluvial" (*Ibid.*).

Named "New Wales" in 1612 by Thomas Button and renamed "Principality of South Wales" nineteen years later by Captain Thomas James (*Encylopedia Canadiana*, VII, p. 326), New South Wales was still largely unexplored in 1811. Traders had occupied its shores since 1683, but they had seldom strayed from its turbulent rivers or from the great windswept marshes which lined its coast. The rivers carried them into the interior of the Northwest; their rapids, shoals, and rocks were very well known, indeed; so, too, were the marshes, for they had been covered on foot many times by the men going from one factory to another; but for the rest: it was largely unknown.

2/ HBC Archives, B. 42b/57, Churchill Correspondence Book [*sic*] (1811-12), sketch map of York Factory area.

3/ Macdonell to Selkirk, York Factory, 1 October 1811, P.A.C. *Report*, 1886.

4/ Coats, *Geography of Hudson Bay*, pp. 38-9.

5/ Macdonell to Selkirk, Nelson Encampment, 29 May 1812, P.A.C. *Report*, 1886, p. ccxvi.

6/ HBC Archives, B. 42a/136a f 6d, W. Auld's Memorandum Book (1810-11).

7/ Macdonell to Selkirk, Nelson Encampment, 29 May 1812, P.A.C. *Report*, 1886, p. ccxvi.

8/ HBC Archives, B. 42a/136a, f 7, W. Auld's Memorandum Book (1810-11).

9/ On 8 January 1811, Mr. Cook, who was then in charge of York Factory, wrote "Our Gentlemen have all tho' rather reluctantly been out at Tents and are there yet. Indeed there is no alternative owing to the wetness of the firewood. I have seen the Doctor twice and the poor Devil appeared to be miserable, from indolence having a habitation that Proserpine herself could not exist in. He declared he was almost blind with smoke but as he saw that I was out myself and braved the smoke like another Pluto I expected he would do the same and make a virtue of necessity. ... " (HBC Archives, B. 42/b/55, f 1d, W. Auld's (Churchill) Correspondence Book (1811), copy of letter from W. Cook at York to Auld at Churchill, 8 January 1811).

10/ HBC Archives, B. 42/b/57, ff 4-4d, Churchill Correspondence Book [*sic*] (1811-12), M. Macdonell from W. Auld. York Factory, 16 October 1811.

11/ Henry Ellis, *Voyage to Hudson's Bay*, p. 154, quoted in *James Isham's Observations on Hudson's Bay*, ed. E. E. Rich, p. 214, fn.

12/ *Ibid.*, p. 91.

13/ Macdonell to Selkirk, Nelson Encampment, 31 May 1812, P.A.C. *Report*, 1886, p. ccxviii.

14/ HBC Archives, B. 42/b/55, f 1, W. Auld's (Churchill) Correspondence Book (1811), copy of a letter from Cook at York to Auld at Churchill, 8 January 1811.

15/ Macdonell to Selkirk, Nelson Encampment, 31 May 1812, P.A.C. *Report*, 1886, p. ccxix.

16/ Hearne, *Journey*, p. 254.

17/ HBC Archives, B. 42/b/55, f 1, W. Auld's (Churchill) Correspondence Book (1811), copy of a letter from Cook at York to Auld at Churchill, 8 January 1811.

18/ Macdonell to Selkirk, Nelson Encampment, 29 May 1812, P.A.C. *Report*, 1886, p. ccxvi.

19/ Umfreville, *Present State*, pp. 6-7, 13-14.

20/ HBC Archives, B. 42a/131, f 1d, Churchill Factory Journal (1805-6).

21/ Two calves, born in the spring, were then at Oxford House. They were to be sent with the colonists to the Red River (HBC Archives, A. 11/18, f 25, London Inward, reply to public letter by William Auld, York Factory, 26 September 1811).

22/Macdonell to Selkirk, Nelson Encampment, 29 May 1812, P.A.C. *Report*, 1886, pp. ccxvi-ccxvii.

23/HBC Archives, B. 42/b/55 f 2, W. Auld's (Churchill) Correspondence Book (1811), copy of a letter from Cook at York to Auld at Churchill, 8 January 1811.

24/HBC Archives, B. 42/b/57, ff 4-4d, Churchill Correspondence Book [*sic*] (1811-12), M. Macdonell from W. Auld. York Factory, 16 October 1811.

25/Macdonell to Selkirk, Nelson Encampment, 29 May 1812, P.A.C. *Report*, 1886, p. ccxvi.

26/Macdonell to William Cook, Governor of York Factory, Nelson Encampment, 30 November 1811, P.A.C. *Report*, 1886, p. cxcviii. Deer hedges were made of trees felled in such a way as to divert the animals to rivers and other places where they might be killed by hunters.

27/HBC Archives, B. 42/b/57, f 4d, Churchill Correspondence Book [*sic*] (1811-12) M. Macdonell from W. Auld. York Factory, 16 October 1811.

28/*Ibid.*

29/HBC Archives, A. 11/16, f 17, London Inward, W. Auld at Churchill to London Committee, 24 August 1811.

30/HBC Archives, B. 239/b/82 f 12, York Correspondence Book (1811-12), M. Macdonell from W. H. Cook. York Factory, 2 January 1812.

31/HBC Archives, B. 42/b/57, f 13d, Churchill Correspondence (1811-12), W. H. Cook at York to W. Auld at Churchill, York Factory, 17 December 1811.

32/HBC Archives, B. 42/b/46, p. 12, Churchill Correspondence Book (1802-3), W. Auld at Churchill to Thomas Thomas, Chief, Severn Factory, 28 December 1802.

33/Coats, *Geography of Hudson Bay*, p. 36.

34/Christopher Middleton,*The Effects of Cold*, ed. John Barrow, pp. 130-1.

35/HBC Archives, B. 239/b/43, f 5d, York Factory Correspondence Book (1783-84), Samuel Hearne at Churchill to Chief at York, 27 December 1783.

36/*Thompson's Narrative*, pp. 12-13.

37/*Ibid.*, p. 9.

38/HBC Archives, B. 42/b/44, f 1d, Churchill Correspondence Book (1783-1801), Committee to Samuel Hearne and Council at Churchill from Hudson's Bay House, London, 21 May 1783.

39/HBC Archives, B. 42/a/131, f 2d, W. Auld in Churchill Factory Journal (1805-6).

40/HBC Archives, B. 42/a/131, ff 2d-3, W. Auld in Churchill Factory Journal (1805-6).

41/William Wales, *Journal of a Voyage Made by Order of the Royal Society to Churchill River*, p. 118.

42/Hearne, *Journey to the Northern Ocean*, p. 134, fn.

43/Wales, *Journal of a Voyage*, p. 118.

44/Hearne, *Journey to the Northern Ocean*, p. 252.

45/HBC Archives, B. 42a/136a, f 10d, W. Auld's Memorandum Book (1810-11).

46/HBC Archives, B. 239/b/75, p. 11, York Factory Correspondence Book (1807-8), W. Auld at Churchill to John McNabb, Chief at York, 9 March 1808.

47/HBC Archives, B. 42/a/132, f 18, Churchill Journal (1806-7).

48/Macdonell to Selkirk, Nelson Encampment, 29 May 1812, P.A.C. *Report*, 1886, pp. ccxvii-ccxviii.

49/Hearne, *Journey to the Northern Ocean*, pp. 225-7.

50/*Ibid.*, pp. 216-17.

51/HBC Archives, B. 42/a/130, ff 1-2, Churchill Journal (1805).

52/HBC Archives, B. 42/a/132, f 18, Churchill Journal (1806-7).

53/Hearne, *Journey to the Northern Ocean*, p. 218.

54/HBC Archives, B. 42/b/55, ff 15d-16, W. Auld's (Churchill) Correspondence Book (1811), W. Auld to T. Thomas at Albany, dated Churchill, 16 August 1811.

55/HBC Archives, A. 11/16, f 18, London Inward, W. Auld at Churchill to London, 24 August 1811.

56/Douglas MacKay, *The Honourable Company*, p. 75; Knight, *Churchill*, p. 90.

57/*Thompson's Narrative*, p. 559.

58/Hearne, *Journey*, p. 115-16.

59/HBC Archives, B. 42/b/51, f 11d, Churchill Correspondence Book (1807-8), W. Auld at Churchill to Hodgson, Thomas and Gladman, 10 August 1808.

60/Little information is available about Fort William in 1811. However, Franchère has left us the following vivid description of the post in 1814, which must have differed little in appearance from 1811 (*Narrative*, 386):

"Fort William has really the appearance of a fort, with its palisade fifteen feet high, and that of a pretty village, from the number of edifices it encloses. In the middle of a spacious square rises a large building elegantly constructed, though of wood, with a long piazza or portico, raised about five feet from the ground, and surmounted by a balcony, extending along the whole front. In the centre is a saloon or hall, sixty feet in length by thirty in width, decorated with several pieces of painting, and some portraits of the leading partners. It is in this hall that the agents, partners, clerks, interpreters and guides, take their meals together, at different tables. At each extremity of the apartment are two rooms; two of these are destined for the two principal agents; the other two to the steward and his department. The kitchen and servants' rooms are in the basement. On either side of this edifice, is another of the same extent, but of less elevation; they are each divided by a corridor running through its length, and contain each, a dozen pretty bed-rooms. One is destined for the wintering partners, the other for the clerks. On the east of the square is another building similar to the last two, and intended for the same use, and a warehouse where the furs are inspected and repacked for shipment. In the rear of these, are the lodging-house of the guides, another fur-warehouse, and finally, a powder magazine. The last is of stone, and has a roof covered with tin. At the angle is a sort of bastion, or lookout place, commanding a view of the lake. On the west side is seen a range of buildings, some of which serve for the stores, and others for workshops; there is one for the equipment of the men, another for the fitting out of the canoes, one for the retail of goods, another where they sell liquors, bread, pork, butter, etc., and where a treat is given to the travellers who arrive. This consists in a white loaf, half a pound of butter, and a gill of rum. The *Voyageurs* give this tavern the name of *Cantine Salope*. Behind all this is another range, where we find the counting-house, a fine square building, and well-lighted; another storehouse of stone, tin-roofed; and a *jail*, not less necessary than the rest. The *Voyageurs* give it the name of *pot au beurre*, the butter-tub. Beyond these we discover the shops of the carpenter, the cooper, the tinsmith, the blacksmith, etc., and spacious yards and sheds for the shelter, reparation, and construction of the canoes. Near the gate of the fort, which is on the south, are the quarters of the physician, and those of the chief clerk. Over the gate is a guard-house."

61/The swamp had been chosen because the surrounding tablelands or spurs of the shield were not suited to building.

CHAPTER 7

1/*Thompson's Narrative*, p. 181.

2/Harmon, *Sixteen Years*, p. 211.

3/Masson, *Les Bourgeois*, II, p. 308.

4/That is, the area where the shield disappears under the broad marine terraces of the bay.

5/Morton, *History of the Canadian West*, p. 440. It includes the whole of the region forming a low saddle in the shield between the bay and the prairies.

6/Mackenzie, *Voyages*, p. lxxvi.

7/Morton, *History of the Canadian West*, p. 449.

8/*Thompson's Narrative*, p. 153.

9/HBC Archives, B. 42/b/50, f 23. Churchill Correspondence Book (1806-7), Circular Letters to Officers and Traders Inland from Churchill Factory by W. Auld, fall of 1807. Even to this day, as a legacy of the need for defence, the Hudson's Bay Company posts have a very compact form.

10/*Thompson's Narrative*, pp. 133-6.

11/HBC Archives, B. 42/b/55, f 6d, W. Auld's (Churchill) Correspondence Book (1811), J. Charles, Inland Master, Clapham House, Deer Lake, to W. Auld, 7 February 1811.

12/*Ibid.*, f 10d.

13/HBC Archives, B. 239/e/1 ff 4-4d, York Factory Report (1815), W. H. Cook to T. Thomas, dated York, 1 September 1815.

14/*Ibid.*, f 4.

15/*Ibid.*, f 5.

16/*Ibid.*, f 4. Ice coming down stream at the deltas and mixing with off-shore pack ice at the bay, helped to delay the spring and shorten the growing season.

17/HBC Archives, B. 42/z/1, f 48d, Churchill Miscellaneous (1797-1803), "Reasons for preferring Churchill River, to York River, for conducting the Northward Trade," London, 29 November 1797.

18/HBC Archives, B. 239/b/68, f 25, York Factory Correspondence (1802-3), from W. Auld to the Chief at York.

19/*Ibid.*, ff 24d-25.

20/HBC Archives, B. 239/b/79, f 10, York Correspondence Book (1794-1809), Colen and Council at York to the London Committee, York Factory, 16 September 1795.

21/HBC Archives, B. 42/b/55, f 5d, W. Auld's (Churchill) Correspondence Book (1811), extract of private letter from W. Holmes, Inland Master of Rat River, dated Bedford House, 12 February 1811.

22/HBC Archives, B. 42/b/55, f 10, W. Auld's (Churchill) Correspondence Book (1811), extract of Letter from Mr. Snoddie, dated Nelson House, 24 February 1811.

23/*Ibid.*, ff 10d-11, W. Auld's remarks (undated) on the above letter.

24/HBC Archives, B. 49/e/1, f 4d, Cumberland House Report (1815), report on the Cumberland District by Alexander Kennedy, addressed to Thomas Thomas, Gov. of Northern District.

25/HBC Archives, B. 89/a/2 (unnumbered), Peter Fidler's Ile-à-la-Crosse Journal, dated 8 June 1811.

26/Mackenzie, *Voyages*, pp. lxxvi-lxxvii.

27/HBC Archives, B. 42/b/55, f 6, W. Auld's (Churchill) Correspondence Book (1811), extract of private letter from W. Holmes, Inland Master of Rat River, dated Bedford House, 12 February 1811.

28/Wallace, *Documents Relating to the North West Company*, pp. 264-5.

29/Harmon, *Sixteen Years*, pp. 113-14.

30/Mackenzie, *Voyages*, p. lxxxi.

31/*Thompson's Narrative*, p. 539.

32/Morton, *History of the Canadian West*, p. 453.

33/HBC Archives, B. 89/a/2, f 1d, Peter Fidler's Ile-à-la-Crosse Journal (1810-11), dated June 1810.

34/Morton, *History of the Canadian West*, pp. 451-2, 453.

35/HBC Archives, B. 89/a/2, 1d, Peter Fidler's Ile-à-la-Crosse Journal (1810-11), dated June 1810.

36/*Ibid.*, f 36d, June 1811.

37/*Journals of Hearne and Turnor*, p. 446.

38/Harmon, *Sixteen Years*, p. 114.

39/Hearne, *Journey*, p. 210.

40/Mackenzie, *Voyages*, p. 404; Hearne, *Journey to the Northern Ocean*, pp. 210-11.

41/Hearne, *Journey*, p. 129.

42/Jenness, *Indians of Canada*, pp. 392-3.

43/Hearne,*Journey*, pp. 210-12, 116-17.

44/HBC Archives, B. 42/b/55, ff 15d-16, W. Auld's (Churchill) Correspondence Book (1811), Auld at Churchill to Thomas Thomas at Albany, 16 August 1811.

45/*Thompson's Narrative*, pp. 16-17.

CHAPTER 8

1/*Thompson's Narrative*, p. 184.

2/Masson, *Les Bourgeois* I, p. 273.

3/HBC Archives, A. 6/18, pp. 28-9, London Outward, instructions addressed to William Sinclair, Winnipeg Factory, dated 31 May 1810.

4/HBC Archives, B. 42/b/57, f 5d, Churchill Correspondence Book (1811-12), William Auld to Thomas Swain, dated York Factory, 28 October 1811.

5/*Journal of Hearne and Turnor*, p. 111.

6/Coues, *New Light*, p. 470.

7/*Journal of Hearne and Turnor*, p. 113.

8/HBC Archives, B. 49/e/1, f 3d, Cumberland House Report (1815), report on Cumberland District by Alexander Kennedy (addressed to Thomas Thomas, Gov. of the Northern District).

9/Coues, *New Light*, p. 483.

10/HBC Archives, B. 49/e/1, f 2, Cumberland House Report (1815), report on Cumberland District by Alexander Kennedy (addressed to Thomas Thomas, Gov. of the Northern District).

11/Coues, *New Light*, pp. 475-6, 477.

12/HBC Archives, B. 49/e/1, f 5, Cumberland House Report (1815), report on Cumberland District by Alexander Kennedy (addressed to Thomas Thomas, Gov. of the Northern District).

13/By 1815, however, the lake was becoming "very unproductive," and "the constant labour of two men with from twelve to twenty nets" was not sufficient to procure one meal per day for all hands for ten months of the year. During the remaining two months, i.e., May and November, there was "generally Sturgeon enough for daily consumption." The dogs required nearly as much fish as the men; HBC Archives, B. 49/e/1, ff 2-2d, Cumberland House Report (1815), report on Cumberland District by Alexander Kennedy (addressed to Thomas Thomas, Gov. of the Northern District).

14/*Ibid.*

15/Coues, *New Light*, p. 476. Agriculture was, however, strictly limited in extent, and was confined to glacial-lake or kame terraces. Beyond, the land was too acid and poorly drained and stony for use.

16/HBC Archives, B. 49/e/1, ff 2-3, Cumberland House Report (1815), report on Cumberland District by Alexander Kennedy (addressed to Thomas Thomas, Gov. of the Northern District).

17/Coues, *New Light*, pp. 475, 483.

18/*Ibid.*, pp. 184, 198, 221, 245, 259, 281, 422, 440.

19/*Thompson's Narrative*, p. 188.

20/*Ibid.*, p. 248.

21/ *Ibid.*, p. 259.

22/ Harmon, *Sixteen Years*, p. 91. This, of course, is the site of present Winnipeg, the largest city in the Northwest, founded by the Selkirk settlers in 1812.

23/ Macdonell to Selkirk, York Fort, 1 October 1811, P.A.C. *Report*, 1886, p. cxcv.

24/ J. B. Tyrrell in *Thompson's Narrative*, p. 188.

25/ Mackenzie, *Voyages*, p. lxix.

26/ Coues, *New Light*, p. 705.

27/ Morton, *History of the Canadian West*, pp. 511-12. It has also been said that the French had had a post (called Fort La Jonquière) on the Bow, near the present Calgary, as early as 1751-2 (Coues, *New Light*, p. 484).

28/ *Thompson's Narrative*, pp. 249, 274.

29/ Mackenzie, *Voyages*, p. lxii.

30/ *Thompson's Narrative*, p. 246.

31/ *Mackenzie, Voyages*, p. lxii.

32/ *Thompson's Narraitve*, p. 253.

33/ *Ibid.*, p. 195.

34/ Harmon, *Sixteen Years*, p. 111.

35/ *Thompson's Narrative*, p. 268.

36/ Harmon, *Sixteen Years*, p. 41.

37/ *Thompson's Narrative*, pp. 235-6.

38/ Coues, *New Light*, pp. 530, 734.

39/ Masson, *Les Bourgeois*, I, pp. 299-340.

40/ *Ibid.*, p. 272.

41/ *Thompson's Narrative*, pp. 212-13.

42/ Masson, *Les Bourgeois*, I, p. 317.

43/ *Ibid.*, p. 270.

44/ *Thompson's Narrative*, p. 245.

45/ Masson, *Les Bourgeois*, I, pp. 268, 274.

46/ Mackenzie, *Voyages*, p. lxiii.

47/ Masson, *Les Bourgeois*, I, p. 257.

48/ *Thompson's Narrative*, pp. 185, 194, 204-6.

49/ Masson, *Les Bourgeois*, I, p. 275.

50/ *Thompson's Narrative*, p. 196.

51/ *Ibid.*, pp. 193-7.

52/ Masson, *Les Bourgeois*, I, p. 275.

53/ Harmon, *Sixteen Years*, p. 36.

54/ Morton, *History of the Canadian West*, p. 439.

55/ Coues, *New Light*, p. 605.

56/ *Ibid.*, pp. 559, 578.

57/ *Ibid.*, p. 540.

58/ *Ibid.*, pp. 500-1.

59/ Masson, *Les Bourgeois*, II, p. 22.

60/ Coues, *New Light*, pp. 585, 603, 746.

61/ *Ibid.*, pp. 604-5, 615-16, 622.

62/ *Ibid.*, pp. 621-3.

63/ *Ibid.*, p. 745.

64/ *Ibid.*, p. 701.

65/ J. B. Tyrrell in *Thompson's Narrative*, p. 88.

66/ Coues, *New Light*, pp. 655, 666, 701.

67/ *Ibid.*, p. 575.

68/ *Ibid.*, p. 737.

69/ *Ibid.*, p. 575-6.

70/*Ibid.*, p. 737.

71/*Ibid.*, p. 530.

72/*Ibid.*, pp. 719-20.

73/Harmon, *Sixteen Years*, p. 115.

74/*Journal of Hearne and Turnor*, p. 454.

75/Harmon, *Sixteen Years*, p. 124.

76/*Ibid.*, p. 116.

77/*Journal of Hearne and Turnor*, pp. 325-493.

78/*Documents of the North West Company*, pp. 264-5.

79/HBC Archives, B. 89/a/2, f 2d-3, Peter Fidler's Ile-à-la-Crosse Journal (1810-11), dated June 1810.

80/Harmon, *Sixteen Years*, p. 115.

81/Mackenzie, *Voyages*, p. 8; *Journals of Hearne and Turnor*, p. 456.

82/Harmon, *Sixteen Years*, p. 124.

83/*Ibid.*, pp. 117-18.

84/Mackenzie, *Voyages*, pp. 123, 145-6.

85/Harmon, *Sixteen Years*, pp. 130, 256.

86/*Ibid.*, p. 132.

87/HBC Archives, B. 42/b/51, f 11d, Churchill Correspondence Book (1807-8), W. Auld at Churchill to Hodgson, Thomas and Gladman, 10 August 1810.

88/HBC Archives, B. 42/a/136a, ff 12-12d, W. Auld's Memorandum Book (1810-11).

89/Mackenzie, *Voyages*, p. xci.

90/HBC Archives, B. 42/b/51, f 11d., Churchill Correspondence Book (1807-8)) , W. Auld at Churchill to Hodgson, Thomas and Gladman, 10 August 1810.

91/HBC Archives, A. 6/18, pp. 32-3, London Outward, instructions to W. Auld and T. Thomas, dated 31 May 1811.

92/Wallace, *Documents of the North West Company*, p. 269.

93/Macdonell to Auld, Nelson Encampment, 25 December 1811, P.A.C. *Report*, 1886, p. cxcxix.

94/Macdonell to Selkirk, Yarmouth, 4 July 1811, P.A.C. *Report*, 1886, pp. clxxxvii-viii.

95/Harmon, *Sixteen Years*, p. 238.

96/Mackenzie, *Voyages*, p. 400.

97/*Thompson's Narrative*, p. 241.

98/Macdonell to Selkirk, York Fort, 1 October 1811, P.A.C. *Report*, 1886, p. cxciv.

99/Umfreville, *Present State*, p. 82.

100/Macdonell to Selkirk, York Fort, 1 October 1811, P.A.C. *Report*, 1886, p. cxciv.

Index

68, 107-8, 114, 124; route to Lake
  Winnipeg, 66
William Henry's House (Red River), 128
William, Hugh, 15
Winnipeg River, 122
Wish-a-cappuca "tea," 80, 81, 89, 90

Yellowknife Indians, 15, 107, 117, 139

York Factory or Fort, 53, 54, 62-3, 78, 86,
  91, 96-101, 122; route to Lake Winni-
  peg, 65; rivalry with Churchill
  Factory, 111-12; shortcut to Upper Red
  River from, 131; to supply Churchill
  Factory, 139-40

xy Company, 36

This book
was designed by
ALLAN FLEMING
with the assistance of
ELLEN HUTCHISON
University of
Toronto
Press